D1557524

Another Hurdle

DAVID HEMERY

Another Hurdle

THE MAKING OF AN OLYMPIC CHAMPION

TAPLINGER PUBLISHING COMPANY
NEW YORK

First published in the United States in 1976 by
TAPLINGER PUBLISHING CO., INC.
New York

Library of Congress Catalog Card Number: 76–364
ISBN 0–8008–0233–0

Frontis. On top of the world, on top of the podium;
a warm and happy feeling inside, an Olympic
gold medal and world record in one

Contents

*Dedicated to my parents, Peter
and Eileen; and to my coaches,
Fred Housden and Billy Smith.*

Illustrations

between pages 88–89

Acknowledgments

Ed Lacey, 1, 2, 3, 4, 11, 12, 14, 16, 20, 26, 27, 33; Tony Duffy, 9, 28; Mark Shearman, 13; Omega, 15; John Hirwood, 18; Sportsworld, 19; Alan Carr-Locke, 22; B.B.C., 29; Moscatel, 30, 31, 32.

CHAPTER 1

Mexico City, October 15th 1968

I pulled the grey matt blanket over myself in an attempt to harbour some warmth, yet at the same moment was afraid of becoming too warm. The blanket weighed heavily on me. In that room, more than at any other time, I became aware of the expression 'cold sweat'. Athletics is a funny sport – you lay yourself bare in public, putting yourself and your training on the line.

John Sherwood and I had been brought to the Olympic stadium at 3.30 p.m., two hours before our event. This was arranged in case a traffic breakdown or other happening might have caused difficulty in arriving on time. Since the warm-up time usually started 45–50 minutes before the event, we went in search of the cell-like medical room assigned to the British team. Four army cots with a long bench at the foot of the beds, were all that furnished this stark, whitewashed room.

John Cooper had been through this before to become the silver medallist in the same event in Tokyo in 1964. He and national coach Denis Watts accompanied John Sherwood and me to the room. The tension was unbearable. Sherwood and I were now two of the top eight men in the world in the 400 metres hurdles final. Americans Ron Whitney and Geoff Vanderstock were joint favourites. West Germans Hennige and Schubert were the new co-holders of the European record at 49·1 seconds. European champion Frinolli of Italy, and the Russian, Skomorokov, completed the top-class field.

I was practically paralytic with fear – John too – although somehow we were able to crack bad jokes in our attempt to relieve the tension, wishing we were anywhere but there at the time. John Cooper and Denis sat at the end of the beds smoking

furiously, and looking, perhaps, even more over-wrought than
Sherwood and myself. My fingers and feet were damp and freezing
cold. I felt weak, my breath was short and I felt a slight constriction
in my throat. The back of my neck ached a bit and my prevailing
thoughts were of impending unpleasantness. Sherwood and I just
wanted to get the whole thing over and done with. Time wasn't
moving! The waiting was agony but my mind, conditioned through
long training and experience, warned 'Wait to warm up! Wait!
Wait!' The greatest temptation is to get on with it. An athlete
gears himself physically and mentally to a peak time and the
waiting is killing. Nevertheless, he must not allow himself to
yield to temptation and warm up too early or he will, literally, be
tired by the time the race commences.

After hours of blank limbo waiting when every minute took
ten to pass, the time for warm-up, 4.45 p.m., finally arrived. There
were fifty minutes to go. The rain of mid-afternoon had stopped
and John and I walked slowly up to the warm-up track, situated
about three hundred yards from the Stadium entrance. I took off
my shoes and jogged around the grass. The damp under my feet
took me back twelve months to the time when I had been running
on the edge of the water along the firm sand of Powder Point – a
beach near Boston in the U.S.A. I tried to recapture some of the
joyful and enthusiastic thoughts and feelings I had then
experienced.

John and I warmed up independently, trying to make this
occasion no different from that of many previous ones throughout
our careers and yet geared to producing our best-ever efforts. It
was good to be starting the familiar routine, jogging, stretching
muscles, striding at a progressively faster speed and flicking my
legs over the hurdles. The speed felt good but then I began to
think how close the time was getting to the Final. Was I really
ready? My mouth was dry again and my throat constricted as I
tried to swallow. I pulled on my track suit to keep in the warmth
and headed towards the check-in point twenty minutes before the
start of the race. My eyes were on the ground watching only
where the next few steps were going. Denis Watts asked if I
would like him to carry my bag but I said, 'No, don't bother',
then immediately felt it weighing so heavily in my hand that I
changed my mind and thankfully handed it over.

Fifty yards from the entrance, I stopped for one last trip to the cloakroom and the chance to splash cold water over my face and the back of my neck and, temporarily at least, to take the dryness out of my mouth. I murmured 'Hi Jim' as Jim Ryun, then world mile record holder, crossed my path, having just finished qualifying in his 1,500 metres heat, but this was no time to talk. I drift-walked on, reporting to the table where a young Mexican girl checked my name, vest number (402), and lane (6). An official checked her work and inspected my spikes to make sure that there were only the regulation six spikes in the sole. After that I was shunted into the pen where we closely resembled caged animals. Despite the close proximity, every eye averted contact. Each of us was in a semi-trance of concentrated thought, fear, and numbness.

It was getting close to 5.30 and, because of the earlier rain, the atmosphere was cool. We would not be allowed on to the track until ten minutes before the race, so we just had to stay where we were for the intervening *ten minutes*. The wooden benches were just wide enough to lie down on and this was exactly what I did, flat on my back, pulling up my knees, folding my arms and putting my head on my track bag, eyes closed, trying to relax every muscle. Whitney started jogging up and down the eight-yard pen, keeping his muscles loose and warm. One by one the other athletes joined him – I wished so much that they would keep still. It was a great temptation to start moving around with them – almost in a ritualistic dance – but I knew that the final ten minutes before the race would be sufficient for the last minute warm-up so I lay still, trying to breathe deeply and attempting to keep my pulse rate under 180!

Ten minutes to go and a maroon-blazered, grey-trilby-hatted official came to escort the Finalists to the track. We were led down a ramp covered with Tartan, the synthetic track surface on which we were to run. I could feel the buzz of the crowd on the surface of my skin: someone yelled in a very loud voice 'Come on Ron'. I tried hard to block out all thoughts except about what I had to do nine minutes from that moment. Absolute concentration was essential: I could not afford to think of the size of the crowd or of the 600 million who would be viewing on television. I was blinkered to photographers and television camera men who were within feet of the side of the track.

The ritual I had undergone so many times already, had to be gone through yet again. Fix your starting blocks the right distance

from the line, aim them at a tangent to the bend; remember your
stride pattern and pace judgment. I talked to myself, repeating
the words of my coach, 'It's your lane, your hurdles, your pace:
all you have to do is to channel your training into less than 50
seconds' effort.' Remember all that has gone into it. Take a trial
run out of the blocks. Hyperventilate and concentrate. Concentrate.
Oh, God, how will it go? Please help me just to do my best. I still
felt weak.

The starter's whistle blew – time to strip off our track suits.
Standing behind my blocks, I put my hands on my knees and
tried to take as deep a breath as I could. I could not completely
fill my lungs. There was a cold constriction between my stomach
and my throat. My mouth and throat were again dry, it was
impossible to swallow. A brief panicking thought – after the gun
goes, supposing a gust of wind blows up, depositing grit on my
contact lenses and forcing me to stop? I wished I could be anywhere
else. Why was I doing this anyway? I had never before felt such
dreadful pressure. I walked forward to put my hands on the track
in front of my blocks. Take your marks! No turning back. I
kicked each leg out and placed it against the block. *Still* I felt
weak. Did I feel ready to run the fastest quarter of my life? I
was not sure.

'Set – stand up, please' – something had gone wrong! I was not
sure if Ron Whitney in lane seven had gone before the gun but I
took a few strides out of the blocks and down the track. A deep
breath, and suddenly my lungs felt full. At last I felt ready – still
weak – but ready and conscious as never before of exactly what I
was aiming to do.

The second time we went to our marks and my legs coiled back
against the starting blocks. I felt as though a spring were actually
inside me. A Spanish command for 'get set' – my ears strained
for the noise: a puff from the gun and a snap into action. Good
effort, fast, stride-length under control, first hurdle came spot on:
sprinting thirteen strides between the hurdles, fast and relaxed. I
felt my legs paw down over hurdle two and I was catching Whitney
outside me. I was sure enough of my own pace to realize that he
was going out quite slowly and I strode out feeling strong and
determined, concentrating fantastically hard on stride-length and
pace judgment.

I passed Whitney by the third hurdle but did not dismiss him from my mind as I had no way of knowing if he was then matching my pace, stride for stride, on my shoulder. John Sherwood, out in lane eight, was now the only man in my vision and moving strongly. Go after him!

The greatest technical problem I had to face was coming up now at the sixth of ten hurdles. I had to change my stride-pattern from thirteen to fifteen; my legs had to accelerate and stride-length shorten without losing momentum. I felt as if I were running in slow motion as I saw every inch of where I had to place my feet. I was vividly conscious of myself, the red Tartan and the hurdles on that final bend. Putting in a great effort to try to hold my speed around that bend, I lost sight of John before the seventh hurdle so for my last 190 yards I was running 'blind'.

Still straining as I neared the end of the second bend, I started to question whether it would be possible to maintain so much effort and not die before the end. For one step my pace eased but instantly a flash came through my mind 'this is the Olympic Final – you can't let up now'. Somewhere on that second bend, I heard a foot splash down in water. It sounded well up on my left side: the adrenal-panic glands joined my conscious mind in renewed effort. I nearly sat on hurdle eight and held my glide slightly longer over the hurdle to make sure of not hitting it. I started yelling at myself 'keep the legs moving, fast legs, work your arms, make sure of ten – the final one, okay'.

Stepping down over the tenth, I immediately recalled that Coach Smith had said, 'Go at the last hurdle as if it were the first of a 110 metres spring hurdle race'. I was upset because I had not remembered this advice in time but tried to make up for it by changing gear into a sprint over the last 45 metres. Maddeningly, my legs just would not change pace. To make matters worse, I was, subconsciously, waiting for the 'ooh' of the crowd when a leader is being caught by a fast finisher and could not understand why there was no crowd noise. With every muscle in me, I forced my stride length and speed to be maintained to the tape. I dipped at the line, and two stride afterwards, tipped my head to the right to see if Whitney was coming by. I could not see him and my hands went to my knees. I had not looked left and was still not 100 per cent sure that I had won.

I think the gradual confirmation came when B.B.C. camera men raced forward for an interview. My eyes searched the sea of faces in the direction where my family was sitting. At that time, it was impossible to pick them out but I waved my acknowledgment and thanks in their general direction. My pervading feelings were a combination of exhaustion, relief, and happiness.

Later I was to hear the comments of those who had watched the race. 'Unbelievable.' 'By a bloody street.' 'Just fantastic.' However, directly following the race, medical officials took my arm to escort me to the dope-testing area.

Between the track and this underground testing place, 100 yards away, I stopped at least five times. I apologized for keeping the attendant waiting but the lack of oxygen in my blood was making me go black behind the eyes, and I was very close to passing out. Sitting in the medical cubicle, with a very flushed face and heavy pulse racing in my head, I panted like a dog for twenty minutes. During this time a medical attendant came in with a scrap of paper on which was written 48·1. I didn't quite associate those figures with what I had just run. I asked him if the one meant that I was first? Only when he confirmed my first place did the three numbers begin to sink in and I started smiling at their significance. *Track and Field News* later wrote: 'Hemery's 48·1 cremates field.' *Athletics Weekly*: 'It wasn't just the time – a staggering 48·1 that made me reach for every superlative in the dictionary . . . even more it was the manner and margin of his victory.' I was told that it was the widest winning margin in that event for forty-four years.

However, from superlatives back to basics. The officials wanted to check that I hadn't used any drugs. But my system was quite dehydrated and most unco-operative. In spite of water, orange, and coke, it was quite impossible to produce the urine sample required by the medicos, so they had to wait until after the medal ceremony.

As I emerged from the medical area to head for the room where the medal winners were to assemble, I was greeted by a jubilant John Cooper with the ecstatic news that John Sherwood had finished third. I headed rapidly to the glass-walled room opposite the victory rostrum, but there I met Gerhard Hennige and Geoff Vanderstock. John Sherwood was sitting on the far side of three women javelin throwers, his elbows on his knees, his chin resting on his hands, as he looked into space. He told me he thought he'd come third. I quickly went to check for him. Confirmation came through that he had, in fact, taken the bronze medal, all three men being credited with the same time, 49 seconds exactly. I couldn't have been happier for John, but at the same time felt really badly for Geoff, the only one of the three who had missed a medal. He was very sporting but, of course, asked if he might see just how close he had been by looking at the photo-finish picture.

Meanwhile, in spite of the persistent rain it was finally decided that, drizzle or no drizzle, we would receive our medals that night. A warm vibration rose inside me as we walked out and I saw the number of Union Jacks and groups of people who had stayed on just to be there when John Sherwood, Gerhard, and I received our medals. The presenter was Lord Burghley, now the Marquess of Exeter, President of the I.A.A.F. who had won the same event in the Olympic Games exactly forty years before. His warm greeting added to my pleasure and we all turned to watch two Union Jacks and one West German flag slowly rising to our National Anthem. I have no idea what the temperature was but the rain felt warm on the back of my neck. We waved to the crowd and walked back towards our waiting friends, and for the first time I saw my parents above the entrance way. The extent of their joy was reflected in their faces – I suspect even more than on mine – and I was glad that they could share my feelings after all they had done to make my achievement possible. They went as far as to say it was the high point of their lives.

Telegrams flowed in – 'tremendously thrilled'; 'heartiest congratulations'; 'just beautiful'; 'proud of you'; 'Britain gasping'; 'fantastic record'; 'the most incredible performance'; 'we were screaming with excitement'; 'it was absolutely wonderful'; 'we loved the short but beautiful 48·1 seconds.' And London Zoo named their rare new-born Mongolian species of wild horse David.

Late on the night of the race my family and I were taken to the television studios to talk to Britain and some of the rest of the world. Mexican technicians struggled vainly to connect our studio to Telstar and another studio 6,000 miles away in London. A brief chat, then a chance to *see* the race on videotape, but while viewers in Britain and those at the far end of the studio ogled at their screens, the one facing my parents, David Coleman, and I remained blank. We were 'live' to London so I couldn't leave my seat, although it took immense self control not to sprint to the other monitor.

Coleman said, 'Play it by ear – they're coming back. Well David, what a race. Had you any idea how far you were ahead of the rest of the field?' I *honestly* replied 'No – no idea. I had no way of knowing, as I was running blind for the second half of the race. For all I knew they could have been right beside me.' And this was so, as far as I still knew.

It was not until the interview with my parents had been completed that *we* had a chance to see it and for the first of many times, I relived every step of that race. Only then did I realize what had happened during the race. Frinolli had been second at the eighth hurdle but faded dramatically to last place. Favourite Ron Whitney had run an almost exactly even-paced race but had left himself too much to catch up at the finish. He had run within two-tenths of his best but was rewarded with only sixth place, catching Schubert on the line in 49·2. The Russian, Skomorokov, who was a year later to become European champion, justified his place in this Final with a time of 49·1. Geoff Vanderstock had moved into second place by the final hurdle and had become the immediate target for the fast-finishing Sherwood and Hennige. It required a photo-finish to separate these three. The thickness of a vest made the difference between silver and bronze.

My eight yards winning margin still shakes me. I have been told that it is the largest winning margin in any Olympic track Final up to and including the 800 metres for the previous eight Olympiads. How on earth was this possible? Why me? What were the factors which contributed to this achievement?

CHAPTER 2

Why Me?

The question how on earth I had reached the top of the podium in Mexico City was to haunt my thoughts for months after the Games. I knew that my coaches and the final years of preparation had played a large part but I tried to go back beyond these more recent years. Where were the foundations laid?

As long as I can remember, I have enjoyed games, whether they were simple puzzles, brain teasers, tests of endurance, or organized sports. My early life seems to have been crammed full of physical and mental stimulus. I have always enjoyed testing my limits. When given a pogo-stick for Christmas, I constantly tried to improve the number of times I could jump. Usually, my jumps for height were over telephone directories. Lengths of the veranda on stilts occupied quite a time after the receipt of another present. Times and distances were always fascinating and I kept a record of athletic bests almost as soon as I could write. My father felt, however, that he had to stop me in my attempts to count to a million when he found me racing through numbers in my sleep!

As recently as my early twenties, I found that I was counting my strides from the dormitory to the classroom but was not aware of doing so until I was interrupted by meeting someone and was trying to remember the number I had reached. When I recall tests of endurance in holding my breath or sitting without a chair, with my legs at right angles against a wall, I realize what a challenge physical activity and its measurement have always been in my life. Everything had to be measurable in terms of time, distance, height, length, or number. At a very early age, I came to believe that man is never satisfied for long and that it is always possible to push one's self one step farther. This factor was to become more real to me than I could have realized while I was on my pogo-stick!

We had a large area of grass at our home in Frinton-on-Sea which served as a multi-sport facility in a small way. At different times, cricket balls were flung into the nets placed at one end of the lawn. High jump stands made of lengths of 2 × 4 inch timber with holes bored in them and clothes pegs were used for height adjustment. Football, cycling and, of course, a confined running track all had their part in different seasons. Occasional swims in the freezing North Sea, long walks with the family on the high sea wall, and standing long jumps from it to the beach below provided considerable physical activity. As a young family, we enjoyed many activities together. I have a sister, Judy, two years older than myself, a brother, John, two years younger, and another sister, Anthea, two years younger than he.

My father and mother spent much time with us during our formative years, passing on many of their values. One was an appreciation of the importance of the health and strength we enjoyed. If we were taken for a walk in the woods, some of the time would be spent gathering wild flowers – bluebells, primroses, or, perhaps, blackberries for some whom were housebound. I am sure that at that age I was not aware just how much influence my parents were to have on my life. By example, perhaps, more than by precept, they have demonstrated what love and considera- tion can provide. We were not particularly well off but life was always full and we were given every possible opportunity within their power to provide. Perhaps the biggest support they gave was in recognizing and accepting each of us children as individuals with whom they tried to be absolutely fair and honest. Their own value system stemmed very much from their faith and, to this day, I respect their beliefs.

My father was an accountant with a private practice and at times when visiting clients the whole family would pile into the car. Sometimes it was a farmer's account and, while the books were being pondered indoors, the farmer's wife showed the rest of us around the farm or put us, briefly, on horseback. On other occa- sions the client might have been in the High Street of a town and mother would prompt a word game or a spell of I spy, twenty questions or who am I? When these became exhausted, the four of us would settle back to hear the endless, intriguing and amusing stories about an imaginary couple of children named Dick and Betty. My mother had the ability to weave incidents which had happened or nearly happened to us into tales which left us helpless with laughter and completely spellbound. The tales would close as our father's hand reached for the car door. In retrospect, I have the greatest admiration for this talent. I know that I would have no chance of keeping going for five minutes non-stop, let alone vary the anecdotes and their duration in according to an unspecified time limit. My pervading recollection of childhood is one of much happiness.

I was certainly no scholar in my early years. One reason may have been that it was not discovered until I was 10 that I needed glasses. Hence, perhaps my early pre-occupation with sport. But some of my running and other sporting talent must, I feel, have been hereditary. My grandfather was a champion sprinter. He emigrated to Australia when my father was 2. At Shore School, my father ran 100 and 220 and long jumped his way into the New South Wales Schoolboy Championships which he won with a jump of 21 feet 2½ inches. Then while still 17, he was compelled by his father to discontinue his athletic career. His family belonged to a narrow religious sect who had very strong views on sport. My father qualified as a Chartered Accountant and then headed back to London. There he met my mother Eileen Price. She was best known as a swimmer but was also a first team player in four sports at the North London Collegiate School. She, like my father, belonged to a family within the same religious sect. This group was founded on study of the Bible and separation from 'worldly' pursuits. Mixing with non-believers was not allowed and pressure to withdraw from sport was exerted as soon as school days were over. As the years progressed, the edicts passed down from the leader of this sect became more and more inhibiting and, in some cases, to my mind, outrageous. Before we four children knew very much about it, my father withdrew us all from the fold.

My parents' strong faith and high valuation of people did not wane. Their lives have been dedicated, firstly to our upbringing and support and secondly to helping others. Education has been at the top of the list of priorities. I use the word education in its broadest sense. Of course, it included formal education but also moral, spiritual, and physical education and the education

which comes through travel and social experience. Without
unlimited resources, they provided us with the widest possible
experience.

When I was 12, my father was offered the job of putting a new
financial system into a company in the United States. It was
typical of him that he made it a joint family decision whether we
would all like to go to America. We went! Fifteen years later I
read in graduate school studies how important it is to allow those
whose lives will be *personally* involved, to be included in important
decision-making.

Following an initial six months' stay in Colorado Springs, we
moved to the north-east coast of the United States. We had been
told that Boston and Los Angeles were the two best educational
areas. At our different levels, Judy, John, Anthea and I started at
the co-educational independent school, Thayer Academy, in
Braintree, Massachusetts. For rugby, I substituted basketball
where I found out that height and arm strength were definite
requirements in order of success. At the age of 13 I was 5 feet
and weighed only 90 pounds. At one of the first basketball prac-
tices, I was told to take a jump shot. This involves a good sense
of timing. The shooter springs high off the floor and, right at the
top of his jump, he pushes the ball towards the basket, hoping
that it will fall through the ring which hovers ten daunting feet
above the ground. I took the ball and leapt into the air but mis-
timed my push. This I did as I was coming back down, with the
result that the ball did not reach the height of 10 feet, let alone the
distance required to make the shot close.

There was no second attempt. The 6 feet 7 inches assistant
coach took it that I was the all-time weakling of the Academy and
I was forthwith banished from the floor in the direction of the
weight training room. Feelings of ignominy and injustice ran
through my head as I obediently went to work. I pressed weights
until I was purple in the face. Of course, my shooting went to
pot because basketball shooting requires quite a delicate touch,
married to controlled power. After some sessions I could not feel
my arms – they had long since lost contact with my nervous
system. However, within a few weeks some of my warm-up shots
were push-shots from the half-way line 75 feet away. Perhaps the
most pleasing ones were those that missed the backboard completely and went over the top: too strong, obviously! Within the

year my speed on defence and willingness to move the ball to the better shooters nudged me back in contention for a spot on the end of the bench.

I could not wait for the track season. Unfortunately, there was no age grouping so, while not yet 14, standing 5 feet 3 inches, and now improved to the massive bulk of 93 pounds I was confronted with the 15–18-year-old American track scene. One starts school at a younger age in the United Kingdom and I was, therefore, a year or two in advance of the American educational age grouping. I was a sprinter. 'Right' said the coach, 'you run the mile'. The difference in power and speed between the age of 13 and 18 is quite considerable. I really had no chance of getting on to the team except as a miler. Few seemed interested in the distance. For me, anything over 100 yards was like cross country. My place finishes ranged between second (three times) and fifth (once) but I always beat someone – even if it was another poor unfortunate whose miling talents were even more deeply hidden than my own. The times varied according to the wind. If your weight is 93 pounds and your shirt acts as a sail, headwinds on any part of the course make the going very strenuous and rather ponderous. My knees may have been coming up – but only to tilt the sail, not to propel me forward at any great rate. Over the month April 22nd to May 20th, my mile time dropped from 5 minutes 44 seconds to 5 minutes 12 seconds. That was progress!

That was 1958. By this time I had my mind truly set on growing. I had received a set of weights for Christmas in 1957 and with the purchase of a couple of extra plates, I had 100 pounds worth in the basement. At various times of the day, I would dive downstairs and heave weights in all directions. If I happened to pass my mother as I rose from the depths, puce and panting like fury, she would invariably warn me not to strain my heart! Since the heart is a muscle, it thrives on work, but, of course I always promised her I wouldn't.

The school started a soccer team soon after I arrived and this pleased me greatly. From a very young age, this was my favourite sport. I started at inside-left and moved to centre-forward after the first season. The team was pretty raw but so was the opposition. I averaged about two goals a game through my last two years of school. The average was greatly helped in one match where the opposition had opted for size in their full-backs. They were the

200 lb, 5 feet 4 inches variety, and had to lift their whole frame up to let one short leg at a time swing through in running form. The long pass proved lethal and I scored my first . . . and last double hat trick, as our side won 10–1.

During my final two years at Thayer, my brother, John, played on the wing and added to the speed and venom of our side's attack. John developed size and strength at a young age – younger than I had – and was holding his own as a sprinter as soon as he joined the senior school's track squad. He and I are of similar basic speed and this proved a great help and challenge in training. Prior to John's arrival at the senior section of the school, I had moved from the mile to the half-mile. The 1960 season was relatively successful as my times came down from 2 minutes 17 seconds in the first race to 2 minutes 08·3 seconds by the last. I won most of these races but found the strain of competing against much older and stronger boys quite traumatic. In later years, I avoided the 800 metres like the plague.

In 1961 my father decided that the school should have hurdles. Without too much thought of whether he could afford such generosity, he donated a complete set to the Academy. I am sure he had no idea what this gift was to reap. A hurdle was put up in the gym and most of the boys had a go at jumping it. Perhaps because of my time at Frinton, where I had hurdled over break-waters on the beach at 5, I took to hurdling like a duck to water. In the 1961 season, I continued to run the half mile, bringing my time down to 2 minutes 05·8 seconds. I ran one 440 timed in 53·9 seconds, competed once in the long jump – 19 feet 2¾ inches, and was unbeaten in the hurdles. My time for 160 yards low hurdles came down from 19·4 to 18·1 seconds; for 80 yards high hurdles from 11·1 to 10·3 seconds, and the 120 yards lows, from 13·7 to 13·5 seconds.

Rumour had it that I was faster over the hurdles than on the flat over the same distance. To me, the hurdles were a pleasant respite from straight running. I thoroughly enjoyed jumping. There is something aesthetically pleasing about going over a hurdle. It is also such a technically and physically demanding action that I found much to occupy my time in learning the skill. To say I never mastered it at school would be an understatement. My best time for the 120 yards highs was 16·5. My brother re-wrote all my school hurdle records after I had left Thayer Academy.

He went on in his senior year to duplicate the award I had received two years before as the school's best all-round sportsman.

Perhaps the most health-giving time of our formative years in America was the summer holidays. My father rented a cottage on the coast in Plymouth, not far from the site of the Pilgrim Fathers' landing place in 1620. The three months from mid-June to mid-September were spent absorbing the sun's rays, running, swimming, and playing tennis. Quite a few young teenagers belonged to the Eel River Beach Club and there endless games of water-tag were played. Young hearts fell in love, and hamburgers and barbecued chicken were devoured to the strains of 'Take good care of my baby' and 'Who put the bomp in the bomp, bomp, bomp, bomp, bomp'. My hair turned whiter in the sun and our bodies resembled mahogany. They were happy and carefree days and I continued to grow.

The cottage where our family stayed was on a headland from which we could run down a 300-yard hill to the swimming and tennis club. A small break in the hedge allowed only one person through at a time. Ready for the pool, clad only in trunks, my brother and I raced from the house one day. Stride for stride, we flew down the hill. Near the bottom, I was about a foot ahead, so John swung wide just before the hedge to come through it at an angle behind me. In the long grass, just inside the hedge, lay a plank with an upstretched nail. John came on to it in bare feet at 20 m.p.h. He yelled and fell to the ground on the other side of the hedge. I turned to see what had happened. The sight shook me rigid. The only way I could describe the bottom of his foot was to compare it to a piece of raw meat which had been cut with a sharp knife. It was open for six inches to a depth of nearly an inch. I told him not to move at all and went back up the hill probably faster than I had come down. Within three minutes, my mother had 'phoned the doctor, brought the car around to the Club, and had John on the way to hospital. The repair job was first class and the speed of his recovery phenomenal. He was off crutches before the end of the summer and within the year had regained his place on the school track team.

My injury problems were far less dramatic than those of my brother. However, they were to haunt me during my athletic career. I was very susceptible to leg muscle tears before, during, and after 'flu. During my last year at Thayer 1962, an early season

training session was a series of flat-out 220s. I was a bit low with a
virus and the front of my thighs became incredibly painful following the session. The cramping and pain continued throughout the
evening and while sitting in a hot bath, I discovered that the tops
of both thigh muscles had separated and the front part of the
quadricept resembled an hour glass. Even today, this formation is
apparent when I step up on a bench. I ran with thigh support
bandages and a fair amount of discomfort for the remainder of the
season.

A further injury occurred while carrying the pole vault standards
out to the equipment cart. Stepping from the gym door, I stumbled
down the step and the front of my foot kicked into the metal base.
It hurt but I soon forgot about it. Weeks later, a red mark appeared
on the top of my foot and running became increasingly uncomfort-
able. I made an effort to train through it but finally started favour-
ing the other leg. An X-ray showed a stress fracture. No plaster
was needed but, I was told, if I ran on it, the injury would take
longer to heal. This was my last season. I ran on.

Taking out the equipment cart became a regular feature of my
afternoon activities. It was study-hall last period and I could
avoid that by doing something relatively constructive and public
spirited. At that stage in my life, studies took a low priority. In
fact, I manoeuvred a further avoidance of these dreaded sessions
of silence, by masterfully volunteering to turn pages for piano
music scholar Phil Gorham. My music reading ability was nil
but my appreciation of fingers flying on the keys was very high.
Phil would nod, I would turn the page and return to the raptures
of audio sensory stimulation. He went on to receive an Open
Scholarship to Oberlin, a top music College. I went on to receive
mediocre academic report cards. My desire to learn caught fire
rather late in my academic life. Throughout my school days, basic
I.Q. and the bare minimum of work allowed me to graduate to
further life.

By the time I finished at Thayer, we had lived in the U.S. for
five years and some of the family looked wistfully towards a return
to England. As my younger sister, Anthea, was completing the
junior school at Thayer and my older sister, Judy, was finishing
her nursing training in the same year, it seemed that this would be
a reasonable time to return. My brother would come back to
start 'A' levels. My father had completed his theological degree

course through Wycliffe College, Canada. This was an astonishing piece of work as he took the degree by correspondence. Following his day's accountancy work and some time with the family, he would go into his den and study. At exam times, he would travel to Toronto and sit with all the students who had been in residence. He received a high honours degree and his intention was to enter the Ministry in the United Kingdom. This, however, was not to be.

In June 1962 we returned to London. A good education was still high on my parents' list of priorities, and independent schools were believed to be a prerequisite, but these were not possible on a curate's salary. In addition to this problem, neither John nor Anthea could settle in England at that time. They had picked up American accents and were told 'go home Yank' and made to feel distinctly unwanted. Their American friends and the informal student–teacher relationships in the States, made them long for that side of the pond. I tend to enjoy life wherever I am, so did not attempt to influence a move one way or another. England was no paradise. But time allows the mind to remember mostly the good things of the past. The cost of living had risen and continued to rise at a rate far faster than wage compensation. A new U.S. job offered to my father tipped the balance and the family headed west again.

Thankfully, this was not before I had met Fred Housden. While in Moor Park, my father asked for the nearest Athletics Club and Ruislip/Northwood, now part of Hillingdon, was named. At the track, Miss Hill, W.A.A.A. walking official, talked with my father and told him to go over to Hurlingham Park track the next day, as an excellent hurdles coach would be there. We went and Fred was asked if he minded watching me hurdle to see whether he thought I was worth coaching. He had me go over a few hurdles without making any comment. I knew that I was 'floating in space' over the hurdles but was trying hard. Fred asked me to think about a single feature of my action. This I did and felt exhilarated. One tip had made a difference. I really hoped he, too, had noticed. Evidently he had as he agreed to take me on as one of his small squad of pupils. For the next few months I worked at the National Westminster Bank. Three evenings a week I trained under Fred until the time when with my family, I returned to Boston.

When we arrived back, my father received quite a shock. The
job he had been told would be waiting for him was only there in
spirit, not in reality. His business 'friend' had meant only that
he would be welcome back in the country but he had sold his
interest in the existing firm. No job was readily available. My
father soon discovered that one can be over-qualified for jobs.
A.C.A., A.C.M.A., A.A.C.C.A., S.Th. – varied experience but
no job for months on end. John and Anthea were studying again
at Thayer Academy while the rest of us rowed in with meagre
incomes to keep the family's body and soul together. A second
bitter setback came in the first attempt at a sizeable investment. A
franchise was purchased for a computerized accounting system
for the medical profession in the Boston area. It turned out to be
a 'phony'. My father was further behind than ever.

Gradually, he began a private practice accounting and
financial consulting. During these eighteen months, I worked in
the computer department of the National Shawmut Bank of
Boston. In the early evening, I took computer programming
courses at Boston University. Thoughts of athletics held a low
priority. Large computers must be run twenty-four hours a day
to make them economically feasible. I worked on the 11 p.m. to
7 a.m. shift and often spent 9 p.m. to 9 a.m. at the Bank. I felt as
though I were keeping this night shift going. The pressure I put
on myself increased daily.

After a year, it was a relief to take a week's holiday with my
brother during college week in Bermuda. My eyes were opened
to the difference in outlook between the young students and me,
now feeling almost like a 40-year-old banker. I started thinking
and wondered exactly where I was heading and what I wanted.
I enjoyed travel, perhaps I should be a pilot. No, poor eyesight
would rule that out. If I could not fly, perhaps aircraft design.
With aeronautical engineering in mind, I discussed the thought
of attending University. I had to sit the college board exams and
started wondering who would have me. My academic school
record was nothing to go by! However the high 80s average I was
now achieving in my University evening courses persuaded me
that I could cope with University level work – if only I were given
the chance. I applied for admission to the School of Engineering
at Boston University, and was accepted.

My school track and basketball coach, Dick Sawyer, was a

genuine friend. He had a fellow coach heading the water-front activities at Thayer's Summer Day Camp. This man taught physical education in the Scituate School system, twenty-five miles south of Boston and coached the Boston University track team. His name was Billy Smith. My meeting with him supplied the third side of a strong athletic triangle two years after I had met Fred Housden in London.

CHAPTER 3

Coach and Athlete

It is unusual for any coach to allow a second coach to work with his athlete. It was to my extreme advantage that I had been put in touch with two unselfish men, Billy Smith and Fred Housden. Neither coach was obsessed with trying to prove himself through me. They worked in close co-operation with each other and with me to allow me to try to fulfil my athletic potential. Without them, I would not have an Olympic medal.

Billy Smith was a half-miler of note in the early 1950s. At the age of 10 I must have seen him competing in the British Games at the White City in June 1954. As I know him now he is tough, almost heartless when he has to be, pulling no punches, always straight talking and, at other times, showing the depths of emotion required in his total involvement in athletics and life. He has a family of three and at the end of weekend athletic trips away, he cannot wait to get back to his wife and children. Over the years in Boston, I came to know his family well and he mine. This probably helped to take our dedicated athletics' relationship out of the isolated intensity required to do well.

After our first meeting in the summer of 1964, I received a long letter from Billy with drawings to illustrate exercises which he said I should start if I wished to become a more flexible and stronger athlete. He stressed that these should begin immediately and continue throughout the year. When I heard of my acceptance by Boston University, I mentioned to Coach Smith my interest in trying out for the crew, and the soccer team, as well as for track and field athletics. Billy did not leave much room for negotiations. He questioned me about my aspirations in athletics. I told him that from the age of 10, when I had watched athletics meetings at the

White City in London, I often thought about the possibility of, one day, getting in the British team. Then I met Fred Housden and his rapid improvement of my hurdling technique, had elevated this dream into the realms of possibility.

Billy quickly stressed the need for specialization. If I intended to reach the Olympic Games, I had to work – and not just for a couple of months in spring and early summer. Since it was the athletics coach talking and as he was already mapping out plans for my first cross-country, I did not appear to have much choice. Actually, the choice was clear and it was mine to make. Either I would drift along, as I had been doing, enjoying each sports season as it came, doing well but not really dedicating myself to any special end, or I could now decide to specialize and, with the help of two coaches, just see how far we could go together. I had never really *worked* at sport before and I rather wondered what it would be like. It was a challenge and this excited me. The decision was made – I would give it a go.

With nostalgia, I looked over my shoulder at the soccer pitch. Ah well, the training could not be too demanding; perhaps I could play inter-mural soccer, basketball, and touch football in my spare time. Wrong again. Time at university is not really spare, especially in the north-east university league where the student must maintain an academic average of 70 per cent or better in order to compete in inter-collegiate sport. I studied, ran and began a social life.

Coach Smith kept a watchful eye on all these areas for each of his athletes. He was not averse to telling any of us to get our tails back to the books, or on to the track, or even into or out of affairs with the opposite sex. As late as the spring of 1972 when I was going through a dull patch, he recommended a search for beauty. He is not your average motivator. In a sense, though, this attitude expresses the depth of Billy's involvement when trying to bring the best out of his athletes.

During the summers of 1966 and 1968, I returned to England to compete and to train under Fred Housden. Fred had been scrum-half for Blackheath and an international pole vaulter and high hurdler shortly after the turn of the century. He graduated from Cambridge University with first class honours in mathematics. I met him eleven years after he retired from teaching mathematics at Harrow. Coaching was his hobby, and he coached small groups of athletes of very mixed abilities. This ability range was *his* choice as he considered this the best way of collecting and studying information invaluable to other athletes. He asked all his 'pupils' to call him Fred as, he said, this helped to cut the generation gap.

He kept himself unbelievably fit and was still demonstrating high jump and hurdle clearance in his late 70s. When he was 76, I spent one year dabbling with the decathlon and one of the exercises he showed me involved using a chinning bar to represent the pole vault pole. The exercise involved hanging from the bar, pulling my feet above my head, lifting the whole of my body up from that position, and shooting my legs towards the ceiling. I found this extremely difficult and Fred very simply demonstrated how it should be done. Not a little impressed, I asked him how many pull-ups he could do and discovered, to my chagrin, that he was at that time able to do two more than I – a total of eighteen!

Even while I was seeing him regularly, Fred would put some of his coaching thoughts into verse which he would send or give me on the next occasion we met. These might have been informative, were usually amusing, and sometimes merely a record of an occasion. However, they gave each of us for whom he wrote, the knowledge that he often thought about us and our training progress. Fred compiled eight volumes of these poems.

Both coaches involved themselves quite closely in my life. Just how a coach–athlete relationship develops depends on a number of factors: the personalities of coach and athlete, the event being attempted, the experience of both parties, how much time each is able and prepared to spend together, and whether the aims of the two coincide. I can only speak from personal experience, which is, of necessity, unique.

It is difficult for me to avoid sounding too effusive about my coaches. I believed both to be exceptional people. As Fred is no longer alive I shall speak of their similarities in the past tense. With Billy all still holds true. Both valued their family life greatly, each had three children while Fred also had a number of grandchildren. Both coaches were true teachers, dedicated to passing on their knowledge and experience to the young. They both read widely in their pursuit of knowledge of their sport but, what is more important, they had the insight and skill to transmit

that knowledge in a usable form to the athlete and knew when it
was most needed.

Each was shy of publicity; neither was particularly tolerant of
the reporter who was after a 'story'. Nor were they keen on the
hail-fellow-well-met approach. They were genuine, sincere
friends who rated personal friendship higher than economic
reward. Both found their reward in seeing improvement in their
athletes. Like Billy, Fred came to know my family quite well,
and I his. Fred said he made a point of this with his athletes as
he liked to know them as complete people. He was happiest to
become a coach, adviser, and friend.

An outstanding feature of both men was their reliability. I
cannot remember either coach missing or being late for a work-out.
It was possible to set your watch by Fred's appearance at a training
session, no matter whether he was being brought, had come by
rail or had driven himself. Perhaps this was another of the unique
qualities of my coaches. Both were always there whenever they
were needed. Where many would not have been bothered, they
were constantly giving of themselves and going through the work-
outs with me, rain or shine.

The best instance of this dedication and involvement came in
the middle of the winter prior to Mexico. I was in my final year
at Boston University. Outside the dormitory block a 160 yard
board track had been set up. If it snowed during the night, the
ground staff would shovel at least a couple of lanes clear of snow
next day. Billy used to arrive at the dormitory at about 3.30 in
the afternoon. In those days the passage to the changing room
area opened on to a car park beside the building. One day a
blizzard started at about noon. By three o'clock quite a lot of
snow had fallen and it was still coming down. I did not really
expect to see Coach Smith that day. However I went down to the
changing area, wandered along the passage and put my shoulder
to the door against the wind. As the door opened there was Billy
coming in.

I asked what he thought I should do – weight training and/or a
few exercises or should I take the day off? He paused, then,
pushing the door back open, said: 'Out there is the road to
Mexico.' I thought he was joking but it quickly became apparent
that he was not. Bundled up against the elements, I went out to
do a series of half-miles on the boards. Coach Smith stood with

his back to the wind, his feet entrenched in the snow, while I strode round and round the track. My feet tramped through the snow on to the grey-painted boards but it was snowing so heavily that by the time I had circled the small track my footprints were again white. I, at least, was running and, in spite of my damp and freezing feet, was keeping warm. How Billy just stood there, I still have no idea. My respect for him, already high, increased tremendously and I hoped that my efforts under such atrocious conditions would help to increase his respect for me.

Although it was impossible for them not to overlap, Fred and Billy tried to keep their roles distinct – Fred working on hurdle technique and Billy concentrating on my strength and stamina development. Apart from this they epitomized, for me, the big difference between an English and an American coach. Fred would never force an athlete to train. Rather, he would encourage and work on the technicalities with him, but leave the rest to the pupil. If I said I was getting tired, he would not be averse to suggesting that we had done enough for that day. Of course, times and attitudes are changing, but for years British coaches have placed insufficient emphasis on sheer hard work. In contrast, however, Billy Smith represents the American's insatiable desire to push through pain barriers and to almost kill one's self to reach towards maximum physical potential. When Billy heard I was writing a book, he jokingly remarked that if I wanted to include anything about moving immovable objects, that is, motivating dead athletes, he would be more than happy to supply some information. I had the feeling that he wasn't really joking.

I remember during one work-out in Boston I was feeling rather tired and mentioned to Coach Smith that my legs hurt. He put his hands on his own legs and said, 'I can't feel a thing – let's get on with the next repetition'. It takes time to understand this attitude. The coach can, from one standpoint, appear heartless. However, Billy could claim that he never asked me to do anything that he had not already attempted himself. Nevertheless, his tremendous drive was tempered with deep concern for each athlete he trained. Like Fred, he believed that coach and athlete must work as a team to bring out the best performance on the track.

This coach–athlete union was invaluable to me, especially when feeling lazy or tired. Very few people have sufficient drive or self discipline to go out and push themselves every day. Before long my own laziness, boredom, or questioning would probably have caused me to ease off, certainly to shorten the distances run. The coach can help the athlete to hold on to what both of them know the athlete must do. Coach Smith left me in no doubt as to what he expected of me, and his expectations and trust developed what I can only term my athletic conscience. Perhaps I absorbed part of Billy's determined spirit but, whatever it was, when I was training alone, perhaps on a long run, churning up sand dunes, or running repetitions on the track, when I got to the point of tiredness and desperately wanted to ease up, I could hear Billy shouting his instructions and encouragement and even feel his eyes on me.

At Lilleshall, in the Easter of 1973, I discovered I was not alone in this experience. Young Steve Ovett had felt much the same, hearing his coach, Harry Wilson, yelling at him, although Harry was not physically present. In 1974, while still 18, Steve won a European silver medal for 800 metres with a time of 1 minute 45·6 seconds. He has the talent to win an Olympic medal too.

Obviously, in such coach–athlete relationships, there is a high degree of compatibility, but the growth of rapport depends, to a great extent, on the level of interest the coach has in his athlete as a human being and on the standard the athlete himself wishes to achieve.

The development of a close working relationship is a gradual process. Patience is needed by both parties. I now appreciate the fact that I was not hurried by either coach – and I was starting from a pretty modest level. Because of my elementary standard of knowledge, both of hurdling technique and what it would take to work my way into shape, I was extremely receptive to guidance from both coaches.

Fred brought his analytical mind to bear with great success on the technicalities of hurdling. Every exercise and movement had to make sense to him before he would pass advice on to his pupils. I was eager to understand the mechanics of what I should be doing in order to improve. Fred's mind-eye was like a movie camera which could break down movement into minute detail, while the athlete was in full speed motion. He was quite brilliant at picking out one fault at a time, patiently working until each small aspect was corrected and the right motions had become second nature to the athlete. Only then would he mention any further fault. In this way, the athlete's mind was neither cluttered, pressured, nor overawed with the task ahead.

During the winter of 1962–63, I spent a lot of time with Fred training at Hurlingham Park in South London with George Tymms and, occasionally, Mike Parker, another British Olympic hurdler. Through hundreds of starts, Fred would hold his home-made clappers, two pieces of wood hinged at one end, which acted as a starting gun. His voice would boom out in a long steady s......e......t! Then a snap of the clappers would send us over the first few high hurdles. Either he or one of his girl athletes would take it in turns starting or timing us up to when our feet touched down over the first hurdle and over the third. Improvement was gradual but constant. Added maturity, step-ups with weights to improve speed and leg strength and Fred's gradual modification of my style reduced my time for 120 yards in the space of one year, from 15·6 seconds over 3 feet 3 inches barriers to 14·7 over 3 feet 6 inches. One second to the layman means very little but to the sprinter it represents a difference of ten yards.

In these early days, Fred encouraged me to take part in various indoor competitions. One arena was at R.A.F. Stanmore just outside London. I did sufficiently well there to earn the opportunity of running in the A.A.A. Indoor Championships at Wembley. Delayed in traffic on my way to the meeting, I raced up the steps of the stadium and told the nearest attendant that I was a competitor in search of the changing rooms. He said: 'You may be fast, mate, but I think you'd stand a better chance over there.' In my hurry to get to the start on time I had presented myself at the greyhound track.

That 14·7 seconds in 1963 took me into the Final of the National Championships at the age of 18 and won me the Wall's trophy for the best performance of an athlete under 21 at the A.A.A. Championships. Eight years later, I was to register 13·6 on a number of occasions, electrically recorded, and one hand-timed 13·4 in Zurich. The important thing about this improvement was that it came over a period of years. Neither of my coaches ever allowed themselves or me to look too far in advance. An instance of what I mean arose during the winter prior to Mexico, on the flight back to Boston after a disastrous U.S. Indoor Nationals where I had been tripped up while in the lead in the 600 yards heats. Determined that the outdoor season would be good, I wrote out a progress chart on my plane ticket starting with 51·5 seconds for 400 metres hurdles, in March and reducing the time by half a second each month, arriving at Mexico City in October with 48·5 or 48·0. Billy took a look at the list, put his pen through all the months after June and just said, 'Let's get the first three months taken care of.'

At some point in his development, a young athlete reaches the stage of maturity where, instead of merely accepting all the coach has to say, he is sufficiently experienced to develop the relationship with his coach into a partnership. Training then becomes a joint venture to produce the best results. In my time at Boston University, one course in Human Relations stressed the importance of each individual's capacity for self-awareness. The students in the course were encouraged to step back, mentally, to look at themselves. Apart from the general insight gained, this exercise had a great effect on my athletic aims. Both Fred and Billy spent much time alone and with me thinking about how this mythical athlete – Hemery of the future – could produce an exceptional time.

Oddly enough, I myself actually felt detached from this character. It was as if a body which, in this case, happened to be mine, was being dissected in a pathology laboratory, the structure examined, its reactions to certain conditions studied, its mental reactions recorded and a plan gradually shaped to make the body develop and grow, in fact, to come alive as a joint creation. Special work-outs were planned to try to eradicate current weaknesses or to enhance strength, memories of which I would carry with me out on to the track.

As in my training under Fred, when my times were reduced by technical improvements, so, under Billy, I achieved a steady progression through increased strength and stamina. Billy had an uncanny feeling for knowing from various training sessions exactly what I was capable of achieving in a race. As each race approached, starting from my first year's indoor meeting, he would be able to tell me to within a few tenths of a second what I was going to run. I usually felt he over-estimated my ability but soon discovered how accurate he was. In the letter he wrote me on October 6th 1968, he told me I would run 48·1 or 48·2 in the Final in Mexico City. On October 15th my time, electrically recorded, was 48·12, and therefore entered in the record book as 48·1!

Fred Housden once wrote: 'It is useless for a coach and athlete to work together unless they have complete confidence in each other.' My confidence in both of them grew as my times improved. Even though I often questioned myself and occasionally doubted my abilities, my faith in *them* was absolute. I valued their frankness and honesty in assessing my training and my race chances. They never expressed any doubts – both had implicit faith in me and this helped me to persist in the upward climb of work and hope towards improvement, new awareness, new confidence, then new levels of work and hope, and new improvement. This was not an unbroken advance. Often doubts, illness, injury, and questioning were set-backs for which recovery periods and re-assessment were necessary.

Billy was brilliant at getting me into top shape by the time of the most important meeting of the year. However, some of the boys who worked under him felt that he was a somewhat heartless slave-driver. I have never met a man who so much lives, eats and sleeps athletics. His thoughts are always concentrated on how to develop the athletic talents of his athletes. It goes far beyond a job for him and is unquestionably his way of life. Many months after Mexico, Billy reviewed my time at Boston and from this I knew just how deeply he had been involved in my exploits. He told me of his tears when I had torn a muscle in the winter of 1967 and his physical sickness through tension before I competed in very high level meetings. This hardly displayed a lack of personal concern. One of the things I value most in my relationship with him is that Billy put personal friendship above nationalism. I was an Englishman studying in the United States but he dedicated himself to getting me on top of the rostrum in Mexico and to a further two medals in Munich. Reaching this level of concern and involvement took a good deal of time and sacrifice.

My transition from a totally receptive beginner to that of a working partner with the coaches was, as I have said before, gradual. The third stage was clear-cut. A definite breaking point in the old relationships dates from October 15th 1968. I no longer existed athletically as a body to be analysed and studied but was a new entity, an Olympic Champion and World Record Holder. Both coaches dealt with me as such and became advisers. Billy told me, prior to my Munich build-up, that he was determined to avoid the split which had occurred between so many other coaches whose athletes had become Olympic champions. There was no shortage of ideas and suggestions about improved training methods but it was left, far more, up to me to agree to the suggestions and to implement them. The task master of before was no longer present. In many ways, I missed the old relationship. I knew that these coaches were far more knowledgeable than I. There may still have been a partnership but I felt out of place being made the senior partner. The closeness and mutual respect were, of course, still present but the pupil–master relationship was gone. In the eyes of the world, I had become a master. In my own eyes, I still felt like an experienced and knowledgeable pupil.

However, attitudes and circumstances had changed: minds had matured and time moved on. I now had to stand in my new position and make the ultimate decision to keep pushing and the coaches would say whether they thought it was too much or too little, instead of the other way around. I learned a lot about myself during the Munich build-up year. I also learned of the humility of my two coaches. They were saying that *I* had made them. I was not at all sure that this was so but I was very sure that *they* had made me. Through them I had discovered that a good coach can be creative – he captures a dream, harnesses a power, moulds a body, directs a will, motivates a mind, and develops a conscience in this athlete.

The coach–athlete relationship can be either the best or the worst relationship in the world. With mutual trust, respect, understanding, sacrifice, co-operation, and good senses of humour a close working partnership can develop. I was incredibly fortunate that this occurred twice.

August 19th 1972 was an emotional time for me. It was the one day in their lives when my coaches met each other. Billy was on his way to Munich and stopped in London. I was leaving for the Munich Games the following day. Both came to watch my final track session. It was a test run over a few hurdles on the back straight at Crystal Palace. Because of a muscle injury, it was to be my first hurdling session for two weeks. It was a strange experience for me to look down the track and see both my coaches. They had kept in touch by mail and through me, but to see them together, watching, made me slightly self-conscious. They leaned on a temporary metal fence beside the track. I can only guess at their level of concern. Months of preparation, discussion, and thought, could all be for naught if my leg would not stand up to the additional pressure of hurdling again. One reasonably good run and no pain. They knew I would be in the Munich Final.

I am indebted to them for their part in my success. The feelings between the three of us goes beyond words. Ten years in an intense mutual endeavour, often under stress, obviously brings closeness. How does one say 'thank you' to two people who have meant so much? I miss the times we had together. It is my hope that I shall be able to pass on to other athletes some of the inspiration, knowledge, encouragement, and concern which they gave so freely to me.

CHAPTER 4

Track Takes Precedence

Entering Boston University in the autumn of 1964 was an exciting prospect. I exercised hard for the first time for over a year – and felt awful. I could not run anywhere near 5 minutes for a mile – something I had done six years before while only 14. I wondered what was wrong with me. I was finding out how great the difference between normal health and true fitness. In the few days between finishing work and starting at the University, I started running. I could not start with a team and not be in some kind of shape. I have always been competitive. One does not necessarily race in training but I always expected to be with whoever was leading and for that I needed to be fit.

Training was fun. A group of reasonably good athletes gathered every afternoon and worked on Smith's 'cards'. During my first autumn term he outlined my weekly schedules. Smith was often with the cross-country team at Franklyn Park, but also frequently oversaw the rest of us training on the gravel dirt track around the football pitch. I started to understand the meaning of hard training: 30 × 100 metres with a 100 metre walk or jog back between each; a 7 mile run; 7 × 200 metres; for me, this was an incredible work load.

Coach Smith gave as he was given. If an athlete did not turn up for training, Billy would not chase him for long. He let each of us know what he wanted and expected that this would be done. If an athlete wanted to drop out, Billy would, likewise, drop interest in him. His approach was straightforward.

On one traumatic occasion for me, Billy subtly tempered this approach. At Christmas 1964, when I had only been with Billy for a few months, I went to a party. My co-captain of track at

Thayer Academy was getting married. He had concocted a fruit punch – with a punch. Only just before midnight did I discover just how spiked it had been. I had no trouble getting home but the next day I felt decidedly green. I had to meet Coach at the old squarish indoor cinder track at Harvard. The training session was four flat-out 300s. I could not back out of training so I dragged myself to the track and started jogging. Even this made me feel bad. Under Coach's watchful eye, I sweated through the warm-up. With great effort, in a slight haze, I started the first 300. It was run completely on memory. Each movement of every muscle had to be thought about. With a supreme effort of co-ordination, one was finished, and so was I. My face turned scarlet and I felt unbelievably hung over. I tottered around for five minutes and was then called on to start number two. Oh no, not already! 'Could I have two more minutes?' Ignominy combined with sickness is an awful feeling. Coach rapped, 'Just get it started'. Alcohol does not carry much oxygen to the muscles and I felt as though my blood stream had been replaced entirely by the previous night's punch. My muscles felt as though they were quite content to ferment in this new fluid. Very few of them were listening to the panic commands coming from my brain and, unfortunately, half my brain was either on strike or trying to reason with my stomach to remain in place.

The few rubbery muscles which had decided they had better try to run, moved me to the start line. With tremendous will power, I flew from the line with the other training athletes. It is no use starting a second repetition when you have totally failed to recover from the first. My knees rose but my thighs were not coming up very high; my lungs heaved but, for some reason, there was no oxygen in the air; my body floated along in a state of shock, attached to my cranium by only a few stringy fibres. It was as though I was on a 1-in-10 hill going up and the 300 metres felt as though it took just over half an hour to complete. The line crawled towards me. I crossed it, staggered towards the high jump pit and lay down. The smell of foam rubber enveloped me and added to my feeling of nausea. Every noise in the cage echoed in my head. I desperately wanted to sleep. Immobility was sporadically relieved by my efforts to lift my fifty-pound throbbing head from the foam sacks to see if the building had stopped moving.

Coach came over and simply asked me: 'David, do you think

you're getting enough to *eat*?' In my very ill state, I made my confession of stupidity, including the fact that I had not known the content of the previous evening's liquid refreshment. That made no difference – the whole point was that I could not train properly. I rarely drank but this session taught me how I would feel if I ever made a habit of it. Billy preached me no sermons; he just left me in no doubt about his attitudes. He knew what was *best* for me. I could take it or leave it. Take it and I would improve. It could be tough but I would improve. Leave it and he could not respect or really help me. To get to the top, the commitment has to be all or nothing. I resolved to choose the 'all'.

I soon found out that the more I did, the more I was capable of doing. My muscles gradually adjusted to the work required of them. This took time and on some occasions my body started fighting back. One reaction was leg cramps, The University offers duplicate courses at various times of the day with different professors. I scheduled to take one Economics course which ran from 6–9 p.m. on Wednesday evenings. I just had time to train, shower, and rapidly descend to the classroom a mile from the track.

One Wednesday I had a longer session than usual and, rather late, I hurried to the class. For some reason, a young and rather attractive nurse was attending this course and was seated not far from the door. The chair next to her was free so I headed towards her, sat down, smiled, quietly said 'hi' and crossed my legs. As I did so one of the all-time great cramps caught me high up on the inside of my crossed thighs. My legs flew out rigid and, with a stifled scream, I found myself half on my feet. She must have wondered if I had ruined myself – or, at the very least, *what* had sat down beside her. Scarlet from pain, I sat down muttering 'cramp' and smiled again. A track man sometimes has difficulty making a cool entrance.

My training started to pay dividends during the first indoor meetings. Competition was limited to other first year University students, but this still proved quite stimulating. I ran the 50 yards dash, 45 yards high hurdles and the anchor leg on the mile relay. I don't think I ever won the dash. I came very close a few times but my basic sprinting speed was never in world class. Once hurdles were thrown in my way, my whole mental outlook changed. I welcomed them as old friends. I didn't lose a hurdle race.

My first University competition was against Brown University in December 1964. I was extremely nervous before the relay and this helped me to run well. The time for my 440 stage was 50·9, three whole seconds faster than my best time at school. In a state of exhaustion, delight, and disbelief at my time, I told one of my relay team mates, Butch Donahue and Coach Smith that I honestly thought I'd never run faster. Neither of them treated the comment seriously. Butch insisted that this was just the start. I was less than convinced but a month later I was given a 50·4 split, and two weeks after that, 49·3. The latter was against my brother who was running for Dartmouth College, one of the Ivy League Universities. In the same match I clocked 7·4 seconds for the 60 yards high hurdles, equalling Mike Parker's British record.

As a result of this, I received a visit from a newspaper correspondent for the *Christian Science Monitor*. He asked about my connection with Fred Housden. In hasty nervousness or temporary confusion, I said, 'Yes, he's my high girdles coach.'

Freshman year came and went. So did I as an engineer. Having sat in a bank behind a desk, pushing a pencil, I could see that I was not moving into a very mobile occupation in my current area of endeavour. In fact, I thought I might wind up sitting behind a desk pushing a pencil for ever. That would be okay for part of the time but if I had any choice, I would like to have travel included in my future. I was not terribly excited by my studies and I was not enjoying the struggle. As my mathematics was quite strong, I enjoyed meeting people, international business sounded as if it might hold interesting possibilities. After some investigations, I made a transfer and during my second year found the studies more to my liking. A B.A. or B.Sc. in the U.S., is a four-year programme. There was still much work to be done, with the books, as well as on the track.

The cost of a University education is high and wanting to help to reduce the burden on my parents I applied for two scholarships. At Boston University there are no 'Athletic' scholarships but the athletics department may back an applicant who is applying for a need scholarship. Billy Smith did so on my behalf and this provided some help. The second type of scholarship was that of an assistant-in-training or resident assistant in the dormitory complex. At the West Campus there are three huge blocks, each with facilities for approximately 550 students. At that time two were for men and one for women. Every floor held fifty students and a resident assistant was responsible to the University administration for that floor. Usually the post was held by a graduate student or senior but as I had worked before going on to University, I was older than the average student and was given the opportunity to act in this role for my last three years.

At the beginning of second year, Coach moved me on to considerably more distance work. Although I did not know it, thoughts of 400 metres hurdles were already established in his mind.

In my first major indoor meeting on January 15th 1966, I ran second in the 600 yards in 71·5 seconds. As this was in the Knights of Columbus Invitational, I was delighted to have finished so well up. January 27th saw our University mile relay team win at the Melrose Games in New York. My anchor leg was a new personal best – 48·5. Two days later, in the B.A.A. Indoor meeting, I ran 5·6 seconds for the 45 yards high hurdles and again competed in a 600 (3¾ laps). I finished second behind Tommy Farrell (U.S. record holder) at 69·5, I set a new British and European record of 69·8, a time which still stands in 1976.

Competitions with the Boston University team came thick and fast and my season was extended through a series of Collegiate and National Championships. I managed to win the I.C.A.A.A.A. Championships 60 yards high hurdles in 7·2 seconds having set another new British record and equalled the European best of 7·1 in my semi-final. I thus qualified to run in the National Collegiate Championships. Perhaps I was too naïve to realize that I would not be expected to make the Final of the U.S. indoor nationals. However, running on many waves of adrenalin, I did make the Final. Certainly, on outdoor times, I was by far the slowest man in the field but it was not the time to think about that. I got away to a fairly good start, flew over the five barriers and leaned forward into the line. To my far left, Jerry Cerulla came past with his upper body parallel to the floor. The Judges took ten minutes to decide from the photo which of us had won. Jerry received the verdict. I, meanwhile, had learned a lesson on how to dip at a finish.

Back at Boston University, the students' newspaper read 'Hemery loses by a nose'. Having looked in the shaving mirror every morning for years and seeing the nature of my proboscis, I felt that their choice of words was, perhaps, misplaced.

The final meeting of the indoor season for me, took place in Hamilton, Ontario for the Canadian Indoor Nationals. There I won the 50 yards hurdles in 6·2 seconds having equalled the then world best with a time of 6·0 seconds in my heat. The occasion was marvellous in any case with all the pageantry of the annual event, but for me, what made the evening was a long discussion with Joe Healey of New York University. I gleaned as much information as I could about 400 metres hurdles, training programmes, stride pattern, and other general matters. My mind was fixed on the thought of making a good try at 400 metres hurdles. Unfortunately, a strained hamstring put a crimp in my training and thoughts of experimenting with the longer hurdles had to be postponed.

During the second year at University, I fell in love with Kathie. Perhaps one of the sad facts of life for an athlete is that athletics, if pursued to the highest level, must have top priority. My training, my weekends away on competition, and my job as a resident assistant quickly brought from her the comment that she was a track widow. Occasionally, however, I did have somebody to help me sort the mail when I was on desk duty. It was also extremely useful that the cafeteria happened to be in the girls' dormitory and no one can study and train *all* the time.

In my third year, however, Kathie moved dormitories, but so did Joanie, an art student who came to fill the void in my social life. After a few weeks of seeing each other, she sculptured my head. Her instructor said he liked the features but that the hair looked rather like a cabbage. Remembering my tousled mop, Joan's honest reply was, 'Well, that's the way it is'.

I remember one evening after dinner when the skies opened in a torrential downpour, Joanie leaped from the doorway, ran across the football field, and up the stadium steps. If there had been a full moon, I would seriously have questioned her sanity and I did this, in any case, when she returned looking half-drowned. Her sheer delight at the feeling of the heavy rain caused me to become more aware of my own feelings and sensations when running in all types of weather.

Between these two academic years, I had my first international competitive experience. In the summer of 1966, the Commonwealth Games were held in Kingston, Jamaica and I had to return to London to prove myself for a place on the team. The first meeting after my return was the Inter-Counties Championships held at the White City. Laurie Taitt and I crossed the line together in the 120 yards high hurdles, both timed in 14·3 seconds. I thereby gained selection for my first G.B. international, the match against the Russians.

It was also my first meeting with Vyacheslav Skomorokov who is both deaf and dumb. He leaves his blocks when he sees the others move. It is an incredible feat for someone with these handicaps to reach international class. I was to meet him on a number of subsequent occasions as he also moved up to the 400 metres hurdles winning the European title in 1969.

However, in this particular race, he was partnered by Anitoliy Mikhailov, the European high hurdles champion and bronze medallist in the 1964 Olympic high hurdles. I was fortunate enough to win this race and shortly thereafter received an invitation to visit Russia for a re-match. Walter Wilkinson, the miler, and I were the only two English athletes to be invited, and our team manager was Dr John Wrighton, who only a few years before had been the European 400 metres champion.

Arriving at the airport in Moscow, I felt extremely conspicuous with a large Union Jack on my blazer. Trying to remain unobtrusive – which is in any case difficult with my features – I casually leaned on a huge street map of Moscow while waiting in the bus queue. It must have been at least twelve feet long and six feet high.

A few seconds later, a funny crunching noise attracted my attention. It came from high above me to my right and as I turned my head to investigate, glass began to fall from the top making its way towards the pavement. As more and more fragments fell about me, every eye in the queue turned, had a look, and presumably thinking I was Britain's new secret weapon, backed themselves into the road. I couldn't move, because my back was holding up a sizeable amount of the glass which remained. Eventually I took a giant leap forward and was chased into the gutter by more piles of shattered glass. I started saying how terribly sorry I was, when a very old man shuffled towards me and, with a heavy accent, said, 'Long live Queen Victoria.' I smiled and thanked him but it was an embarrassing start to my international travel career and my opportunity to promote international understanding through sport.

On his home ground, Mikhailov turned the tables. I landed

badly over the final hurdle and was beaten on the run in, but I
did establish a personal best and equalled Mike Parker's national
record of 13·9.

Back in London the A.A.A. Championships followed this event
and at that time I wrote two versions of how I saw this race. The
first was as I recalled my run through 120 yards in the new
British national record of 14 seconds, the fastest time by a Briton
on home soil. The second was an attempt at imagery.

The first: 'Six men went to the line for the Final of the 1966
A.A.A. Championship 120 yards high hurdles. I was a few weeks
away from my 21st birthday. I had beaten Laurie Taitt in my
heat. He was on my left and would be swinging his lead arm away
from me. On his left was a South African. I smiled and wished
him good luck. I noticed his 6 feet 4 inches stature but that did
not bother me – it was the fact that he had run 13·8 which did.
However, I felt some comfort from his 14·6 heat time. No one
slows down that much. On my right was another South African
whose best was 14·0 seconds but, again, I tried to undermine the
threat of losing – after all, Mike Parker had said 'Sure, downhill in
Durban!' On the second South African's right was Mike Parker,
co-holder of the U.K. record. He could have been trouble but I
wished him good luck anyway and likewise to Andy Todd. I
sympathized with Andy, remembering my feeling of running in
the A.A.A. Senior Championships for the first time three years
before. Knowing that one is the slowest man in the field by three
yards was not comforting – even if you're only 18.

We went to our marks and waited an interminable time. On
'set', Parker rolled into view and we all stood up. Another look
down the track. Putting my hands on my knees, I saw the tops of
the hurdles appear to be a solid strip to run down. I tried to think
'speed' and with a couple of deep breaths, moved back to the
line; 'set' . . . the gun had fired and I had reacted before being
conscious of doing so. By the time my vision was up, it was time
to take the first hurdle, fifteen yards from the start. I was with
Taitt and a figure in white was to my right, probably Parker. Over
the first hurdle, I sailed a bit and forgot all about my arms. 'How
do I speed up?' . . . 'Stay on your toes.' – I was now at six –
'and try to spring'. I thought it was working but at the eighth I
caught my knee. Was it all over? Would Laurie come flying by?
No, he was still six inches behind in spite of my collision with

the hurdle. I had to pick up my pace again. Over the ninth, I concentrated on forward lean and away from ten, sprinted for the line. My hand felt the white cotton of the finishing tape trail between my first finger and thumb; what a wonderful relief.

The lid then came off the vacuum in my ears and the crowd was cheering loudly and Laurie laughing happily. He was delighted to have run so well from behind. He had equalled his personal best and was jubilant. He said, 'that was fast' and I replied, 'Yes, 14 flat, I think.' Then he and I walked back to the start together and I realized that it was drizzling, there was a little breeze, and I had enjoyed racing this man. I felt glad that he was happy even in defeat. I felt sorry for Mike who finished out of the top three for the first time for years. He told me he was worried about his place on the team for Jamaica. I was sure he would go. I thought all three of us would be in the Final there and very much hoped so. This was in fact to be.

A few days after this race I felt the need to write again of this struggle and competition. It came out as follows – 'A sea of hurdles! A metallic voice speaking through a microphone commanded us to move to a line. Six heavily breathing figures obeyed. Slowly they knelt. The weight of each body rested on one knee. The cinders bit in angry reply. Two arms fell to relieve the burden and the forms settled on their tripods. Each looked in front of himself before he knelt. An ocean was in view. White caps followed every trough, and each of these men had volunteered to pass through the billows. On the tripod the view was different. There was a tunnel under this ocean and the view was now clear. The distance did not look as great but the converging lines hypnotized. Each head drooped as if to receive a blow and until they finished, they would not know if it were to be knighthood or decapitation! Movement was nil until the voice again commanded motion. Then the figures half rose like animals ready to spring, a bow pulled taut at the back of each thigh.

A whip cracked and the animals sprang as if attacking this sea in force. A small spray was left in their wake as they flew over the first crest. One did not clear it completely and the force of the tide buffeted him. He was stunned but already numb, blindly flew on in pursuit of the others. The men were not only defying the sea but also trying to ignore it – to treat it with respect but with the least possible interest. Their object was to move through it faster than they, or anyone else, had ever done before. They battled on, not given time to think, every muscle moving – straining! Legs kicked out viciously: arms slashed the air but left no mark.

'They were treading water between the crests again, rising and falling as if swelled by the tide. After a few seconds, their unison of cadence changed and a couple were left to break the way. Finally, from the depths of the ocean, the leader emerged, hair tousled, clothes wet but skimming like an arrow on to the land. The tug of a small thin line brought him back to reality and time, which had been suspended, started again. The world stopped moving and the sounds of life came back to his ears. He had gone through a great mental and physical strain. If he had lost concentration, he could have drowned. Runners may temporarily disrupt the sea but it never changes and will always be there for any and all to try to overcome again and again. No one sails on the crest of the waves for long. Toll on spirit and body is too demanding but while one has a chance it is worth trying. Constant return to this challenge is inevitable – man, striving for the infinite.'

Jamaica, the Commonwealth Games venue, was humid and sticky, but I thoroughly enjoyed training in the early evening. The practice track was grass and the practice pool was within fifty yards. Following training, the British track boys headed for the water. My swimming and table tennis improved tremendously during my stay. Two days before the high hurdles Final, John Sherwood and I were hit with a virus infection. Unfortunately, John's heat for the 400 metres hurdles was on the day he went down. He was out of the Games. I was sick three or four times in the night and remained in pretty rotten condition for a couple of days. Although very shaky and feeling rather weak, for the high hurdle heats and semi-finals, I did qualify for the Final, and went back to bed. Mike Parker and Laurie Taitt had both reached the Final with me.

Our race was in the early evening under floodlights. Walking and jogging to the track, I felt clammy inside my tracksuit. I just kept thinking – it's only 14 seconds – you're not *that* weak. I didn't get a particularly good start and most of the way was screaming at myself to stay on my toes, move my arms and sprint. I only caught Mike Parker, the leader, between the eighth and ninth hurdles and was a few inches ahead by the tenth. I desperately

sprinted for the line and dipped less than a foot ahead of Mike.
Gold and silver for England. In third place was Raziq of Pakistan,
Murray of Jamaica was fourth, Laurie Taitt fifth, and the time
only 14·1 seconds.

Obviously, if I were going to place in the European Championships, I had to work on my speed. For three weeks I did nothing
but short sprints and sharpening up work. I felt I had never been
faster but I was to learn another lesson. While sprinting without
hurdles, my stride length increased a few inches. With hurdles
back in the way, I kept getting too close to them. In the semi-finals
at Budapest I came so close to hurdles seven, eight, and nine that
I had to put on the brakes before each to save myself from smash-
ing into them. My deceleration was just sufficient to allow four
people to go by in the last fifteen yards. I was out of the Final and
felt awful.

Mike Parker and Laurie Taitt suffered a similar fate in the
preliminaries. I do not think the following incident had anything
to do with our mutual demise. I had been invited by Martin
Winbolt Lewis's parents to join them in Budapest for a meal. The
last train back to the athletes' village left Budapest at 11 p.m. On
the same platform, Martin and I met Laurie and Mike and we all
shared a carriage as we headed back to our hotel. In the pitch
blackness, it was very difficult to recognize our station so after we
had been travelling for approximately half an hour, we started
searching for station names. One looked slightly familiar but someone spotted a large sign, which was not the name of our village, so
the two who had alighted from the train quickly jumped back on
board. The next station was definitely not familiar and we did not
stop again for another twenty minutes. At this point, we were sure
we must have passed our station. We showed our identification
cards to a train official, but he could not understand what we had
said before the train moved on again. When the chap finally
understood our plight, he told us to stay on the train for two more
stops when we would be at a large junction. From there, we could
make our way back. However at this 'large' junction, there was no
'phone, no taxi, no one who spoke English and very few people
who were still awake. The only suggestion made was that the next
train was the 5 a.m. local and we were shown a draughty waiting
room in which several bodies already lay on the wooden benches.
This would be no way to prepare for a race so Mike headed for the

only manned vehicle at the junction and with much gesticulation
ordered him to take us back to Godollo. With the help of the very
confused stationmaster, the persuasion of four determined
athletes and the assistance of a few English cigarettes from my
hurdling friends, the driver and stoker agreed to take us back. So
at one o'clock in the morning, six men stood in the cab of a flying
engine, for all we knew heading for the Baltic. Finally we arrived
and with great relief retired to our beds. The team official who
listened in disbelief to our tale may not have been as happy as
we were just to be back.

Following these Games, I returned to Boston University. My
lack of success in combining my full speed stride into the high
hurdle pattern convinced me that I would like to make a serious
attempt on the 400 metres hurdles in 1967. As I was still in fine
speed condition at the time of my return, I badgered Billy Smith
into allowing me a trial run over five 400 metres hurdles to see if
thirteen strides between the hurdles were possible. The experiment
was a resounding success and I contentedly headed into my first
ever competitive cross-country season.

Cross-country is one of those activities in which the individual
is left for prolonged periods with little to think about, bar the
nagging question of whether or not to slow down or even stop and
walk, just for a little while. On long runs I have often had a crav-
ing for chocolate and inevitably a drink. One can try various ways
of delaying these agonies. It can be a pleasant distraction to simply
view the countryside as it passes one by. This, however, is not
conducive to fast times. Another tactic is to settle into a stride and
breathing rhythm which may not be broken unless confronted by
wild animals, unfriendly terrain, or chronic internal disorders
any of which may warrant special detours, or pace modification.

Unfortunately no matter what one does, the human system
creates noises in enough parts of the body eventually to force the
mind to listen. Then the struggle begins:

Q : Shall I ease off? *A :* You can't you'll be passed . . . again.
Q : Who will know? *A :* The coach – he's holding a watch.
Q : Am I really tired? *A :* What a bloody foolish question.
Q : Was it something I ate, the sleep missed; or am I really not
cut out for this sort of thing? *A :* Probably all of these.
Q : Am I going to die soon? *A :* No such luck.

The only truly rewarding feeling is finishing and finding out that your time for the course is a few seconds faster than your previous effort. My only previous cross-country experience was at the age of 11 in Endsleigh School, Colchester. All male pupils ran in the schools $2\frac{1}{2}$ mile cross-country race. The youngest in the school started first, with 2 seconds head start for every month of age, that is, 24 seconds for each year. My time of 16 minutes 57 seconds brought me home first, just 5 seconds ahead of the school's 17-year-old athletics captain.

I was never very good at distance running, but it was going to be fun trying again now ten years later. Training was progressing reasonably but with only one race completed I headed for sick bay. At the end of October, I caught a cold but decided to train anyway. It proved to be a bad decision. A session of half-miles into strong icy wind on the tow path by the frozen Charles River provided a perfect formula for developing pneumonia. With a temperature of 103 degrees, I entered the University infirmary and came out just in time to sit the end of term exams.

From this very low state, I had practically no time to beat myself into shape for the indoor season. Following a night of little sleep due to cramming for an exam, I wrote my reactions to a very tough session. It may appear slightly incoherent but it is virtually as it was written while on desk duty the same evening . . . a stream of consciousness.

'December 1st, 1966: Four hours sleep last night – but I must practice. Desk duty at 5 o'clock so no time to lie down: better go and start. No one in the locker room. Oh yes, the coach gets here late today – well, I'll do a good hurdle session first. It's cold, well below freezing, and I'm stiff from working fast and hard to get back in shape – only a week to the first University indoor athletics meeting. I know I'm well behind the others on conditioning. I'll do a lot of exercises. I jog a half – I'm still stiff. Try to remember last year's exercise sheet. You're out of shape – work! Forty sit ups – the last ten hurt – stretch: thirty push ups and every one I work but I'm warming up. Five runs over three high hurdles. Take off sweatpants for greater freedom. The air feels cold on my legs – but I'm warm. I think . . . Not much chance of a pull. Five faster runs over the three;

then four, flat out, from a crouch start. Smith arrived during
these last runs so I'd better stop. What's the work-out? Back-
to-back quarters, one lap walk between; three sets, the quarters
in 59·0. It sounds bad but I hope I'm okay for 59s. The board
track is 160 yards round, so 2¾ laps to the quarter. I'm to do
them with Butch Donahue. (New England schoolboy half-
mile champion also in his third year at University.) At least it's
not Hoss who is in great stamina-shape right now. I lead off
and Butch says "move it up". I do and manage to stride through
it. It must have been 58 or a bit under; time 59·6. My speed
timing is off – the effort was 58 or even better. I walk the lap;
at least I'm feeling recovered enough to get it started. The only
place I feel I'm fading is the last 70 yards but I do feel the
fading. I'm not in shape – 60·4. I'm quite tight but I know I can
make one more set. Coach makes a quick trip to his office. I
have a good recovery time. But when he comes back I am still
late to start. Butch is stripping down and we're starting. Butch
pushes the pace a little as I see his shadow swing wide on the
upper turn; I try to hold pace but still fade slightly for a 59·0.
It had felt like 57·5. Damn: walk a lap – slowly after moderate
delay with hands on knees. This fourth one will hurt: my legs
are getting tired. "Come on, Hemery, let's get this going."
I move it out at a moderate pace; run the first bend well,
2¼ to go; 2 to go and it's not too easy: 1½ to go and I'm fighting
a bit. The last lap will be rough. I can feel Butch is fading too
but it's not terribly fast; I must try to hold some sort of pace.
Only half a lap left but I'm down on my heels and very tired;
my thighs are stiffening; 5 yards to go and I drop effort. A step
after the line, I'm dead stopped, and down on to my knees.
The backs of my thighs and my seat hurt. I get up but every
couple of steps stop, hands on knees. My hands are so cold, it
takes a great effort not to let them slip off. Gripping I rock
back and forth a couple of times, then stagger on, trying to
move my dead legs. The backs of my thighs feel as if they've
been hit across the middle by a steel bar. All I can do is groan
out my breath. I don't want anyone to hear so I groggily stumble
east – past the high jump pit. My head is throbbing and I
feel sick. I turn back and find the football line machine, hang
my elbows on that and make an effort to lift each knee repeatedly,
to try to work the muscles again. Slowly life comes back and

I try to jog. Twenty yards, then a walk and back, hands on
knees but I know I'll be able to run at least one more moderate
quarter-mile. The coach allows a little more time than necessary
then urges us to begin the last set. It's 4.45 and I ought to be
on the desk at 5.00. I'm going to be late. I'd better get this
over with but I don't feel as if I can do a set – "If I do it in
just under 58 can I just run a quarter?" "Do the set." "What
pace?" "The same . . . get it started." I'm on the line – "ready
Butch" and we're off and I know it'll be a long $2\frac{3}{4}$ laps. I have
little life, or stride-length; some guys are watching on the far
turn – for a second my mind's off the distance and I move
round the bend quite well; – $1\frac{3}{4}$ to go and Butch is up and
pushing my pace slightly. I fight to keep the lead and there's
one lap to go. You can always make one lap but I can hear
Butch is right on me. No let up – but I'm on my heels and
very tired, but running right through to the finish; no idea of
the time. I'm hands on knees every two steps with long pauses;
how can I make another? 59·8 – hell – why did Butch push the
2nd to last. He's quarter of a lap ahead walking. I walk very
slowly on. By half-way round, Butch is back to the start. His
recovery is so much better than mine right now. Will the coach
let him go? I know if I hurry at all I'll never make the last one.
I don't know if I'm going to tie up. My stomach and heart feel
rotten. The field lights blaze on but it doesn't wake me up at
all. I'm in a daze. I come 20 yards from the line and rest,
hands on knees again and coach clears his throat. I come
close to the line and the coach says all I have to do is start and
I ask if we can slow it down at all. "Just the same" he nods,
and I start and coach yells at the head of the turn, "Don't let
Hemery slow it down". I realize I can put out more and there's
$2\frac{1}{4}$ laps to go. The guys are again on the far turn; I'm numb
and, with $1\frac{3}{4}$ to go, Butch moves to my shoulder. I still have
life but he's making a prolonged effort to pass. Into the turn
and all the way round but I'm still ahead out of the turn fighting
hard – then relax a bit and feel a drop in pace. Into the turn
running fairly well. It's a long straight and Butch is close. I'm
on my heels again, but have a moderate pace heavy-footed
stride; I've been told to relax my upper body. Now only a
straight and on to the middle of the bend. Butch is there
and I'm not giving in. Only 60 yards to go – hang on – into the

turn and finished. I crumple to my knees, my head near my knees and the track; my thighs hurt and my seat hurts and I involuntarily rock forward and back, almost like writhing. Coach says, "Are you going to vote for me as the good guy of the year?" I'm hurting too much to laugh or make a come-back. I'm blank to all but my physical feelings. I get to my feet and totter forward only conscious that I'm late for the desk and I hurt, my head aches and is throbbing. I have no strength to put on my sweats. I lean on the hurdles where they are. I feel sick and I'm wishing I could sleep but I have five hours on the desk and I'm late. I grip my sweats and drag them towards the coach who tells me to jog tomorrow. That sounds great. I trudge toward the locker room and inside the building entrance I sit to take off my shoes. My fingers hurt from the cold, my head hurts even more if I bend forward. I'm panting faster than a dog. I sip some water and meet a couple of guys who say I look terrible. In the locker room I sit on the bench to get my locker open. It's 5.07 and I'm late. I slide my long johns off and reach for my towel while still seated, but I can't move, my head weighs heavy. My brain is pounding, throbbing and my face is scarlet. I drift, stagger, to the shower. More comments on how awful I look. I can smile and wise-crack. I'm recovering, but slowly. It takes me till 5.23 to reach the desk. The dormitory resident Director is there but sees the shape I'm in and understands why I'm late, thank God; he stays a few minutes. I feel a fool; when I take a deep breath it comes out in a shuddering vibration. My hands are shaking and my eyes are misty and bloodshot but I'm recovering. The Director hears why I have to kill myself; only a week to the Brown University match and I've only trained four days so far – but what a four days. 11.30 p.m. I'm fully recovered; not even stiff, but I need to sleep.'

Eight weeks later, I ran within a step of Martin McGrady of the U.S. 69·9 to 70·0 seconds over 600 yards and left Bill Bruckel (Cornell) and Bill Crothers (Canada) in third and fourth place. McGrady was the world record holder for this distance. Crothers was an Olympic 800 metres silver medallist in Tokyo Olympic 800 metres. I had a number of encounters with McGrady none of which proved successful. The Olympic 400 metres champion, Lee Evans, was to have similar problems in the years to follow. McGrady was supreme on the boards.

In the New York Knights of Columbus meeting on February 3rd, I was invited to run 500 yards. Jim Kemp burned out from the start and, leading all the way, won in 56·2. I came very close to catching Vince Matthews on the line – both of us being given the same time, 56·7. Five years later, Vince was to win the gold medal for the 400 metres in the Munich Olympics.

Occasionally, I was the only athlete invited from Boston University and Billy Smith joined me as my Coach. Once, while walking through one airport a *fabulous*-looking stewardess took my breath away. She half-smiled and I think I practically stopped in my tracks. Billy, also a connoisseur of the fairer sex, saw my shell-shocked state and laughed. My heartfelt comment about ships that pass in the night became a much-repeated phrase on future trips.

On February 11th 1967 I competed in my first hurdle race since Budapest. The venue was an indoor cinder track at Tufts University and to provide more space, the 45 yard hurdles were run diagonally. At the finish line in the far right-hand lane, there was a sudden dip in the ground before the edge of the circular track. In a desperate lean to ensure first place, my outstretched left leg found the depression and my hamstring tore like a piece of rope. I shot up into the air and stopped within two paces. The size of the thud inside my leg and the dull ache over a large area at the top of my left hamstring told me that quite a sizeable number of fibres had separated. I was taken round to the medical room. Lying on my stomach having ice packs applied to the torn area, I leaned forward and picked up some dumb-bells, jesting with the coach that I could at least now concentrate on my arm strength. But seriously, I wondered whether I would ever compete again.

A few hours later, my leg began to discolour, the back of the thigh turning purple and black. Over a period of months the Boston University trainer, Tony Dougall, worked with me to get my leg back into shape. For the first ten days, I did arm exercises only and limped my way to classes. During the second week, I started very gradual jogging and, two-and-a-half weeks after the injury, I tried striding through a quarter-mile. Although the pace was only just under 60 seconds, the fibres had not knit sufficiently and, with some pain, I re-strained the area. Almost as regular as clockwork, I attempted to come back every two weeks with the

same disastrous results, a dull thud arising in the same place any
time I moved from a jog into a stride.

Towards the latter part of April, it seemed as though the problem
was beaten as I was able to cope with 5 × 400 metres averaging
about 57 seconds and a couple of half-miles at around 2 minutes
4·0 seconds. These were not great times but gave me confidence
that my leg would now stand up to some work. However, there is a
great difference between an even-paced quarter-mile and the
demands put on a thigh running at full speed over high hurdles.

At the New England championships on May 20th, with my leg
still heavily strapped, I ran a painful second place in the 120 yards
hurdles (14·6). Billy took my arm and walked me away from the
crowd, telling me to forget about competition and even training
for the rest of the summer. It was time to give my leg injury,
which had become chronic, a very long recovery period. From late
August, we could start a concerted drive towards Mexico.

My emotions were very mixed. I was relieved at the thought of
having the pressure removed but also frustrated and disappointed
that this season, so badly needed for experimenting in the 400
metres hurdles, had come to nothing. Strong resolution and
determination had to be fostered during the summer as I nursed
my hamstring and thought about the dedication required for the
year ahead. As I was missing the summer competition in Europe,
I returned to the National Shawmut Bank's computing department for summer work. Throughout that long summer one question nagged interminably. Would I ever again be top class?

CHAPTER 5

The Road to Mexico

In late August, while the summer sun still held some warmth, I started jogging on the Duxbury sand bar known as Powder Point. Running in eighteen inches of water had three merits: I learned to lift my knees, and therefore the jar on my hamstrings, was carefully cushioned on landing, and perhaps most important, my speed was restricted. The last thing I wanted was to tear another muscle. The week prior to the start of my final year at Boston University I ran miles across the sands. Confidence in the knowledge that my leg had healed grew steadily. It was great to be running again. I accelerated into full-blooded strides for hundreds of yards along the water's edge. I had to do all in my power to insure against any further muscle pulls. The only way to do this was to build up the strength of the area around the injury. I purchased two metal plates (weight boots) which could be strapped to my shoes. Weights were attached, a total of 17 pounds for each foot. Daily exercise began.

My programme for the year was heavy. I had to study hard to make sure of receiving a good degree in June. I still held dormitory responsibilities and was a member of the Judicial Committee. I was also on the committee which ran the student activities at Trinity Church in the City of Boston and I wanted to run. The last was my top priority because contained in that simple desire was the aim to run the 400 metres hurdles in the Olympics at Mexico City. This desire consumed me for the following thirteen months. With all my other commitments, my social life suffered. Over the summer, Joanie and I had drifted apart. Consequently, I determined that, although I would go out, I would begin no serious relationship with any girl during my senior year.

From the first week in September 1967, I started pre-breakfast runs. The only way of getting myself out was to set out my kit before I went to sleep. As soon as the alarm rang, my feet hit the floor and I felt for my clothes. My eyes scarcely opened until I had been running for five minutes. Four to five miles were covered at a good stride with a number of other track men living at West Campus. Afternoon sessions varied – some days on the track, others in the park, as well as some weight training sessions. Cross-country was, for me, a means to an end. I accepted it, tolerated it, and enjoyed watching the improvement in my time. I sympathized and half-identified with the fellow who, on finishing last, made the following statement: 'I was running along, all alone, in my underwear, with acorns hitting me on the head and cold rain rolling down my neck and all I could think was, "what the heck am I doing here?"'

During the two-month cross-country season, my time over the five mile course dropped by a minute-and-a-half, while my weight dropped by 10 pounds, and my esteem for one of our University newspaper reporters dropped into oblivion! I was visited for an interview which ran along the following lines: 'When's your next race?' . . . 'Tomorrow.' 'Are you going to win?' . . . 'Of course not. I'm a sprinter not a cross-country runner.' 'What are you doing in training?' 'Hills, dunes, weights, track work, and up to ten mile runs.' 'Well, if you can run ten miles, why aren't you going to win tomorrow?' 'That is like suggesting Bob Hayes should be able to win the Marathon just because he can currently move faster than anyone else over 100 metres.' I waited for 'Bob who?' to come out but, instead, he decided to return to ask some more questions at 7 p.m. In the meantime, I wrote out a few bits about my past at Boston University and aims for the 1968 season which I handed to the fellow when he came back. He said 'Oh *thank* you, that's the easiest interview I've ever had . . . do you always give these out?' I felt like saying 'No, only to idiots!'

With great faith my parents decided during November 1967 that the following October, they would take the family to the Mexico Olympics. I only hoped I would make the team.

From the middle of December, indoor competitions came nearly every weekend. It took me quite a while to change gear. Five-minute-mile pace and sub-50 seconds quarter-mile pace, are poles apart. For most indoor meetings the coach asked me to run the 600 yards and anchor the mile relay. Occasionally, 1,000 yards was thrown in for good measure. Sprint hurdles were omitted to avoid a repeat of the 1966 pull. This was a courageous decision on the part of Coach Smith as he was forgoing easy points in all our dual meetings. Straight from the country, my first 600 yards was 75 seconds, two weeks later, I ran 72·7, but it took me two more months to reach 70·2 – a time which had come relatively easily during the previous two years.

This was not a happy season for me. Because of the volume of stamina training, I lacked sharpness and, as a consequence, found myself being boxed in during early races. A bad cold eliminated nearly a week of training. Then in the Greater Boston Championships, my shoe ripped right along the seam of the sole. My bare foot came out on to the cinders on the corners and I was forced to stop. Finally, to culminate the chapter of accidents, I was tripped from behind while leading, near the finish of my heat in the National Collegiates Indoor Championships. Next day the title went to a man I had beaten by more than five yards in the Eastern Championships the week before.

Following that meeting, I looked towards the outdoor season with burning determination. All the way from Detroit to Boston, I pestered the coach about how we should proceed from there, mid-March to Mexico in mid-October. I was impatient and resolute. In the plane, apart from mapping out my time aims, I wrote myself the following, to be read and re-read during the build up to the 1968 Games:

(1) Something has to give . . . and it's not going to be me.
(2) Second place is as bad as no place. *Only* firsts count.
(3) The difference between first and second is very small.
(4) You have to work hard.
(5) You have to think positively.
(6) Run one race at a time.
(7) You won't and mustn't forget – pulled muscles, torn shoes, and being tripped in the National Collegiate Championships.
(8) Be strong, *mentally, morally,* and *physically.* Attack *now*!

My jaw was set and so was my will. The outdoor season would be different. On March 19th, three days after returning from Detroit, I pulled up with a slight strain in my right thigh. The soreness lasted through the final indoor meeting but following a few days' rest between sessions, I was able to train properly again. This settled one thing in Billy's mind; I would not do any full-speed short sprints on the flat. All my work under 440 yards would be over hurdles. He reasoned that this was a built-in control. He proved to be right. I had no more hamstring trouble that year.

In the first outdoor meeting on April 10th, I ran 14·0 for the 120 yards high hurdles and equalled my personal best in the 440 yards hurdles – 51·8 secs. On April 19th, I reduced this to 50·7, a new British record. The next day I led off the sprint medley relay with 46·9 seconds. The winter's training was paying off. Week by week, I trimmed off a tenth of a second from my best. April 26th, 50·7 again; May 1st, 50·6, and 13·9 for the highs. May 25th 50·5, June 1st 50·4. On May 25th at the New England Championships I was kept busy. In the morning, 120 yards hurdles heats, 14·4; 440 yards hurdles heats 52·8. After lunch, 120 yards hurdles semi-final 14·1, followed by the 120 yards hurdle Final in 13·9, the Final of the 440 yards hurdles in 50·5, and an anchor leg in the relay, 47·7. May 26th was a day off.

On June 11th, Coach Smith and I – again travelling as the only two from Boston University – headed for the National Collegiates being held in Berkeley, California. Apart from Ron Whitney, almost all the other top contenders for the U.S. Olympic Team would be taking part. The Californian climate is superb and Billy and I drove in a hired car along the spectacular coastline. I love the sea and felt at home taking a short jog by the water's edge. As in the Olympics, the 400 metres hurdle heats, semi-finals, and Finals were held on consecutive days. I won my heat in 50·9 and watched the other rounds to assess the opposition. It was strange, half of me did not want to know, the other half would have died of curiosity and fear of the unknown if I had not watched.

Information came in that I was drawn in lane one for the semi-final. Few hurdlers enjoy this lane – the bend is more sharp and the kerb on the inside edge is usually raised. The big advantage, though, is that one can see all the opposition. I won my semi-final in 50·2. Geoff Vanderstock won the other in 50·3. The Final would be close. I was worried. Again I was drawn in lane one. Once given it, there is nothing one can do about it so I mentally ordered a pair of blinkers. I found it quite hard going but I set a personal best of 49·8 in winning the Final. Vanderstock was eight yards behind in third place, Big Bob Gittens was second in 50·5. I was pleased but knew that there were still four months to the Olympic Games and 49·8 probably wouldn't win a place.

Unbeaten and in first-class condition, Billy Smith handed me on to Fred Housden. On June 18th, I flew back to London. It was good to see Fred again and we immediately began work on the technical problem of my 'change down'. When sprinting at full speed, I take thirteen strides between the intermediate hurdles. No one can run at full speed for long, no matter how fit he is. As a consequence of slowing down one's stride length becomes shorter. In order to clear a hurdle fast and smothly, an athlete must take off an exact distance from the barrier. All this means is that at some point in the race an extra stride or two must go in between each set of hurdles. One extra, and the hurdler must take off from his other leg; two extra and he will be leaping from the same leg. My hurdling was less than adequate from my left leg. I, therefore, had to go for two extra, that is, fifteen strides, from about half way through the race. Fred and I worked on angles of approach, running wide round the second bend, and shortening strides in the middle part between hurdles. This work continued and improvements were devised until I left for Mexico City.

The A.A.A. Championships were held at the White City on July 12th and 13th. The Queen honoured us by attending and presenting the trophies. The results of the 440 yards hurdles determined the places on the U.K. Olympic Team for Mexico:

(1)	David Hemery	50·2 (49·8 at 400 metres)
(2)	John Sherwood	50·9
(3)	John Cooper	51·3
(4)	Ralph Mann (U.S.A.)	52·1
(5)	Andy Todd	52·6

I was to see more of the young fourth place finisher four years later.

Once qualified, I moved away from track work. I had been training hard for ten months and still had three months to go. My training was moved into parks and on to hills. Sprinting 300 metres up hill sent my pulse rate sky high! On waking my pulse rate is about 48–52 per minute. On separate hill training days, at the end of the third and fourth runs, my pulse reached 64 and 63 beats in 15 seconds, a rate of 256 and 252 a minute. I am told that the most blood is pumped at about 180 beats to the minute and faster than that the heart cannot act efficiently, as the volume pushed through to oxygenate the muscles is reduced. It did take time to recover between each of the runs! I have no idea of the volume being pumped through my system at that time but I never cease to be amazed by the extent to which the human body can be driven and successfully adapt itself.

At the end of July, I caught a 'flu virus which put me off training for eight days. This worried me. How much would it detract from my overall fitness? Evidently, one does not lose all of ten months training in a week. On August 24th, I ran a personal best 400 metres hurdles of 49·6 at Crystal Palace. I was disturbed, though; only two-tenths of a second improvement over my time of two months before in Berkeley. I wrote a worried letter to Billy Smith who immediately reminded me that August 24th was not October 15th (the date of the Olympic Final), and he urged me not to give in to thoughts of pure speed work. He suggested I should stay on the hills a while longer.

In the meantime, the Americans were setting the track at South Lake Tahoe alight with their times in the U.S. Olympic Trials. Geoff Vanderstock ran an unofficial world record of 48·8 seconds, not ratified because he wore the illegal brush spikes. Bob Gittens and Ron Witney followed him in, running 49·0 and 49·1. Geoff was quoted as saying that the U.S.A. would finish 1, 2, and 3 in Mexico City and if they could take five, they would finish in the first five places. As he had finished eight yards behind me in Berkeley, I found this rather unbelievable. The apparent arrogance of the statement toughened my determination. I still thought that in a one-to-one race, I could beat him.

On September 9th, one week before leaving for Mexico, I was elated by the results of a training session at Crystal Palace. I had put up twelve hurdles, the eleventh came just before the 400 metres finish line, and the twelfth several yards before the start, out in lane six. Quarter-miler Colin Campbell ran in the lane inside me, without hurdles, for pacing assistance. The aim was to go through 400 metres in about 50.8 then run on to 500 yards, where a track suit top was placed. I hit the 11th hurdle and knocked it down but still passed 400 metres in 49·8, completing the 500 yards in 58·3. This was only 0·7 outside the official world record for 400 metres hurdles, and was accomplished during a training run over eleven hurdles, on the way to 500 yards. I could not believe it. A time of 48·8–48·9 in Mexico City did not seem out of range. I really felt in with a strong chance of winning. I was excited but also apprehensive about the unknowns – I had never raced Whitney and who knows what is going to happen in an Olympic Final, if I could reach it, although, somehow, I was quietly confident about that.

Mexico City is built on a plateau 7,500 feet above sea level. There is 25 per cent less air resistance and 6 per cent less oxygen. The latter, to say the least, makes it a problematic place to hold the Olympic Games. For all those who had to compete for longer than two minutes, i.e. events in which oxygen taken in during the event was used, it provided an abnormal situation and was in *no* sense a competition equivalent to one at sea level. Men born at altitude have heart and lung systems adapted to perform at 7,500 feet almost as the rest of us perform at sea level. I could remember failing in an attempt to run all the way home from school in Colorado Springs when I was 12. That was only two miles at 6,000 feet but I felt strangely breathless and weak. Now, in the light of research carried out at Mexico City, I understood why I had felt that way.

All members of the British Team running in the 400 metres and longer distances were given the opportunity of going to Mexico four weeks before the start of the Games in order to acclimatize. Our arrival there was prefaced by the most hair-raising electrical storm. Clouds were lit up on either side of the plane. Temporarily, my thoughts were distracted from the purpose of our visit. Mexico is a country of contrasts: mountains and plains, wealth and poverty, fear and fiesta. Now, she was host to the Games where individuals' hopes and dreams were to be fulfilled or dashed. As everyone knows, the Olympics have an aura – something special, romantic, and challenging. Mexico is a colourful, emotional country and the people were extremely proud to be staging the Games. They were eager to welcome all foreigners, whether athletes or spectators. Their uninhibited enthusiasm and desire to please created an infectious fiesta-like atmosphere.

Apart from this, however, there is something intangible, high-spirited, and emotional in a gathering of the world's greatest athletes. Men and women, representatives of some 120 countries, had made incredible sacrifices and worked intensely hard to reach the top of their particular sport and now they had won the opportunity to compete against each other. All the years of thinking about reaching the Olympic Games had now to be channelled into achieving maximum efforts.

It took me ten days to feel completely settled as, in addition to the altitude change, we had to adjust to the time shift. After this initial period, the sore throats and the panting after walking up a flight of stairs were gone.

The Duke of Edinburgh came out to see the Games and spent one lunch time with the team. He attempted to encourage the Britons to think positively concerning the altitude problem. After all, he had played polo there the year before and had not felt a thing, to which long jumper Lynn Davies replied, 'with respect, Sir, did you ask the horse?'

Five restaurant areas provided catering for the various national blocks in self-service restaurants. Unfortunately for the restaurant manager and for the Swiss, Austrians, New Zealanders, and anyone else who followed the British athletes and hockey players, the menu being offered became unrecognizable. The reason for this was that the board, posted at shoulder height, had individual white plastic letters pressed on to a black felt board. And in their own version of the game of scrabble, the British squad amused themselves making changes in the available choices. It started quite innocuously with Cream of Tomato Soup becoming Scream of Tomato and Mushroom Soup reading Mashroom Soap. Matters progressed as the days wore on. Cold Buffet on various days read Cold Feet, Cold Tuffet, or Cold Muffet; Roast Turkey with Cranberry Jelly became Roast Turk with Cranberry Belly; Desserts changed to Desert Boots; Hot Vegetables stooped to Hot Getables; and Roast Chicken Livers descended to Raped Chicken Lovers. As matters rapidly became out of hand, a new official was appointed – chief menu watcher!

In the British squad, we also discovered some very talented musicians. John Whetton who was to finish fifth in the 1,500 metres, and win the European championships in 1969, is a good clarinettist: Clive Longe, our big decathlete friend from Guiana, was hot on the trombone, and Welshman Howard Davies accompanied on the piano. The International Centre rocked to the strains of the Beatles' 'Hey Jude' which was topping the charts at the time. This Centre provided draughts and chess sets, table tennis, and soft drinks.

Conversation was sometimes quite limited in the village which contained such a variety of languages. Also, at this time, few wanted to talk along the common interest lines of training. Inner tensions became increasingly apparent as the days wore on. Looking around the restaurant at meal times, one could see some athletes sitting, trance-like, not touching their food for minutes on end. Outside, it was impossible to go anywhere without seeing someone practising some sport or other.

The most trying time of all was at the practice tracks. Day after day, one was forced into close proximity with one's rivals. All of them looked very good, powerful, strong, and fast. I tried to keep my mind on what I had been asked to do. I found that the altitude caused me to reduce the number of repetitions I had planned. It was taking me twice as long as at sea level to recover from flat-out efforts. However, the reduced work-load, shorter sprints, and rarefied atmosphere, provided the speed my legs had been lacking. For a couple of training sessions, John Cooper kindly oriented his training around mine. On one occasion, we ran 2 × 200 metres; he ran on the flat, I over the first half of the 400 metres hurdles course. The first run was as fast as I could make it; time 22·2 seconds. The second was fast but relaxed, perhaps at about race pace. Time 22·8 seconds. Cooper enthused, timer and National Coach John le Masurier was impressed, and I was delighted. I felt totally under control and full of power.

Only a couple of times in my life have I felt in such condition that my mind and body worked almost as one. This was one of those times. My limbs reacted as my mind was thinking: *total control, which resulted in absolute freedom.* Instead of forcing and working my legs, they responded with the speed and in the motions that were being asked of them.

There were more spectators at the practice track than coaches and athletes. One day I was visited by a representative of a sports shoe company. If I just wore their spikes, they would make it worth my while. I was not intending to change my shoes but asked what they meant. I was told I could receive in the region of £1,000.

For a student, that sum sounded astronomical, but one thing stood in the way – my conscience. I knew myself. If I switched, all I would have thought about would have been my shoes. I would have been on my marks in the Final with my mind at my feet rather than on the race. Also, although I would welcome changes in amateur rules, while they were as they were, I would stay inside them. The decision was made – I was there to run. Nevertheless, those figures danced in my head for months to come.

I tried to bring my thoughts to bear on the real task at hand. Waiting can be one of the worst agonies of life, and man seems to spend much of his time in this role. Prior to the Final, I must have run the race more than a hundred times in my head. Every evening, after dinner, I walked down the bank from the restaurant to the practice track and, in the semi-darkness, walked round the track burning into my mind the pace-judgment, stride-pattern, and effort-distribution which would be necessary at each part of the track. Occasionally, I was joined by my friend, Martin Winbolt Lewis, 400 metres runner and team mate in the 4 × 400 metres relay. We would talk over our relay chances and exchange general thoughts about athletics and life. In the dormitory, I had my training diary for the past year. I studied the work that had been completed in the effort to get to Mexico. On separate sheets of paper, I drew pictures of the track and wrote down exactly what I wanted to do in the heats, semi-final, and Final. Every time I thought of those, my pulse rate rose and after a few minutes, I would lie back on the bed with a mild case of nervous exhaustion.

The testing time of my life had come. I tried hard to remain calm and to tell myself that, after all, this was just another athletics meeting. This was difficult, if not impossible. The intensive training of the previous thirteen months and the gradual preparation throughout my twenty-four years were coming to a climax. Everything, was to be compressed into less than fifty seconds. Uncertain thoughts again flickered across my mind, what was I doing there? The pressure was building up as the days before the competition ran out. Telegrams arrived from well-wishers, letters from friends, and special morale-boosters from my coaches, Fred Housden who sat in London, and Billy Smith in Boston.

An air-letter arrived from Fred, then aged 78. In his usual fashion, it was in rhyme:

October 8th 1968:
> When others quail
> And Geoff looks pale
> And Ronnie's* – knees are quaking,
> Then is the time
> To heed my rhyme
> And take to record making.
> You know the point
> Where out of joint
> Your chopping may go wonky,
> So don't lose speed
> But keep the lead,
> Each clearance honky-tonky!
>
> Come off H. ten
> With speed and then
> Sprint like the devil's own,
> If you'd be great,
> Just *concentrate*
> And be the first man home.
> Then, should you win the highest stand,
> It won't be good, it will be grand!
>
> All the best, Fred.'

On October 6th 1968, nine days before the final, Billy's air letter read:

'Time is approaching ... everything is okay – speed seems fine on the basis of those runs over six hurdles. 24 seconds for the final 220 of that 1 min. 18 secs. 600 metres indicates the speed stamina is great. The heat should shake out the cobwebs if there are any ... everything seems great ... just don't get too excited – but you've been through tough situations before. Just another 13 steps – 15 steps good run ... you'll run 48·1 or 48·2 and no one else can do that ... the others are 1000 hills and sand dunes behind you ... and it is too late to catch up ... Your preparation has been perfect ... It seems like we've been through and over this whole thing one hundred times – but we know we're right ... might be the only two people

---

* Geoff Vanderstock and Ron Whitney, ranked one and two in the world prior to the Olympics for the 400 metres hurdles.

in the world to know it but it is true ... smile! as ever, Bill.'

I read and re-read these positive, encouraging letters. The belief the coaches and others had in me, I had to *feel*. I had to convince myself over and over again. I *was* in with a good chance. Lying on my bed while reading, I found myself frequently dozing off to sleep, probably trying to avoid the pressure – the thought of the fearful and threatening competition in which I was committed to taking part.

All athletes enjoy running or they would not run. To an extent, they must enjoy competing but, in all honesty, as the days progressed, the desire to take part dwindled with every passing minute. Food became tasteless and my appetite started to decline. It was, in many ways, a relief to get on with the first run.

October 13th: The Heats. I travelled to the stadium by bus and felt very much alone. It was now all left up to me. I knew that I had sufficient strength to qualify at least for the semi-final but if an athlete gives 100 per cent during a qualifying run, it may not be possible for him to come up with this again in a semi-final and a Final. The concentration and effort of producing such a high level of performance can drain the soul out of a competitor.

The plan for the heat was merely to try to qualify with the minimal expenditure of effort. But I had to run fast enough to maintain thirteen between hurdles. I had to decide at which hurdle I would consciously change my stride-length so that I would be able to clear the next barrier without stutter-stepping in front of the hurdle. I decided to change to a fifteen-strides pattern at 200 metres, and from there to the finish try to relax as much as possible.

In my heat, Italy's Roberto Frinolli, European champion, set off extremely fast. As four men were to qualify, I let him go and concentrated on getting to 200 metres as pre-planned, in 24·2 seconds. Managing to hit it exactly right, I then relaxed and held my stride, trying to remain as aware as possible where the rest of the field were. What rather surprised me was that no one was coming past, so, on landing over the tenth and final hurdle, I took a quick look to my right. To my horror, three fast-moving athletes were clearing the final barrier less than six feet behind me! Adrenalin flew through my system and I very nearly caught

Frinolli in my frantic sprint for the tape. My time of 50·3 was unimportant. One round was safely out of the way but I'd scared myself and my family to pieces.

In the other heats, John Sherwood came through with 50·2 and John Cooper in 51·4. Ron Whitney, the favourite in this event, ran an astonishing time of 49·0, bettering the old world record by a tenth of a second as he edged out Schubert of West Germany who set a new European best of 49·1. These times were eight to ten yards faster than John Sherwood and I were running. John was impressed because Whitney didn't lie down or even put his hands on his knees. He just waved to the crowd, picked up his kit and strode out of the Stadium. Having lived in the U.S. for a number of years, I took it that Ron had pulled off a masterly psyche-out performance. However I guessed that if he were really capable of breaking a world record *so* easily, then surely he would have done so previously during his many years of active competition. I wondered at what stage this effort would hit him like a sledge hammer. While passing on my knowledge of some of America's psyche-out routines to John Sherwood, I'm sure I was trying just as hard to convince myself and keep my own fears under control. My aim was still to get through to the Final with the least possible output of energy. There would be no sense in trying to prove how fast I could run in the semi-final if this would be detrimental to my performance in the Final. However, the semi-final would not be easy. I could just as easily leave so much in reserve as to never be able to reach the Final. When down to the last sixteen in the world, all competitors are more on a par, all having worked extremely hard and all having a fair degree of competitive experience. In the second semi-final, I was drawn in lane six with Ron Whitney and West German Gerhard Hennige in the two lanes outside me. My 200 metres target was lowered to 23·5 which meant putting in effort which would closely resemble that required in the Final.

October 14th: The Semi-Finals. As in the heat, the half-way time came exactly as planned. Then around the second bend, I tried to move my legs faster in the change of stride pattern. So far so good. Now coast. Just maintain pace for the last 120 metres. Whitney and Hennige started to move away gradually 80 metres from home and although I had a little in reserve I let them go, keeping my left eye open to make sure I was not passed by anybody else. On my left, a great struggle was going on between Garry Knoke of Australia and Skomorokov of Russia. Both crossed the line in 49·6 seconds, the Soviet athlete getting home *just* ahead. In the other semi-final, Frinolli and Vanderstock clocked 49·2. John Sherwood set a Commonwealth best of 49·3 and Schubert of West Germany completed the final eight, also being credited with 49·3.

Once the other afternoon races were completed, I joined my family outside the stadium. A slight feeling of elation welled within me as I realized that I had, in fact, reached the Olympic Final and had still not run flat out. But again the interminable questioning, 'Were the others in the same boat? How much did they have in reserve for the next day's final?' However this was not a time to fret. It comes down to you, your own lane, and your own pace judgment. Tension and elation were inseparably fused.

October 15th: The Final. *Finally, it was the day*, a day in which one race was to prove a changing point in my life. Although I had a good night's sleep, nerves were getting to me and I was only able to nibble at my lunch.

The finalists had personal bests within 0·8 seconds of each other. The field was drawn in the following lane order:

(1) Rainer Schubert (W. Germany)   49·1
(2) Gerhard Hennige (W. Germany)   49·1
(3) Geoff Vanderstock (U.S.A.)   48·8
(4) Roberto Frinolli (Italy)   49·2
(5) Vyacheslav Skomorokov (U.S.S.R.) 49·6
(6) David Hemery (G.B.)   49·3
(7) Ron Whitney (U.S.A.)   49·0
(8) John Sherwood (G.B.)   49·3

I would have been terribly disappointed if I had not won and perhaps that accounted for the degree of my terror and uncertainty before the race. Training had been geared for a peak on this day. The excitement of Olympic competition made my adrenalin flow and I ran scared for 48·1 seconds. Reaching a mental and physical peak and having everything go right cannot happen very often in one's lifetime. On October 15th, 1968, it happened for me. From the gun, I raced for the gold. Throughout the run, I held the fear of being passed. I followed my race plan to the letter. A few days

AN ANALYSIS OF THE 1968 MEXICO OLYMPIC 400 METRES HURDLES FINAL
Taken from B.B.C.-T.V. Video Tapes by David Hemery

Hurdle	Lane 1 Schubert (W. Germany) Secs.	Place	Lane 2 Hennige (W. Germany) Secs.	Place	Lane 3 Vanderstock (U.S.A.) Secs.	Place	Lane 4 Frinolli (Italy) Secs.	Place	Lane 5 Skomorokhov (U.S.S.R.) Secs.	Place	Lane 6 Hemery (G.B.) Secs.	Place	Lane 7 Whitney (U.S.A.) Secs.	Place	Lane 8 Sherwood (G.B.) Secs.	Place
1	6·0	3	6·0	3	5·9	2	5·8	1	6·1	7	6·0	3	6·1	7	6·0	3
2	9·8 (3·8)	3	9·9 (3·9)	6	9·7 (3·8)	1	9·7 (3·9)	1	9·9 (3·8)	6	9·8 (3·8)	3	10·3 (4·2)	8	9·8 (3·8)	3
3	13·7 (3·9)	3	13·8 (3·9)	6	13·8 (4·1)	6	13·6 (3·9)	1	13·7 (3·8)	3	13·6 (3·8)	1	14·2 (3·9)	8	13·7 (3·9)	3
4	17·7 (4·0)	4	17·8 (4·0)	6	17·8 (4·0)	6	17·5 (3·9)	1	17·5 (3·8)	3	17·5 (3·9)	1	18·2 (4·0)	8	17·7 (4·0)	4
5	21·8 (4·1)	4	21·9 (4·1)	7	21·8 (4·0)	4	21·5 (4·0)	1	21·5 (4·0)	1	21·5 (4·0)	1	22·4 (4·2)	8	21·8 (4·1)	4
1st 200	23·7		23·8		23·7		23·4		23·4		23·3		24·3		23·7	
6	25·9 (4·1)	4	26·1 (4·2)	7	25·9 (4·1)	4	25·6 (4·1)	2	25·6 (4·1)	2	25·4 (3·9)	1	26·6 (4·2)	8	26·0 (4·2)	6
7	30·3 (4·4)	6	30·5 (4·4)	7	30·2 (4·3)	4	29·9 (4·3)	2	30·0 (4·4)	3	29·6 (4·2)	1	30·8 (4·2)	8	30·2 (4·2)	4
8	34·8 (4·5)	6	34·9 (4·4)	7	34·5 (4·3)	3	34·3 (4·4)	2	34·6 (4·6)	4	33·9 (4·3)	1	35·1 (4·3)	8	34·7 (4·5)	5
9	39·3 (4·5)	5	39·4 (4·5)	6	38·9 (4·4)	2	38·9 (4·6)	2	39·2 (4·6)	4	38·3 (4·4)	1	39·5 (4·4)	8	39·4 (4·7)	6
10	44·0 (4·7)	6	44·0 (4·6)	6	43·5 (4·6)	2	43·9 (5·0)	4	43·8 (4·6)	3	42·8 (4·5)	1	44·0 (4·5)	6	43·9 (4·5)	4
Run in	5·2		5·0		5·5		6·2		5·3		5·3		5·2		5·1	
Finish	49·2	7	49·0	2	49·0	4	50·1	8	49·1	5	48·1	1	49·2	6		3
2nd 200	25·5		25·2		25·3		26·7		25·7		24·8		24·9		25·3	
Difference between 1st and 2nd 200	1·8		1·4		1·6		3·3		2·3		1·5		0·6		1·6	

before I had thought 48·4 might be possible but rain and a cool evening, made me doubt that I would run as fast as that. The fact that Whitney started so cautiously in the lane outside me made it appear that I took a very early lead. In fact, Frinolli, Skomorokov and I were joint leaders at hurdle five, just before half-way, Schubert, Vanderstock and Sherwood, were together. Hennige at this point was seventh and Whitney four yards behind him! Around the second bend, Fred Housden's work was put to the test. From the fifth hurdle, to the finish, I gained at least a yard on the field between and over each hurdle. Frinolli held second place at the eighth hurdle but his strength and stamina failed him and he faded badly in the last 80 metres finishing eighth. Vanderstock ran strongly up to the final hurdle but could not hold his place over the remaining 45 metres. In contrast, Sherwood and Hennige ran for their lives from the last hurdle to the tape. Both dipped well and each came up with a medal. Skomorokov ran well throughout and, although fifth, was only three feet away from a silver medal. Whitney and Schubert were both given the same time of 49·2 seconds in sixth and seventh places. Two-tenths of a second, a distance of about five feet, separated six men from second to seventh place!

At the *Track and Field News* Banquet following the event, the two Americans were asked to comment on their performances. Vanderstock said that, for him, the race was eight yards in front. He had been out for gold, and it was not there. Whitney said, simply, '48·1 is impossible the way I run'. He hurdles from his left foot only and must, therefore, run wide around both bends because if a runner's trailing leg does not go over the hurdle, he may be disqualified. Also, Whitney was a big man, chopping for each of the ten hurdles, as he had not learned to take thirteen strides between. When I saw him across the cafeteria the following day, I felt really bad and embarrassed for him in that I had taken what he so badly wanted. However, I would not have changed places for anything.

Not since 1924 had Britain won two medals in the same Olympic event. When you consider that Sherwood won an Olympic bronze, followed by a European silver in 1969 and Commonwealth gold 1970; Andy Todd, won a European bronze in 1969; John Cooper an Olympic silver in 1964, and Alan Pascoe a Commonwealth and European gold in 1974, Britain must rival America as the strongest nation in the world in the 400 metres hurdles. I once jested with John Sherwood that it was a pity that there is no 4 × 400 metres hurdles relay event as I would have backed Britain to win.

Mexico City was good for the Sherwoods, as John's wife, Sheila, won a silver medal in the long jump the day before John won his bronze. John and Sheila are a fine couple and I have greatly enjoyed travelling with them.

John and I could not get too carried away with celebrations as we were both in the relay squad competing four days later. However, during these intervening days, I went to watch some other athletic events. Lynn Davies was competing in the long jump so my brother and I found our way to the pit side. We were near the front, at ground level, a very poor angle for perspective. However, one man made this word irrelevant. Bob Beaman, a fellow described as having 10-feet legs with a head on top, came down the runway for his first jump. Everything was going well for him, warm weather, a 2-metre following wind (the exact legal limit), and his 9·6 100-yard speed. He hit the take-off board exactly right. Legs and body rose high into the air; his feet were held so high that a head-on photograph showed them on either side of his face. The world record stood at 27 feet 5 inches. Usually, jump records are nudged up an inch, or even a centimetre, at a time Beaman missed out 28 feet completely. The new calibrated viewing device fixed in cement could not be adjusted enough to bring his point of landing into view. The old-fashioned steel tape had to be found and, finally, the scoreboard flashed up 8·90 metres, 29 feet $2\frac{1}{2}$ inches. Truly an extraordinary jump. It will take a few more years before another athlete comes along with equal or greater talent and puts it all together as Bob did in that unique jump.

While officials were measuring Bob's leap, the skies clouded and a cold rain started. The spell was broken as were the spirits of most of the other competitors. How *could* anyone follow such a performance?

Lynn Davies came in for some criticism following these games. He had tried to explain how he had wanted to leave the stadium. Lynn was a supreme competitor and his only aim was gold. In this case, it was taken from him before he had a single chance. It was like having the opportunity to fight Muhammad Ali for the heavyweight crown with him given the first swing and you not even allowed to cover up. In fact, Lynn did jump and jumped well, but for him, the fire for gold had been extinguished.

Another character at Mexico was gold medallist Amos Biwott of Kenya. In the steeplechase, he jumped high from the top of the water jump barrier and landed on the same foot as he had put on the barrier. That means he hopped over the twelve-feet water. While all the others were getting wet, Biwott sailed through space and went on his way dry-footed. One rumour ventured that he had not wanted to wet his new shoes! The Australian 800 metres winner, Ralph Doubell, jokingly suggested that perhaps Amos thought there was no mixed bathing. The truth is that the method is fast and effective, even if demanding and relatively untried. I was to benefit from its use in the Superstars contest in 1973.

Britain's 4 × 400 metres relay effort was an example of 'so near and yet so far'. Martin Winbolt Lewis, Colin Campbell, myself, and John Sherwood ran legs of 45·6, 44·9, 44·6, and 45·5, which should have been good enough for a medal. All of us gave everything we had and ended up in exhaustion. This feeling can be relieved by the knowledge of having gained a medal but we had nothing tangible to show for our efforts. Although our endeavours set a new United Kingdom record they were just not good enough, but a great deal can be gained through losing, sometimes perhaps even more than winning.

The track and field competition finished before most of the other sports, and many athletes, myself included, headed for a couple of days to Acapulco. The water temperature there was 80° F (27° C) and I spent twenty-four of the forty-eight hours in the water. At times the surf was up enough to do some body surfing. If the waves are caught right, the whole upper half of the body can be suspended in space while the wave is carrying one to the shore. The only problem in attempting this by moonlight was not being able to see the beach. A good wave sent me on to dry land at some speed, stomach first. One or two such rapid applications of sand and pebbles and I started cutting down on the long trips!

Back to Mexico City and for the closing ceremony, I was given the honour of carrying the British flag. This I did with a great sense of pleasure, not the least of which was the opportunity of dissolving into the crowd afterwards, still in possession of one huge Union Jack. As the flag bearers solemnly left the track, flag poles aloft, I, in the midst, had one hand on the pole while with the other I untied the cords holding the flag. Outside, the Mexican official was handed a lovely white staff and I headed into the gloom of night with a bulging blazer. This trophy accompanied me home and now has a stand of its own in my parents' home.

The Games village rapidly became a ghost town and I joined the general exodus to the airport. I could not have imagined what was in store for me when I returned. The pressure of Olympic competition ended, but the post-Olympic social engagements still to face were a different type of pressure, one which I had yet to experience.

CHAPTER 6

Moving into the Goldfish Bowl

On my return from Mexico I discovered what a sport-mad country Britain is. The Olympics had been broadcast live, often in the middle of the night and half the country was watching, and falling asleep at work the next day. I was told on my return that my race had been repeated over twenty times, so that even people who were not sports fans recognized me in the street. My features are unusual which mean that people sometimes stare at me anyway but this was unbelievable. I found out what movie stars and pop idols go through. My feelings were mixed. On the one hand it was nice; everyone likes to be liked, and recognized at times. I had won for them and it was good to have their warm acknowledgments. On the other hand I felt I was living in a goldfish bowl. It was not possible to go anywhere without being stopped for a comment or an autograph or just being stared at. There was no longer privacy in public places. At least the greetings were friendly, or amusing. I discovered how avidly Italian restaurant owners follow athletics. Bottles of wine frequently arrived at my table, compliments of the management.

I was interested to discover that television awareness of a person breaks down many of the inhibitions which people have in talking to a stranger. I suppose it's because I was no longer a stranger to them. People felt they knew me. Once in a while that placed me in an embarrassing situation. Someone might come up with warm greetings and say 'Hello David' and I wouldn't know if we had met before or not, and wasn't sure if I was supposed to recognize them. T.V. does another strange thing to people. When they see someone they recognize they act as if the T.V. screen were still there and the individual unable to hear them. Quite often I have had people standing with their finger pointing in my face and saying in a loud voice to their friend, 'Look it's David Hemery'. I usually just smile and say something like, 'Hi! I gather you follow sport.'

I was always sensitive and often would rather not have had the ballyhoo. I had also been somewhat shy and being thrust into a speech-making role in front of hundreds of people was not initially an enjoyable task. For the six weeks after my return from the Games invitations flooded in, by mail, phone and in person. Interviews, luncheons, talks, prize-givings, cocktail receptions, dinners, dances; for charities, religions, commercial companies, athletic organizations, and friends. I tried never to say no and this resulted in two to five appointments every day for this period. Sometimes I was on the go for sixteen hours a day. I don't really enjoy too many of these dos but I felt that a lot of people and companies support Britain's sportsmen and I wanted to say thank you, to give back what I could to them.

One task which wasn't too painful for me and some other Olympians was attending an informal buffet at the Sportsman Club, to host the Miss World candidates before their contest. There I met Penny Plummer. If you believe in love at first sight, that's what I had. She was truly lovely, not only attractive but refreshingly natural. She had, in fact, only entered the Miss Australia contest to see the big city, Canberra. Not having lived in Britain for a few years I needed partners for the dinner functions I was attending in my new social whirl and she accepted my invitation to join me at a couple of engagements.

Unfortunately for me she was crowned Miss World 1968 a day or two later. I received the news with very mixed feelings. I was happy for her and for the opportunities which it might open to her, on the other hand she was going to be thrust on to a similar treadmill to mine and I thought she might like it even less than I did. I was also sorry that any chance I had of getting to know her would never get off the ground as the contest sponsers, Mecca, would have a full schedule of public appearances all mapped out. I philosophically tried to put my heart back in place.

I then had one of my few encounters of pressmen out for a story. Somehow they had heard that I had asked Penny out. While at an informal athletics gathering I think I had said how nice I thought she was and hoped to see her again. Some athletics correspondents present must have picked that up and passed it to their social columnists so that prior to any outings with me, Penny was bombarded and hounded at her hotel with questions of our engagement or marriage. Penny had a boyfriend in a law school in Australia. His parents had relatives in Ireland and had given Penny some financial help to go to see them. Obviously this sort of press story put her into an impossible situation. By coincidence I had been asked to escort whoever became Miss World to dinner the night after the contest. So that reporters could not make anything more of 'us' we were seated on opposite sides of the table. Even so I could see reporters I recognized hovering around, so I excused myself from the table and went to take the bull by the horns. I told them that there was no story. I thought Penny was extremely nice, but she had a boyfriend and that was that. To my disgust the front page of the *Sunday Express* the next day had a lovely picture of Penny with a headline reading 'Miss World shatters Dave Hemery's hopes'. Under the article was a picture of me at the end of a 400 metres hurdles race looking rather shattered. The article went on to state that I had asked Mecca if I could be her official 'boyfriend'. (At that time I needed an official 'girlfriend'!) This kind of fabrication, in order to sell papers, made me considerably wary of what I said to non-athletic correspondents.

I thought the matter of Penny had ended but evidently it had really been played up in Australia. A few weeks after the Miss World contest the B.B.C.-T.V. Sports Review of the Year took place. I had the honour of becoming the Sportsview Personality of 1968, and Australia's great distance runner, Ron Clarke, presented me with the award. Apart from his congratulations, he asked, 'what's this about you and Miss Australia?' He went on to relate that the publicity had been so widespread with rumours of our romance, that a private aeroplane company had flown Penny's boyfriend to England, to rescue her from me! People should not believe everything they read.

In early December the summer and winter Olympic teams were invited to a buffet luncheon at Buckingham Palace. This was also the time when the film of the Royal Family was being made. It couldn't have been terribly pleasant for them constantly to have microphones, cameras and lights around inside their home, in addition to the constant requirements of duty outside. I felt it was extremely considerate when, following a chat with Princess Anne, she apologized for the fact that the camera men had hounded us during our conversation. Only three years later Princess Anne was to win the B.B.C. Sports Personality award for her outstanding equestrian efforts.

The Olympic medal winners were introduced to all the members of the Royal Family who were present. I was impressed by the genuine friendship and human interest which they expressed. With the number of functions and meetings which they must attend it would be understandable if they had lost some personal warmth. Their role is unenviable and demanding and I was pleased to feel a touch of informality and naturalness. Princess Margaret went as far as to say that the excitement of the race (shown at 2 a.m. in Britain) had nearly caused her to jump out of bed.

The social functions varied tremendously. One that was quite formal provided me with a good deal of embarrassment. I was living from day to day and almost running between appointments. Usually the invitations requested or expected me to bring a partner. This occasion was the Centenary Dinner of the Press Association. It seemed as if thousands were present including the Prime Minister, the Archbishop of Canterbury, and other highly notable personages. I arrived with a young lady, bringing the total female population into double figures. The others were there in their own right as editors of National Magazines, Head of the Red Cross, Lady M.P.s, etc. The host at our round table graciously inserted one extra place.

It was quite refreshing at times to meet people who were totally out of touch with sport. I had been asked to speech day at a London school and was introduced to the local Lady Mayoress. She looked at my blazer pocket and said, 'How do you do? I think I've seen you compete. Don't you swim?' A gentleman from the school quickly interjected, 'This is David Hemery. He won the 400 metres hurdles in the last Olympic Games.' The Lady Mayoress, half to him and half to me, said, 'Really, what clever boys you have at this school.'

A quite opposite sort of reaction comes from some people for whom television makes an individual slightly inhuman. For example, when in a launderette, I've been asked, 'What are *you* doing in here?' as if my clothes never became dirty.

Appearing on television is considered an achievement in itself to many youngsters. A small boy comments, 'I've seen you on television' and his friends will often say, 'Ooh, have you really been on tele? What's it like?' I asked them if they've ever had their photo taken, because it's just like that, except that instead of you seeing the picture, on a piece of paper, the picture comes out on the screens in people's homes.

Perhaps the greatest cause of pressure, following the Games was the fact that I hadn't learned how to say no. I didn't particularly want to say no to anyone who asked for anything, from giving an autograph to addressing a large gathering, but at times I probably should have. By the end of six weeks of signing and talking and responding to questions, sixteen hours a day, I was delighted at the prospect of a trip home to Boston for Christmas. This was accomplished by accepting an invitation to run in an indoor meeting in Los Angeles and breaking my journey halfway. Unfortunately my whirl of engagements had left no time for training and my leg muscles were far from being in top shape. In the sixty yards hurdles my mind demanded full speed and a hamstring painfully gave way under the strain.

Back in Boston it was good to slow down. A day or two after arriving I was stuck in a traffic jam. The fellow whose car window was adjacent to mine turned his head lazily in my direction, then back to the road. The fact that his head didn't snap back to take a clarifying look, made me appreciate my anonymity on that side of the pond.

In spite of my break at home I had no hope of catching up on my correspondence. I wanted to reply to everyone who had sent telegrams and letters but the influx was too great to keep pace. It was not until 1971 that I finally sought secretarial assistance from an able and charming lady named Mrs Green. During the year she helped me to answer over two thousand letters. With many requests from around the world for autographed photographs, this proved expensive. I had not kept a count of the number of letters I had answered by hand in the first two years. Despite these efforts a few of the post-Mexico letters were being answered at the time of the Munich Games!

One air letter which I received during that Christmas in Boston came from California. Apart from his return address on the cover the letter was completely blank. I had some fun with my brother and sisters composing the following:

'Dear Jim,

I don't know how to reply to you. Your letter leaves me without words. I have heard of men of few words but don't you think this is carrying it to an excess? However, I wish everyone could express all their thoughts so concisely.

Seriously, though, your letter carried more impact than any I received during the summer. If you have had any more thoughts on the subject, I would love to hear from you again. I shall, of course, keep the personal nature of your letter confidential. Eagerly awaiting your next envelope.

You're 's confused as I am,
David Hemery.'

I'm thankful to relate that he took my reply in the humorous spirit in which it was written and explained that he had merely intended to ask for an autograph.

Signing autographs can become a problem. It is subject to the snowball effect. If there is a queue of people at an athletics match or school function and one person decides to ask for autographs for brothers and sisters, then the next person will usually do the same. If I was signing "To Jonathan, best wishes, David Hemery', with half a dozen different names for each hunter the task became prodigious. However, if there were only a few hunters they might get a drawing of my stick man, going over a hurdle. I usually had to explain what it was, as I had been asked on several occasions what the Chinese symbol meant! My art talent is well hidden.

One day while waiting in Ewell, Surrey, I was standing at the entrance of a new and very exquisite civic centre. Some school boys asked for my autograph and while I was signing, two more boys arrived and asked 'Are you the architect then?' Recognition or lack of it has provided other incidents which I found amusing. During the opening of the K. G. Sports shop near Crystal Palace, two nippers entered. One grabbed his friend's arm and said, 'Look over there, it's David Hemery'. His friend turned and looking straight at me and said 'Where?' I was duly pointed out again and at that the friend came back with, 'Oh, which team does he play for?'

While sitting waiting for the start of a film in London, someone behind me said, 'You know, the fellow in front looks like David Hemery.' I half-turned, half-smiled to let them say hello if they wanted to, when he added, 'Ah no, it's not'.

One little old lady must have taken a closer look because she confidently told my sister, 'You know, I've seen him on telly. He looks just like his face.'

Mistaken name identity has also been frequent. While waiting for a friend an old boy passed by me and stopped a few strides farther on. Coming back he gave me a knowing smile and said, 'You're 'im, ain't yer? You're Dick Emery.' This talented comedian's name is the one most often wrongly attributed to me. However it has not stopped there. At a party in Oxford a young girl came up and said, 'No offence, but someone told me that David Hemery was coming, I thought they meant David Hemmings. I think *he's* super.'

A similar disappointment was suffered by a young fellow who told me at a cocktail party, 'You know last night I was doing some work on Ernest Hemingway and when someone said that David Hemery would be here today, I thought it was his son David and I was so thrilled. But it's nice to meet you, anyway.'

I am never offended by this sort of mistaken identity or of people never having heard of me. I am often more concerned at the way all of us too often identify people only with labels. 'Oh, you're David Hemery, the hurdler.' This can be nice to hear as it is a point of contact, recognition and acceptance. However I sometimes wonder whether that places me in a box marked Athlete. We inevitably place labels on everything to help us to categorize and simplify life, but I am extremely aware of the need to see people as more than just their labels, Black, White, Communist, Catholic, Banker, or Miner. Each person must be allowed to be themselves, a unique individual, of many parts.

I had an early lesson in not allowing athletic success to get out of perspective. During my first Commonwealth Games, in Kingston, Jamaica in 1966, Neil Duggan, a 3 minute 56·8 seconds miler and I walked some way to take a close look at the grounds of a fabulous home on the coast. A lovely old English lady of about 80 standing all of 4 feet 8 inches tall came to the top of her steps and smiled benignly on us. We told her that we were over for the Games and talked with her about England. Neil then told her that I had just won the gold medal for the 120 yards high hurdles. She turned to me and said, 'What a clever little boy'. Neil was rather embarrassed on my behalf, but having just turned 22 I thought it amusing and rather delightful.

The Mexico aftermath culminated in a visit to Buckingham Palace to receive an M.B.E. for services to the Country through sport. I firmly believe in the value of international exchange through sport, so was honoured by this recognition.

It may be a natural mistake but a lot of people equate being well known with being well off. Well, let me assure the reader that in the case of most amateur sportsmen you see on your television, this is not the case. Right after Mexico I probably could have found a pretty well-paid job in public relations, as a representative for a large company. But that wasn't what I wanted. My head was turned towards education. I believed that audio and visual aids were an extremely important part of mass education for the future. The key word is *aid*. The teacher is released for closer personal contact with the students. To find a job in this area was not easy. For a couple of months I lived close to the bread line. At this time Rank Audio Visual were looking into the possible uses of audio and visual aids for pupils and students of all ages in education and industry. I joined the small research group in early 1969. One investigatory trip took me to Oxford's Department of Education. Part of the Diploma of Education course there centred on educational uses of audio and visual aids. The ready market for Rank was on the industrial side. My interests lay in education, with the students.

I thought seriously about my future. For me the choice was not difficult, if I could gain admission to further studies I would centre in education rather than industry. I made application and in due course was accepted for the following October.

Every day after work during my months with Rank, I travelled to Crystal Palace for training. Training? What on earth for? Where do you go after a world record and an Olympic gold medal?

CHAPTER 7

A New Challenge

Many people could not understand my desire to continue after reaching the summit in athletics. I was 24 and that, to me, was young. I enjoyed athletics and all it entailed, the striving, the excitement, the travel, the friends, the zest for improvement and development. The sport is simple in its aims, the people as diverse and complex as you'll find, but there is an intangible bond between them, an understanding among travellers, a mutual respect for each other's efforts. I didn't want to throw this away. I had gained much from athletics but there was so much more to learn. How fast could I run the high hurdles? Couldn't I spend some time learning how to master a few more events, ones I had dabbled at in school and at university? The decathlon had always fascinated me. This would be a new step into the sport, a new challenge.

Challenge is part of the enticement of sport. Man against the elements and himself, men pitted against men. 'Against' is an inappropriate word. It is truly a contest but it's in the same direction. One person gets farther than another in distance or in time. Much of the reward is in the trying. A decathlon is ten events rolled into one. Athletes compete in three flat races (100 metres, 400 metres, and 1,500 metres), one hurdle race (110 metres high hurdles), three throws (shot, discus, and javelin), and three jumps (high jump, long jump, and pole vault). Where you finish in each event is not terribly important, as points are won according to how close you are to the world best. A scale has been established in which all the world records, at the top of the table score between 1,000 and 1,200 points. Filbert Bayi, for example, running 3 minutes 31 seconds for 1,500 metres would score top points, whereas someone taking over 6 minutes would not score more than one or two points. Therefore, the object is to attain a consistently competent level in all events.

In order to do well in the throws, I had to gain strength and weight. I asked how to do this without drugs. I was told to lift hard, three days every week and to eat more than usual. For two months I worked with weights, sometimes half-squatting with three times my body weight. I could feel my upper body gaining power, but some people burn up so much energy inside that they remain thin. I am one of those people. At the end of the two months I had lost two pounds.

Relatively undaunted, I went to work with the heavy implements. In the short circle I discovered that my double-jointed fingers lay back to cushion half the thrust I gave it. A throw of 38 feet 6 inches wasn't going to set Geoff Capes's heart beating any faster. On the javelin runway, my dislocated shoulders came into play and in all three throws I never mastered anchoring my left foot and working my body over that leg as I threw. My problems didn't end there. I had never pole vaulted in my life. To begin with, observers of my efforts thought I might go higher without the pole. The difficulty for me was twofold. One was to do with hurdling, the other, fear of heights. The take-off point for hurdles, is seven to eight feet from the hurdle, the take-off for the pole vault is twelve to thirteen feet from the box. My mind and legs ran somewhere in between the two. I'd hold the pole high, run down towards the pit and, once it hit the box, I would push it out high in front of me. If you do it right and swing your legs at the sky, theoretically the pole comes up to the vertical with you on the end of it . . . theoretically. Well, if you run in to within eight feet of the box, you can swing yourself right into the pole on the way up. I had a blue hip bone several times to prove this point. If you only graze the pole as you pass, it is possible to swing out parallel with the ground. Once I was told that I looked as if I was practising levitation as I came over the bar, feet first, on my back parallel to the ground. To get anywhere near 10 feet with this style probably deserves special mention in the *Guinness Book of Records*.

Needless to say I ran and jumped with desperate fervour to make up for the deficits sustained in the vault and throws. Using the Fosbury flop technique I managed to go over my own height at 6 feet 2 inches and came close to 24 feet in the long jump.

With reasonable speed and stamina for the running events I went into battle. The British record at that time was 7,392 points by Clive Longe. In my first attempt I amassed 6,500 and gained a place on the British squad competing in Holland. The Belgian competitors made it a twelve-man triangular match.

The weather was sunny and warm. I set seven personal bests and scored just under 7,000 points. Without Peter Gabbett or Clive Longe competing, I was the first Briton home, finishing third behind the number-one man from the other two countries, De Hertoge of Belgium and Ed Norlander of the Netherlands. The 1969 European Championships qualifying standard was 7,400 points and there were no more meets on Tartan tracks or in warm conditions. I had greatly enjoyed my brief encounter with this two-day classic event. It had a charm and challenge all its own. But if I was to compete in Athens, I had to concentrate on hurdling. A rapid injection of speed work in my training might tune me up for the high hurdles in time.

Back as a high hurdler I was selected to take part in the G.B. versus Czechoslovakia match in Brno. It is an occasion which will live in every competitor's memory for years to come, but not necessarily for the competition there. We had all been warned not to drink the water and this presented problems as the temperature was in the 90s. At the end of the second day of the competition, the athletes were asked to hurry from the track to the hotel so that they could change before heading into the country for a traditional banquet following the match. There was no time to find liquid refreshment for the relief of our dehydration problems. Coaches left the hotel promptly and drove for what seemed like hours into the country. Parched throats and empty stomachs reminded us how far we were from civilization.

Eventually, on arrival, we were greeted by traditionally costumed folk dancers outside a large chalet. Following their dance, local inhabitants formed an avenue down which we had to pass in order to get into the building. At the door, we were all required to take a drink of Slivovich, the local speciality of pear wine, before entering. The drink is akin to pure alcohol. Those who entered first were unable to warn those following, as they had no voices with which to call. The banquet was held in the loft of the building. The main course, which turned out to be the only course, was a small mixed salad. White wine was the only plentiful item. It was, in fact, the only drink available. Waiters, also in traditional costume, patrolled the tables topping up the glasses. The wine was in containers of a very unusual shape, made of glass, the main volume being carried on the waiter's back with a glass funnel coming down over the shoulders to arm's length. The end of the funnel was kept closed by one finger which, when removed, caused the wine to flow. Most of the athletes were so dehydrated that their bodies acted like sponges and it was not long before a few disappeared off the back of their benches heading rapidly for the floor.

No further food being available, the majority of both teams went to the outdoor dance floor. With the team management enjoying the festivities to the full, whirling round the dance floor with swinging athletes, I was reminded of Nero fiddling while Rome burned. The night air hastened the effect of so much alcohol in the blood and bodies started falling into the surrounding bushes. Within an hour, most of the teams were badly under the weather or completely out cold.

The various states of inebriation produced some comic spectacles in what rapidly appeared to resemble a battle-ground. Some became melancholy, crying over tender memories. One of the very large athletes became invincible and tried to put his fist through an immense barrel. The Management felt he ought to be knocked cold before he did himself or anyone else any damage. No one volunteered to perform this operation and, fortunately, the wine did it for us. The problem then arose as to how many more or less sober people were available to carry his and other carcasses to the waiting buses.

It was amusing to watch one old and staid athlete doing gymnastic turns using the steel posts inside one of the buses. Another a glass-eyed, frail figure starting to fall off the bus seat. As two helpful comrades groggily sprang to his assistance, they bumped heads and all three bodies sank to the floor. It might have been appropriate to have had Red Cross painted on the side of the returning vehicles. The body-ferrying service had to be continued when we reached the hotel. One half-inebriated thrower tried to help a very wobbly-kneed steeplechaser but lost his grip at the top of a flight of marble steps. The descending body floated gently, in a rippling motion, over every step until it reached the foot of the stairs. Unbelievably, the athlete concerned had no memory afterwards of having fallen and was in no way hurt. A case of absolute relaxation paying off.

Alan Pascoe and I spent a great deal of time putting athletes in bed. A couple of sprinters were determined to head out again, although they would have had trouble even finding the stairs. They did manage to re-dress themselves and one made it half-way down the corridor before all the lights went out in his head.

Breakfast the next morning was a tragi-comedy of noises. A fork dropped on to the tile floor and half a dozen hung-over athletes clamped their hands over their ears.

I had to remain in Czechoslovakia after the débâcle as, for the first time, European Sports writers and other athletic specialists had initiated a Golden Shoe Award for the best European track performance of the year. My run in Mexico had made me the only male European to win a track gold and they felt that this performance warranted awarding me the trophy.

One of the Selection Committee was the Czech athlete, Emil Zatopek. As an 11-year-old, I had watched him running at the White City and had struggled to the Czech team bus after the meeting to get his autograph. It seemed almost unreal to me that now this man was voting for me as the best runner in Europe. Zatopek was a hero to his fellow countrymen, not only because he was one of the world's greatest distance runners, winning four gold medals in two Olympic Games but also as an Army officer and strong independent Nationalist. He was one of the most outspoken when Russia moved into Czechoslovakia in 1969.

Our match with the Czechs took place soon after this occupation and as our coaches left the stadium, Zatopek was there with other officials, to say 'goodbye'. From both our coaches, the chant of 'Zatopek . . . Zatopek' rose in a symbolic tribute to this great man and all he represented. The crowd reacted in a touchingly warm farewell, waving and throwing flowers. It was an unforgettable occasion.

My training for the high hurdles continued in earnest as the European Championships approached. A number of men were good but the man to beat would be Eddie Ottoz of Italy, who had split the Americans to gain an Olympic bronze medal in the high hurdles in Mexico City. He was fast and a technically brilliant hurdler.

When the team arrived at our hotel in Athens, we hovered

around in the lobby, waiting for our room assignment. On most international trips, the room accommodation is for two persons and occasionally more. In Athens, I was again to share with Martin Winbolt Lewis. We received our room number and a key. Friends we may have been,but you can imagine how taken aback we were on finding that the room contained one large double bed. While we were agreeing that this was not on, through the same door came Andy Todd closely followed by Howard Payne and his wife. Accommodation may have been scarce but this was ridiculous. Martin, Andy and I retired to a three-bedded room down the hall.

These Championships were made memorable by Lillian Board's double gold, first in the 800 metres and a breath-taking anchor leg in the relay, catching in the last yard, her Olympic rival and friend Collette Besson. My other recollection is of Ian Stewart's absolute dominance in the 5,000 metres. When he had led for a time and no one else would take over, he actually slowed to a walk in lane three, to ensure that the field would move up. He packed in with them and then unleashed such pace at the end that no one could stay with him. Britain has some incredible middle and long distance champions in her honour roll. In the Rome European Championships, the same kind of dominance and disdain was shown by Brendan Foster in his striking 5,000 metres victory.

My encounter with Ottoz was less than striking, unless one refers to my contact with the second hurdle. Ottoz was usually first over the first hurdle. In the Final, I managed an exceptionally good start – and I was, I believe, six inches ahead of him over the first hurdle. My speed carried me too close to the second and I hit it hard. It was my only mistake in the race – but a costly one. Ottoz gained a few feet and held the advantage to the finish. I did not enjoy finishing second and felt bad hearing the Italian National Anthem being played. Some compensation was the fact that Alan Pascoe had come through to take the bronze.

I met Ottoz again six months later – but this time at a conference for European Hurdles Coaches, organized by his great coach, Professor Calvesi. Eddie and I were there to demonstrate and to answer questions. He gave me a ride to our hotel in his very low sports car. As I unwound from our parking spot on a hill, a little Italian lady coming up the slope stopped in her tracks. In both hands she carried shopping bags which made her appear almost as wide as she was high. Perhaps because of the incline, she seemed a little amazed at my stature! Eddie stepped from his side of the car and told her that I was a visitor from Britain and the current Olympic Champion, holding the world record in 400 metres hurdles. Her face remained completely blank and she turned and asked, 'How tall is he?' Eddie converted 6 feet 2 inches to 1 metre 89 for her. Immediately, her face broke into a bright smile as she beamed her praise 'Oh, bravo, bravo'.

Some of my most enjoyable athletic journeys have been to invitational meetings where a few athletes travel together for three or four days. I remember one of these very clearly, both for its enjoyment and humour. In the early summer of 1968, Romania invited some British athletes to compete in their National Championships. The group consisted of three girls, Della James (now Pascoe), Val Peat and Joan Page (now Allison), and four men John Boulter (1,500 metres), Ralph Banthorpe (200 metres), Stuart Storey (110 metres hurdles) and myself competing in the 400 metres hurdles.

The trip started unfortunately for Stuart. We arrived at Bucharest International Airport and decided to freshen up. Just as nature called Stu, so had hunger called the workmen who were fixing the pipe from the wall urinal. Poor Stu discovered too late that the outfall pipe had been left unconnected so that it emptied directly on his own shoes and socks!

Bill Toomey, U.S. decathlon champion and his huge team mate Russ Hodge shared this competition. I discovered that Bill has a never-ending flow of stories and jokes, most of which are highly amusing. I remember the line on one of his postcards, 'Having a wonderful time – wish you were her'.

During this meeting the four U.K. men started talking about a 4 × 400 metres relay team. Relays are for me the most exciting part of athletics. There is a science as to how you balance a relay team. Some people run best on the first leg, others at position two or three. Most of my college days I had spent on the anchor, or final leg. Extreme tension can build up if one is waiting for the baton and can see a deficit building up. All you need is to be in with a chance. Anything under 15 yards in a quarter is worth having a go at, because a slight error in the opponents' pace-judgment can make that much difference. If you're in the lead, going out too slowly, thinking you've got it made can be fatal. You can be caught and even passed, by half-way. The sight of an opponent coming back, brings a crowd to its feet and can inspire an exhausted chasing runner.

Each of the British boys had at one time or another been a part of a 4 × 400 metres relay squad. Ralph was in the best speed shape and it was decided that he should lead off. Stu was the most worried about lasting a full 400 as he was trained as a 110 metres hurdler. His aim was just to stay in contact. John was to run third and I would do my best at the finish. The night before the relay we discussed the folly of our entry – the Romanian and Cuban national teams were entered – and we had pulled together a team of four men out of a choice of four.

Talking with the girls, I told them one of the problems of a 400 metres runner: that is, if you are in good shape you can run really fast for about 300 metres and then you find out if you've run a little too fast. If you have, or if you're not in really good shape, at around 300 metres you can run into rigor mortis, better known as rig. It's as if a bear jumps on you, or there's an invisible wall in your lane and you run right into it. The movie camera slows down, all your limbs gain ten pounds, and you float down the home straight. Your mind demands fast pace but no matter what you do the ease of movement has gone.

Some people increase their stride speed and their feet become a blur of six-inch shuffles. Others try lifting their knees higher but it takes two minutes for each knee to come down. It can be like running away in a dream; all the mental effort is there but you can't get going. The girls seemed to enjoy the rig syndrome and told me that they'd give me a yell at 300 metres.

The time of the race drew near and the chicken talk began. 'How did we get into this . . . voluntarily?' 'Why have we inflicted such unnecessary additional anxiety on ourselves?' As it turned out our performance was creditable. Ralph ran a fine lead off leg in about 47·8 seconds. We were in with all the teams and in fact ahead of some of the 'B' teams. Stu took the baton and looked fine up to 110 metres. I feared for him as he went down the back straight but I'm sure no more than he feared for himself. The length of the race started to tell and some ground was being lost but he came home gallantly with a time in the 49s, very creditable, and we were holding our own. John still had sight of the whole field bar the Cubans who had decided to break the Romanian all-comers' record and were many yards clear. John had to convert much of his stamina training into an all-out speed effort to get under 50 seconds. This he did with room to spare running in the low 48s. We were still in touch.

I grabbed the baton and felt good. The adrenalin had been building up as I waited to get the baton and now that it was stuck to my hand, all the pent-up energy and emotion could flow out in my stride. I caught one team, passed them and soon found myself at the 300 metres mark edging into second place. Just as promised, a chorus rang out; Della and Val in perfect duet yelled 'Come on Rig'. My mind jumped and I didn't know whether to laugh or cry. 'Come on, Rig? Concentrate.' I yelled to myself and held on to second place, covering my split in the low 46s. Our pick-up team had beaten the Romanian 'A' Team with a combined time around 3 minutes 11 seconds. We were rather proud of ourselves but the Cubans' winning margin of well over ten yards was enough to keep our heads from swelling.

The impromptu use of man power is rare at International level but not so rare for clubs, especially since the inception of the National League. This has proved to be a fine idea. It has helped to produce team spirit and to make a second string pole-vaulter as valuable to the club as their number two miler. The early search for talent produced some interesting and sometimes desperate spectacles, not the least of which I witnessed at the second league match of the 1969 season held at Sale. At the time Hillingdon, my club, and Achilles, Martin Winbolt Lewis's club, were in the same division. On this particular occasion, Martin was contributing on other fronts than his 400/800 metres specialities. Few knew that he had talents in the hammer; even fewer knew when he came out. The hammer circle is only 7 feet in diameter. National Champions make three complete turns with the hammer. A few exceptional technicians are experimenting with four turns. On his first throw Winbolt used six. This effort was not legal, however, as the hammer landed out of the sector, barely missing the recording judge standing beside the retaining cage. I was transfixed by his second effort. While his feet were planted firmly in the middle of the circle, he started swinging the 16 pounds metal ball. A few times it whistled over his head, then barely missed his shoes. With great effort, its path was modified and he started spinning in the middle of the circle. His arms, now parallel with the ground, appeared to be lengthening at every turn, as his speeding feet shuffled in ever-increasing circles. I lost count of the number of turns he made. The voice of an official yelled 'Release it' or 'Now' each time he faced the right direction. At last the flying ball shot from his hand. It seemed incredible – he was only eight inches short of the world record ... for the long jump, 28 feet 6 inches a personal best and one more point for his club. A triumph for matter over man. Thank God he could run so well.

There was not a great deal of travelling required for Martin or any of the British Team in the 1970 Commonwealth Games as they were held in Edinburgh, Scotland. My hopes of attempting the decathlon in these Games had been brought to an end during the Winter at Oxford. While competing in a meeting at Iffley Road on a cool November day, I hurdled, long jumped, pole vaulted and then, without a track suit, waited to long jump again. Unknown to me, the low temperature had tightened up my leg muscles and a determined effort to get over 24 feet proved too much for my right hamstring, which gave way on take-off. This injury, coupled with a sprained ankle in the early spring, forced me to centre my attention on speed work in order to have a good year of high hurdling. If all went well, I hoped to defend my Commonwealth high hurdles title.

My biggest opposition was going to come from Alan Pascoe. Alan had fine 200 metres speed, 20·9. He and I had several races down to the wire but throughout 1969 Alan had never beaten me. In spite of this, he retained the belief that he *could* win and this is what helps to make a Champion: never to admit defeat before you begin. Not long before the Commonwealth Games, Alan finally turned the tables winning the Sward Trophy Meeting at Crystal Palace. I congratulated him but could not help telling him that that would be the last time it happened. It was, but not the way I wanted it. Alan suffered an injury during the Commonwealth Games Final and never finished the race. This must have made his 1974 Commonwealth Games 400 metres hurdles victory that much sweeter. He is a worthy successor.

It so happened that the day of the 110 metres Hurdles Final in Edinburgh, July 18th, coincided with my 26th birthday. Following my 13·6 seconds win, there was the traditional medal ceremony with the English Anthem – but once this was completed, the Guards Band struck up 'Happy Birthday'. I really appreciated the gesture, not only of the band but also the 30,000 spectators who sang so heartily.

The Games were good for the Scottish distance fans. Lachie Stewart won the 10,000 metres on the first day and Ian Stewart and Ian McCafferty held off Kip Keino in the 5,000 metres on the last day. The closing ceremony held an uninhibited charm all its own. High-Jumper Mike Campbell made an impressively formal march past the Royal Box; presented arms and then planted a sign which read 'Reserved for Official Party'. A large Canadian athlete on a children's tricycle, doffed his sun hat, placed it over his heart and bowed his head in humble salute as he pedalled past. Athletes of all nations linked arms and danced or jogged around the track. Some moved to the infield and snaked up and down the lines of Bandsmen. Spirits were light and joyful: this family of nations – bound by common language, but more by sport than anything else. Spectators and athletes alike joined in the feeling of this climax to a good Games.

If any competition could be called friendly, then these Games achieved that quality. There are always those who look for unrest, trouble, and dissatisfaction. It would be wrong to say that during the two weeks there were no incidents. However, there were fewer problems by far, than in any other comparably sized community living in close quarters for two weeks at a time of stress. Because of the goodwill from most people, I was angered by the headline in the Scottish *Daily Express* which read 'Black Power Shock'. The writer claimed that all flags were taken down and a black power flag raised. English athletes actually watched the supposed black power flag-raising ceremony. The flag was a blanket – and a pair of ladies underwear. The group consisted of Australians, Bermudians, and others. They circled the pole in the darkness singing 'Waltzing Matilda'.

How does such an erroneous headline reach a front page? Is it the dark fear within one reporter that makes him believe, or want to believe, that the world is hostile? Or is it someone higher up wanting to exploit the public to sell his newspaper? In general our British papers are good. They report as accurately as possible, allowing that most people have some bias towards any event or situation. However, this kind of misrepresentation of fact is inexcusable.

For me, the last major Championships of 1970 were the World

Student Games being held in Turin, Italy. At these Games, I was honoured by being named Captain of the Team for all Sports. The job of Captain has never been clearly defined. I suppose each person handles this as he/she sees fit, and in the manner that different teams and time call for. Usually, there is a full meeting of the team and at that time it is possible to welcome newcomers; to encourage a relatively serious and strong approach and, hopefully, to help increase team unity. This speaking opportunity I passed up at the Commonwealth Games, not because I didn't have anything to say, but because it was not a full team meeting and I had imagined there would be more than one gathering. But, in my opinion, this is not the most important part of the role. Far more, I believe that an individual can set an example, on and off the track. It was my feeling that if I competed well, and won, then it would allow others who had not yet competed to believe that they too could win.

I enjoy most sports and all events in the track and field programme. Because of my genuine interest in each event and in the people taking part, I spent much time just talking with athletes before or after their competition. I am sorry that the B.A.A.B. officials have seen fit to discontinue the role of Captain. I realize that a good team manager and coach may be able to perform a comparable function. However, a peer may well be able to empathize more and even bring general matters to the attention of the management. I fear that the role may have been discontinued, more from a feeling of threat than the non-function of this position. An articulate spokesman on behalf of 100 independent internationals is too powerful a voice to the press. Any number of single individual voices can be written off as 'rebels'.

The World Student Games was even more of a challenge than the Commonwealth. Ron Draper from America, Gunter Nickel of West Germany and a number of other top international high hurdlers were assembled in this hot bowl of Northern Italy. It had been a good season for me and this competition was to be my last Games high hurdles. I was so high on my own adrenalin and hyperventilation plus the 90 degrees heat in the stadium, that I felt quite light-headed. Alan Pascoe had recovered from his injury sufficiently to make the Final but the man in best form seemed to be Gunter Nickel. His sprinting speed was so good that he was on the German sprint relay team and he had run 13·5 during the season. I had two or three 13·6s, one or two on electric timing which is usually worth ·2 compared with hand timing, so I felt I was in with a chance. Ron Draper who had a 13·4 to his credit had not shown his hand.

After two false starts, my ears strained for the noise of the gun waiting to pull my hands off the line and dive at the first hurdle. Over the first few hurdles no one pulled ahead, but Nickel and I were among the leaders. I strained to make my legs move faster between hurdles thrashing the air with my arms on each landing. I could feel the tension in me as I screamed in my head, 'faster', 'faster', 'toes', 'sprint'. By the ninth hurdle I could still see Nickel out of the corner of my left eye, but he was the only one. I knew he'd be fastest from the last hurdle to the tape. By the tenth I couldn't see him and I lunged for the tape and again out of the corner of my eye Nickel came into view. Had he nipped in for first? I didn't know and had to wait for the photo. That waiting time was awful, I so badly wanted to leave high hurdling on a top note. The winning time was 13·8. On the scoreboard appeared the message, first D. Hemery GBR. I felt joyful relief. Alan's lack of work due to the injury limited him to seventh. However, on the same afternoon, Martin Reynolds brought a second gold to Britain by winning the 200 metres in fine style. And in a courageous front running 800 metres Martin Winbolt Lewis nearly held off the great finisher Franz Joseph Kemper (West Germany). With Alan Lerwill winning the long jump the British contingent went home with a strong showing of athletic medals.

My season closed with another 13·6 run, so I figured that my ceiling in the high hurdles had just about been reached. With a 13·4 hand-timed in Zurich and four runs of 13·6, I quite happily hung up my shoes as a high hurdler.

1. I enjoyed the feeling of running from the age of five. This snapshot was taken during a race with my elder sister, Judy.

2. Start of a cross-country race at Endsleigh School, Colchester. Because the handicaps were graded according to age I managed to finish first. That's me on the left with my tongue out!

3. Seated in the centre of the front row, I was, at 13, the least likely candidate for future Olympic honours.

4. Still a raw talent, only a year after meeting Fred Housden, I won the A.A.A. Junior high hurdles at Hurlingham in 1963.

5. My first Games title. The last hurdle in the 120 yards hurdles Final at the Commonwealth Games in Kingston, Jamaica in 1966. I was closely followed by Mike Parker with Ghulam Raziq of Pakistan (*nearest the camera*) third.

CHAPTER 8

A Winter of Adversity

Should I go on? Do I really want to? I think I ought to. It'll be a long year – you'd better be sure. You may not win again. Is that a factor? Are you too old? No, damn it. I'm sure I can get even fitter than in 1968. These questions were gradually answered. I'll try to do my best in Munich. If I get a gold again – great. If not, it won't be for lack of effort.

The decision to continue was only the first step. I believed that, this time around, training for the Olympics was to be an intense and serious project. My best chance for success would be to go back under my Boston University coach, Billy Smith. However, graduate students in the U.S. cannot run for a University and I was also applying to study at Harvard. Billy stepped beyond the confines of his own University and, out of personal friendship, again agreed to work with me. Only now, when coaching others myself, do I realize how much is asked of an individual who coaches. It is an energy and time-consuming commitment. Billy's interest and enthusiasm seemed to be limitless.

Okay, one sure factor settled, the coach. Now I have to discuss the idea with my Headmaster at Millfield, Colin Atkinson. I was heavily committed at the school and it meant they had to find tutors and a housemaster to take over my role for the academic year 1971–72. Colin has played cricket at top level, captaining Somerset, and therefore lent a sympathetic ear to my request for leave. The pace, pressures, and obligations of total involvement in a residential school are not conducive to preparing for an Olympics. The school kindly put nothing in my way.

Two obstacles remained – gaining acceptance to study for a Masters degree in education at Harvard and finding the finance for the year. Harvard came through but the money didn't. If the worst came to the worst I'd borrow it. I didn't know who would lend me the kind of money which was necessary but I was now resolved. In sixteen months I'd be in the best shape of my life.

At the start, my intensity knew no bounds. Daily I pounded the Somerset roads, gradually bringing my mile times down and my total mileage up. When the school term ended I moved to the Crystal Palace. My summer job was to be Meeting Director for the 1971 I.A.C./Coca Cola international meeting. At some time each day I would vigorously attack my session. Billy had asked me to reach Boston in reasonable shape. He felt that sit-ups and press-ups were good conditioners, to go along with the running and asked me to work up to 300 of each every day. I wasn't content to simply reach this target; I had to devise a way of doing more. After a few days, I settled on a routine of 50 press-ups and 50 sit-ups followed by half-a-mile striding. This was repeated until I had reached my target for the day. By the end of six weeks I had reached 550 sit-ups and press-ups, five to six miles running and a flat behind. Also, just as the motion of a heavy sea stays with a passenger after disembarking from his ship, so I felt I was going up and down while at meals. Sometimes my bacon and eggs seemed to be coming towards me, and then floating back to the table again.

All through the summer weeks I continued my search for finance. I wrote to special funds, which I discovered had become extinct; to groups such as Round Table and Rotary, firms, friends, and the governing body of athletics. I drew a blank on all fronts. I found this hard to believe. How can a British youth expect to gain assistance if an Olympic champion can't find any? I was the only 1968 Olympic track gold medallist from the whole of Europe and my cause was to get back to Boston under the same coach to try and do it again. When it reached the point of being nail-bitingly close to taking a sizeable loan, a friend asked me if I'd applied for a Winston Churchill Fellowship. I wasn't sure what that was, or whether I'd be eligible. To my eternal gratitude I discovered that this fund enables British individuals from various fields to travel to other countries to learn more about their interest. They are travelling ambassadors for Britain and bring back the knowledge they have gained to put to good use on their return. I hope always to remain involved with sport and education through coaching, teaching, and administration, so this task was central to my future. Following an interview by one of the Trustees, Lord Byers, I was awarded a dual purpose Fellowship, to study for a Masters degree in education and to study training techniques, in America.

With the major part of the finance found I felt a great sense of relief but at the same time I thought it wrong that the governing body of my sport could not make any contribution. After all, they pay for athletes' travel, training, and living expenses on trips to altitude training or competition abroad. I was going to Boston specifically to prepare for the Olympics. A large part of my expenses would be on travel, to the U.S., to training venues, and occasionally to competition.

Publicity had been given to the fact that Kraft had generously contributed £25,000 specifically for Olympic preparation. The official reply from the B.A.A.B. to me was that the main purpose of my visit was academic and therefore they could not help. By chance, a friend of mine knew the managing director of Kraft and talked to him, off the record, about my request to the Board for any contribution. I had £200 in savings but on top of that I needed about £400 more to live at subsistence level until I returned to Britain in the summer of 1972. I never heard what happened between Kraft and the Board but a letter came from the Board officers saying that they had re-considered my case and were prepared to make a contribution of £400 towards my year, as long as the money was spent for legitimate athletic purposes, which would comply with the amateur rules. There was no question in my mind about that. I wrote sincere thanks to them, *and to Kraft*.

At the beginning of September, I left for Boston. Initially, everything was fine. The mornings were warm and this made the pre-breakfast runs a pleasure. I re-acquainted myself with the Scituate sand dunes, Franklin Park hills, and the tow path of the Charles River. My body gradually adapted to two sessions a day. The blisters cleared. The aches disappeared. The amazing human body will gradually adapt to any demand if not asked for too much, too fast.

For twelve hours a day I studied, read, wrote, and went to classes, in addition to training. This left time to eat and sleep. Gradually the work-load and the toll on my body started to tell on my spirit. The theme 'run for fun' was unfortunately missing.

During this time I occasionally jotted my thoughts down on scraps of paper. Not long into the winter, I recorded that my mental staleness and lack of desire to run, dogged my every step. On one 10 mile run my strides became slower and slower, until I finally could not force myself another step. A run became a jog, then a walk. I was 5 miles from the dormitory at the far end of the Charles River. I was so tired I was at crying point. Turning into the wind, I looked back across the frozen water and sat down. I was still very warm, so the icy wind was quite refreshing. The setting sun was a ball of orange, red, and purple fire and its reflection on the white ice was startlingly beautiful. The ripples raised on the river's surface by the wind had frozen solid. Filaments of ice covered the twigs of a bush on the embankment. Enjoying all this beauty and tranquillity so far removed from my struggle, I wished I had with me a camera and pencil and paper, to capture the scene for always. I think that I briefly understood why mountaineers are sometimes found dead on a climb. Like them, I was too exhausted to want to move. Before my circulation seized up completely, I rose and tried to work my legs back to a trot, turning again to face the wind all the way back to the dormitory.

Many times during the winter I badly wanted to stop. I had become totally involved in my studies and running just didn't inspire me. Sometimes I'd pull my body from the library, back to the dormitory, change, and go through the motions of a 10 mile run. I could feel the down happening but I didn't know how to regain my fire and eagerness. I talked to my father and to Coach Smith. My dad wrote me a letter trying to lift me back on to the spiritual plateau of peace and clear direction, knowing what is right and where I was heading, 'to reach out and touch a new dimension and for a moment to live there'. Smithie told me, 'This is your time in purgatory' and 'summer isn't the time to get too excited about Christmas'. I understood them both theoretically but there was little change in my spirit. I was depressed and it felt like a vicious circle. Coach told me it was natural and that if I hadn't been studying so hard, it would have hit me two weeks before. He decided I needed a third interest to take my mind off the work. He told me to find a girlfriend. Unfortunately most of the time I was too tired to talk, let alone be animating. In fact, I went out only half a dozen times during my nine months in Boston.

One evening encounter with the fairer sex was somewhat

unscheduled. It happened during my first attempt at a winter run after dark. Deep snow had been thrown on the city but I still began my run on the towpath of the river. I was not impressed by the start. Not a hundred yards down the path, nature made its first attack by lowering a branch into my skull. After apologizing to the tree, I staggered on down the path like a drunk. Within a mile I had regained my composure, only to suffer a further onslaught. This time, a twig leaned out and poked me in the eye. There was worse to come. Out of the gloom, along the same narrow path, came a liberated young woman pedalling her bike as if she were a suicide pilot. She bore down on me at high speed. I was thankful for my hurdling ability, for without it, I fear, I might now be talking in a voice at least an octave higher. Running after dark did not continue.

Snow is a fact of Boston winters. Even the morning runs were problematic. My weak ankles twisted on the icy ground. My eyes burned from the snow glare and, when it was snowing, frost and ice caked my sideburns and hair. Often it was too cold to leave without two tracksuits on. During the run my body would heat up, soaking the first track suit and the sleet and snow would drench the outside suit. I'd get back to the dorm several pounds lighter and my clothes several pounds heavier. My normal racing weight settles around 165–168 pounds but during this distance running time, I dropped as low as 152; which is pretty light for someone of 6 feet 2 inches.

I am still not fully aware of the cause of the down which held on to my head. Perhaps it was just that I had flogged my mind and body for several months and my battery was dead – but I kept pushing right through the winter. Coach Smith believed that I was putting so much in, it had to come out later. This wasn't the time to get excited about the Games. Once the warm weather and track work came into sight all would be well.

At the beginning of March I took a four-day break between phases and for the first time had an exciting feeling of the chance of winning in Munich, twenty-six weeks hence. But . . . March 8th 6.10 p.m. 'So this is track. I'm sitting in bed, shaking, shivering as I got in, just back from my first day back on the track, my feet are soaking and frozen. My throat is sore from being sick. My head aches, my eyes are bloodshot, my neck is stiff, my fingers inflexible, and my thighs are in a state of cramp. My stomach is upset and

I'm late for dinner with friends. 15 × 220 yards, 25·9 seconds
150 yards jog between – okay for openers, I guess. 36 degrees and
water on the track. Tom Beatty, B.U.'s track captain predicted
I'd have trouble getting up tomorrow morning. . . . I told him
"any morning" but he may be right. Time for a hot shower – Oh
bliss.'

March 9th 8.20 a.m. 'Eyes tired, neck and shoulder muscles
stiff, calves and thighs a little stiff. Not bad considering yesterday's
feelings, but I could sure do without six hours of classes.'

With over 1,200 miles and as many hills and sand dunes behind
me, the track actually looked small. However, after a few sessions
it quickly assumed its normal proportions. I wanted to hurdle but
the weather remained cold, well into April. I felt as though time
was running out. The Penn Relays was to be my first run on
April 28th and I hadn't any specific hurdle endurance. On April
23rd I felt pretty ropy, heavy headed, and lethargic. I didn't
realize it then, but it was the beginning of 'flu. I shouldn't have
been at the track at all but I read it as another 'down', to be
pushed through. I warmed up, sweating profusely and ran my
trail leg over a few high hurdles gradually increasing the speed.
I felt terribly tired.

The next run down, something popped painfully, high up on the
inside of the right thigh. I jogged a couple of miles and stopped
for the day. The dull ache persisted. The 'flu ran its course and I
tried jogging. The Penn Relays was my first competition for
eighteen months, I couldn't miss it. But I had doubts. My right
thigh hurt even when walking and I was still weak.

I went to the Relays and when warming up didn't feel too bad.
I started fast, not heeding Smith's cautionary advice to take it
steady. All went fine for two-thirds of the distance, then I felt as
though 'the bear' and his family had jumped on to my back. At the
last hurdle I arrived too far away for fifteen strides and too close
for sixteen. My right foot hit the middle of the hurdle top and at
full speed I started going through the air head first. I have never
fallen over a 400 metres hurdle before or since but I made it a good
one – right over on to my back. I got to my feet and finished
second, badly shaken and my leg pain was joined by a wrenched
stomach muscle. I phoned Smithie apologizing and letting him
know what had happened.That night I was to be inducted into the
Boston University Hall of Fame. This was not the time for that.

I wanted to crawl away and recover. My body ached and I was low.

April 29th. 'No current inspiration to write, two term papers due. Cold in my body, cotton wool in my head, sweat on the surface, and nothing on the page. There goes that sleep again. It's corner-squashing time. Fifteen weeks to the Munich final. Right lower stomach wincingly painful doing sit-ups, and inside of the right thigh sore in sprints and hurdles. Tired body, fed up brain, rainy weather, and all's right with the world.'

The right thigh trouble turned out to be an adductor muscle tear. Because it was at the origin high up in the groin it was very slow to heal. Sitting down and pressing my knees together, gave a reasonable test of its condition. Unfortunately, this muscle is used to bring the trail leg over the hurdle. It was seven months later, November 1972, when the pain finally cleared. However, it was not hard to keep my troubles in perspective. During the week of the Penn Relays my mother was on duty, when a 19-year-old lad was transferred to Boston Children's Hospital. He had come off his motor-bike when someone over-ran a red light. Gas gangrene had set in, and so far he'd lost his right leg and buttock. Apart from being heart-breaking, that reminder helped me again to appreciate my health and strength. In fact, visiting the paraplegic sports and meeting some of the talented wheelchair participants had played a part in my decision to continue. Many of these men and women take part and follow sport with as much interest and enthusiasm as can be seen anywhere. The fact that they would have given anything to be in my position, made me feel somehow duty bound to press on towards the next Games.

The feeling that I ought to go on was also strongly influenced by the death of Lillian Board. Contrary to popular belief I was not her fiancé. He was David Emery, the journalist. However, I knew Lillian well, as our international careers began together in 1966. She was a warm and genuine person. Through her congratulations after my victory in Mexico, I knew that she was one of the few people who could fully understand the personal, emotional, and public pressure, as well as the work involved in attaining that level. She had come within a foot of gold over 400 metres in Mexico and it was her resolve to reach that gold in 1972. Following her decisive 800 metres victory in the 1969 European Championships and a fabulous winning relay run against her

Olympic rival, Colette Besson of France, there seemed a strong
possibility of her aim for Olympic gold coming true. However,
by mid 1970 she was unwell, and cancer was diagnosed. She fought
until December 26th 1970. Ironically enough Lillian died in
Munich less than two years before the Games there. The Germans
honoured her by naming one of the Olympic Village roads Lillian
Board Way. The feeling of loss at her unjust death at 22 was
universal. One headline read 'Lillian the Brave'. Her struggle
for life, through intolerable suffering was an inspiration to many,
myself included. The fact that death had so cruelly taken away
her Olympic chances, helped to firm my resolve to try while I
still had my health and strength, in part, on her behalf.

Because of my leg trouble, which prevented practice over
hurdles, Coach Smith started talking positively about fitness for
800 metres. I had sufficient background mileage to consider this
as a possibility, if hurdling was 'off the menu' for much longer.
I avoided taking this decision. I had run half miles in high school
against boys many years my senior and although I usually won,
either the strain of the inequality or the distance involved had left
me with a traumatic dislike of contesting this event. Track training
continued and my flat running times dropped consistently.
Repeats of 5 × 880 yards averaging 2 minutes 01 came down to
2 × 880 yards in 1 minute 54 and 1 minute 52 in cold and rain
(aiming for 1 minute 56 and 1 minute 54); 6 × 660 yards averaging 89 seconds came down to 4 × 660 yards in 83 seconds
average and finally one 660 in 75·9 seconds. Faster than before
Mexico!

One element of Billy's preparation was to build a good base in
the winter, then gradually to reduce the repetitions and increase
the speed as the time of summer competitions approaches. In
this latter phase of maximum efforts, I would take a couple of
laps slow walk recovery between runs. Shortly before leaving
Boston for the Olympic trials Coach Smith asked me to run
3 × 500 yards going through 400 metres inside 50 seconds.
With two completed in the low 49s and while trying to recover for
the third, one of the Boston University athletes passed on a conversation he had overheard. A schoolboy from the local area had
noticed that I was at the track and said to his friend, 'Gee, I'd
like to see David Hemery run.' His coach turned to the youngster
and said, 'You won't – I'm here every day and he only walks

round the track'. On my third one I went through the quarter in 48·8.

My mind ran back to a time in London immediately before I left for Boston, when I had just completed my 500th press-up and sit-up. A small boy walked past and commented to me, 'My Dad says you don't have to train. It's just natural.' What could I say? I smiled and tried to assure the youngster that no one gets anywhere without quite a bit of hard work. Why is one always hit with remarks like this, at times when it is almost impossible to stand up, and when too tired to have the right reply at hand.

Papers and final exams at Harvard were successfully completed by the first week of June, but before returning to Britain, I had one more competition on American soil, the New England A.A.U. Championships. The pain from the adductor had not completely cleared, but it had had long enough, if it was going to. From now on, it had to be ignored. The race went okay. My winning time of 50·2 for 440 yards hurdles provided me with an Olympic qualifying time, but I could feel that my specific hurdling endurance was sadly lacking. Even though I was in the best running condition of my life hurdling practice had been absent.

And so to London and to work specifically on that area. Training was to be aimed at the technical problem of hurdling off either leg. I had spent a little time with Fred Housden before leaving for Boston. I reported to him that prior to my April tear I had run a test, 2 × 120 yards over eleven (one extra) 3 feet 6 inches hurdles in 15·2 and 15·3 seconds, off my wrong leg. This meant that the hurdling wasn't *too* bad but he understood that there had been no more hurdling experiments for the intervening months, because of the adductor muscle problem.

I hurdle better when I take off from my right foot. It is possible to maintain a long running stride for at least half of a 400 metres hurdle race. In this early part of the race I maintained thirteen strides between each hurdle. (The landing step is not counted as a stride.) However by half-way through a race, fatigue begins to set in and a runner's stride-length becomes shorter. Sooner or later the hurdler will be too far away from the hurdle to clear it after thirteen strides. If he can learn to hurdle from his other leg, then he simply takes a fourteenth stride and continues. Unfortunately it is not quite so simple, just to use the other leg. It's like trying to write or serve a tennis ball with the other hand. It's possible but it takes a heck of a lot of practice to even look natural, let alone feel comfortable. In Mexico, I'd stayed on my right-foot take off and put in two extra strides, going from thirteen to fifteen. This meant dropping my running stride length by about a foot every stride, at this changing point in the race. Obviously taking one less stride takes less time, so the experiment to move from thirteen to *fourteen* had to be pursued in the name of progress.

Back in England, I didn't see a track for the first eight days. Alan Carr-Locke, another English athlete who had been studying at Boston University, and I tried in vain to find accommodation. We started searching in the general area of Crystal Palace. For over a week, from 9 a.m. to 5 p.m. we walked and talked to estate agents and landlords. Flat hunting is not a good way to prepare for the Games. As the search went farther afield, we finally opted for a place within running distance of Richmond Park.

With two weeks to go to the A.A.A. National Championships I received word that John Akii-Bua would be running. My hurdles partnership with Fred Housden re-started as he was celebrating his 80th birthday. Together we crammed in a few 'wrong-lead-leg' sessions during the remaining time. Akii had promised to be more than a threat since he thrashed the Americans in the U.S.A. Pan Africa match in the U.S. At that time he ran 49·0 and afterwards was quoted '48·0 easy'. He had felt so good he believed he could beat my world best of 48·1. Akii had Ugandan support to travel and train throughout the pre-Olympic year. In London he came to test out Hemery. We both qualified for the Final, running in different heats. The Final was the next afternoon. By then a strong head wind faced us in the back straight and I had to work hard to hold thirteen strides. Around the second bend I made my first competitive attempt to hurdle from my wrong foot. Fatigue played a part in accounting for the feeling of awkwardness. I lost ground but worked hard into the home straight. Akii had been drawn inside me and I still hadn't seen him. Over the last hurdle, and I heard the crowd 'oooh!' At the finish line Akii came flying past. He had made up three yards from the last hurdle. The photo-finish picture gave me the verdict in 49·7 seconds, but the sight of Akii going on round the bend was a hint of things to come.

My brother, John, watched with agony my final 50 yards to the tape. He saw my tiredness, my lack of zip – even a seeming lack of hunger to ensure getting to the finish first. We are very close and he wrote me a long soul-searching letter trying to help me look at my Munich target with some of my old fire re-kindled. The overall feeling of exhaustion was still very much with me. But with John's letter in hand, I tried to take a final grip of my situation. I received permission to move into the Crystal Palace and concentrated on resolving my stride problems, I could not afford to be unsure in the middle of my race. My strides had to be settled and flowing. I'd have another go in the international match against Finland on July 25th.

What a disaster! I hit hurdles four and seven and my strides on hurdles six to ten read thirteen, fourteen, sixteen, fifteen. I crossed the line shaking my head. Unbelievably the time was 49·3 seconds, a best for the year so far. I decided to have a final attempt at Crystal Palace on August 5th, two weeks before leaving for Munich. The strides were finally successful thirteen to hurdle six, fourteen to the finish, but I cleared the last hurdle with my wrong leg, as if I was stile jumping – arms and legs wind-milled, and my time was only 49·9 seconds. I had run out of time to practise and experiment. A firm decision was made to abandon any further attempts to hurdle from my left foot. I would return to my thirteen-to-fifteen pattern which had been successful in Mexico.

With that settled I felt the desperate need for leg speed. In order not to lose ground on Akii, who *had* mastered hurdling from either leg, I had to be taking fifteen strides as fast as he could take fourteen. So for a few days I trained with Lynn Davies and found my sprinting ability improving daily. One excellent practice was to sprint 100 metres with a marker about 40 metres from the start. We reached the marker travelling at full speed and from then to the finish we consciously accelerated our stride speed – almost tapping the ground with our feet at an extremely rapid rate.

I was really pleased with the way my leg speed was rounding into shape when, on August 10th, three weeks to the day before my heat of the 400 metres hurdles in Munich, I pulled something in the back of my right thigh. I was on my third build-up 100 metres and my legs were moving faster and faster when I felt a thud half-way up my hamstring. I couldn't believe it. I knew what it was, as I'd pulled so many times before. I was tempted to phone the B.A.A.B. immediately and withdraw from the team. I first phoned home, then both coaches. Their instant reaction was:

don't withdraw, get immediate treatment. My brother had suffered a similar tear not long before the 'Varsity match and had received excellent help from Dr John Williams. Colin Campbell, now training for 800 metres, was going to see Dr Williams the following day and a phone call enabled me to join him. Two shots of hydrocortisone and novocaine, one either end of the tear, eased the pain and my mind. At least something was now at work.

My leg remained pretty sore but two days later I was slowly jogging on grass. On the third day I started physiotherapy and ran after hours in the children's wading pool at Crystal Palace. This enabled me to do some leg work without moving them very fast. Two more days and I was able to stride. On August 18th, the day before I left for Munich, Billy Smith flew in from Boston on, his way to the Games. This was the only day that Fred and Billy were to meet and it was my first attempt to go over a hurdle since the pull. My action was cautious as the leg was still painful. However, the hurdling made it no worse and I knew I'd be running in the heats thirteen days later. That night we shared a cordial meal together in London.

CHAPTER 9

Munich 1972

Few people knew I'd been injured just before the Games. One who did was Peter Hildreth, athletics correspondent of the *Sunday Telegraph*. Peter was an Olympic hurdler who once held the British record for 110 metres hurdles which later became mine. He is a man to be trusted. He had followed my build-up almost daily and there was no way of hiding my injury from him. I truly appreciated the fact that he placed personal friendship and integrity higher on his list than a scoop. The last thing I wanted at that time was to have to explain to public and press that I was struggling back to fitness.

A whole year's training is not entirely lost in ten days but doubts did creep in as I was so close to the Games. I continued physiotherapy in the Olympic Village and worked-out at a track away from the crowds and my opposition.

Nothing is ever quite the same the second time around. Perhaps it is unfair even to attempt to compare two Olympics – the countries are different, the structures are updated. Even the few athletes who reach another Games are four years older. The Games are for the young, the uninhibited, who dedicate themselves to become briefly the best of mankind in the strive for excellence. For me the Games will always be about people, their involvement in life, and their struggle to reach for their best, when it really counts. Some things seemed out of balance in Munich, the brilliant architecture, the precision measuring devices, and computer seeding of heats, all conspired to draw press and public attention away from the joys and talents of youth. Certainly advancements in technology are welcomed by the participants but these should be assets to enhance man, rather than to detract from or replace him. The machinery of a big event can sometimes over-shadow the people for whom it was set up. The sportsmen want to compete. The public want to see them. That is the crux of the situation. Then the contractors, promoters, manufacturers, officials at all levels – from local government to international sports bodies, planners, press and media men of all descriptions, plus a host of others from government representatives to drink vendors, involve themselves. It has become too big, too expensive, too political, too commercial, too inhuman, an unfortunate reflection of the world today. The Games have lost their simplicity and to an extent their purity. But more on this later.

The Olympic Village itself is really more like a small city. Within the village various modes of entertainment had been provided for the 10,000 inhabitants. In the open air recreation plaza there were giant walkabout draughts games and chess sets. One morning I had a two-hour chess game with the American, Ralph Mann. Ralph was one of my top rivals in the 400 metres hurdles. I took an early lead in the game but it took me ages to finally win. I told Coach Smith that I had learned a lot about Ralph during the game. He's stubborn, tough and will hang on against the odds. His competitive record bears this out.

The day of the heats drew closer and John Akii-Bua dropped a couple of tit-bits my way. 'I had three runs over the hurdles today, 49·7, 49·9 and 49·8.' Someone else overheard this and asked me why he hadn't run better than 49·7 during the season if he could do that in training. A couple of days later he mentioned a time trial of 48·8. Having experienced Whitney in Mexico and attempts by numerous other athletes and coaches to psyche-out – mentally shatter – their opponents, I didn't take these comments seriously, especially as unknowledgeable spectators often provide athletes with incredible and erroneous timings taken on their wrist watches.

I had my own time-trial planned for three days before the heats. In a quiet lunch hour at the Dante Stadium two miles from the Village, I ran 400 metres going over hurdles during only the second half of the distance. My brother, John, ran in from half-way to help me hold my pace. I relaxed on the first 200 metres then worked hard. It felt good and I was encouraged, since three watches had 47·5, a second-and-a-half faster than the same time-trial in Mexico. Was it all going to come right in the end?

The next day was the final track running session. A couple of

300 metres, with no hurdles, aiming at a reasonably fast and relaxed 34 seconds. My first run was 33·0. Billy didn't want any chances of further injury. He and I agreed it seemed to be all systems go. Just loosen up on the grass, the next day, gently striding, gaining the feeling of relaxation, a building up of power. The state of Limbo was reached. Nothing more could be done, by me, or any of my competitors, only time to wait, worry, and wonder.

One contender who seemed to be beaten before the start was Kenya's William Koskei who had produced some outstanding times, including 49·0, on poor cinder tracks earlier in the year. He told me, 'If the race was to be held at altitude on a dirt track I would be a top contender. I cannot find my rhythm on Tartan, and I'm having difficulty with the sea level atmosphere.' William had also had malaria between his fine runs and the Games. Who knows what factors influence a mind to conclude 'it's not possible for me', but once it's there, it will be reflected in the running.

William was eliminated in my heat, running 50·58. I was drawn in lane five, a good lane. I felt comfortable and was staggered to find my winning time was 49·72. It was so easy. My Australian friend Gary Knoke came through second in 50·10. In one of the later heats, I watched my Mexico team mate John Sherwood. He too had had injury problems before the Games. Perhaps the reduced amount of training had left him vulnerable under pressure. At the third hurdle he tore a calf muscle and was forced to stop. I ran over to him. He was very upset. What can one say. His wife Sheila arrived and helped him walk from the track. It takes so little to be ruled out of contention.

Down to the last sixteen, it was possible to start seeing the top contenders. West Germany's Dieter Buttner had won his heat in 49·78. He and Rainer Schubert could be lifted by the German crowd willing them and requiring them to do well. Rudolph from East Germany won the third heat in 50·00. John Akii-Bua won the fourth heat in 50·35 and the Russian Yevgenij Gavrilenko, won the fifth in 49·73. The previous year at the pre-Olympic meeting I had watched Gavrilenko run away from Akii over the final two hurdles. He could be strong. The Americans have always had strength and depth in this event. Ralph Mann still showed as their top man, but Jim Seymour was also running well.

The semi-final lane draw came out that night and I read some of the names off to Coach Smith. Mann (U.S.A.) Akii-Bua (Uganda),

Savchenko (U.S.S.R.), and Schubert (W. Germany), were all in
my semi-final. 'Well coach,' I said, 'if I can't get in the first four in
a semi-final then the gold medal is out of the question. All I have
to do is make sure of being in the first four.'

In this semi-final Akii went at it hard. I tried to play it the same
as in Mexico, work for two-thirds, then coast in, but the coast
wasn't there. My legs felt quite tired, and although I wasn't in
danger of failing to qualify, the run did nothing to instil great
confidence. John's winning time 49·25. Mann placed second in
49·53, I came third in 49·66, and Rainer Schubert, seventh place
finisher in the Mexico Final, came through to the Final again with a
time of 49·80. I'd run the same time as in my heat, but it hadn't
come as easily. Had I lost some of my stamina?

The second semi-final saw the tragic elimination of two good
men. Rudolph cleared the tenth hurdle in fatigue but in the lead.
As he turned to assess his rivals, his body turn caused his spikes to
catch the ground and he fell, right in the path of Buttner, who
crashed to the ground over the top of him. Both men were out.
Jim Seymour went on to win in 49·33 from Gavrilenko (U.S.S.R.)
in 49·34. The young Russian Yuriy Zorin, gained the third spot in
49·60, and Stavros Tziortzis (Greece) completed the list of
Finalists with 50·06.

I had watched that race with sadness. At the start Gary Knoke
was right out in lane eight. Loud speakers were in every starting
block so that the noise of the gun would be relayed instantly for
each man. Gary heard the instant relay, then the sound of the gun
and thought it was a recall shot, for a false start. He jogged a few
strides, turned, only to see everyone else on their way. He made a
gallant attempt but at this level, one false move and you've had it.

The lane draw came out for the Final. (1) Akii-Bua; (2) Gavrilenko; (3) Zorin; (4) Seymour; (5) Hemery; (6) Mann; (7) Schubert; (8) Tziortzis. Lane five again, all three rounds!

Over the twenty hours before the Final I waited for the feeling
of terror which had accompanied me in Mexico. I slept well and
woke very aware of the day, but with no sense of emotion. No fear,
no forboding, little tension, certainly not as much as before the
heats. I treated my day according to plan. It could be termed
planned trivia. Eat, a short rest, a short walk, nothing to excess.

Tension started building towards the time of the mini-bus ride
to the warm-up area, but where was all the adrenalin? I talked to

myself, 'Don't you realize that this is the Olympic Final?' A placid answer came back. 'Yes and I'm going to try to do my best.' 'But for heaven sake, why don't you get nervous?' 'I don't know, but there's nothing you can do about it. Just get on with it.'

How could I not be nervous? It wouldn't be accurate to say I wasn't at all nervous, but for an Olympic Final, I was ridiculously calm. Surely, right now I should be afraid of the possibility of not winning. No, that I had maturely faced eighteen months before. I desperately wanted to win, but I was not afraid of not winning and that subtle distinction seemed to be taking care of my flow of adrenalin. The only thing is that adrenalin gives an incredible boost for 'fight or flight'. It gives a life-saving flow in emergency situations. At the time when deciding to go on to Munich, it had taken me two months of anguished inner struggle to face the possibility of losing. Up to that time not winning had been unthinkable. I faced the facts that I had had a good innings, I was older, I could be injured, and maybe someone else could come along. I had asked myself whether I would be shattered if I didn't win again. At the end of this long inner turmoil, I felt I had reached a mature decision. If I went on and won I would be delighted, if I didn't win it would not be the end of everything for me, but I would certainly do all in my power to win again. Now, eighteen months later, I was at the start of my second Olympic Final, looking at the 100,000 capacity crowd and pressing my nails into my palms to try and awaken dormant fears that no longer existed.

In previous big races my adrenalin count was so high that I would have to hold myself back from flying down the back straight and blowing up and running out of steam in the home straight.

Now there was nothing to hold back and with the race under way I remembered, 'this is where you normally fly'. So down went my foot on my mental accelerator and I surged into the powerful headwind. I felt the whole field come back towards me. I reached the 200 metre mark in 22·8 seconds, four yards faster than my Mexico Final. Twenty yards later I started to really work the change down from thirteen to fifteen. It was at this point that John Akii-Bua won the race. I had two yards on him at the fifth hurdle and three by the sixth. John told me later that for a split second, he told himself, 'There goes the gold!' But his reaction was not 'Okay I'll settle for silver.' This demonstrated the true character of the man as a competitor. At that stage in an Olympic

Final, he might well have been justified in holding his own pace
and making sure of a place, but with determination and obvious
confidence in his own ability, he dug into his immense resources
and headed out after me. I could see neither this nor the fact that
Ralph Mann, whom I had just passed, now had his eyes on my
tail and was not going to let go. John doing fourteens to my fifteens
took back a yard between each barrier.

In the middle of the second bend I really rapped my left hand
on the top of the seventh hurdle. I remember being instantly
furious with myself for making a mistake. As I landed over the
eighth hurdle, John came into vision. I was pretty shaken to see
him. I'd pushed my first 300 metres as never before and here he
was with me. I tried to keep my leg speed going between eight and
nine, John was a yard up. 'Don't give up,' I yelled to myself,
'maybe he'll fade; leg speed,' but my legs weren't responding. My
mind was on John who was moving away. I knew that my legs
were tired, so in order not to hit the tenth hurdle I sat back, just
a little, but enough to cause a slight loss of momentum. Less than
a yard behind me Ralph landed over the last hurdle and he had
carried his momentum. By the time I realized he was there and
responded with another desperate dig for an extra foot of speed,
he was past me. Time and distance was too short. I felt as if I was
catching him again on the dip but he also dipped well. I knew I
hadn't caught him. By two or three inches he had the silver medal.
The photo-timer separated us by one-hundredth of a second.

Coming up from my dip I had a brief view of Akii going on
round the bend. My hands went to my knees and I gasped for
oxygen. Mary Peters put a congratulatory and consoling hand on
my heaving back. A few seconds later I straightened up and had a
look at the time – 47·82. It took a second or two to take it in. Yes,
it was a new world record, beating mine by 0·3 of a second. My
mouth closed and I drew my lower lip into my mouth and nodded,
well done Akii, well done. I was tired and wanted to put my hands
back on my knees, but forced myself to stay erect and head towards
the man who deserved all the congratulations anyone could give
him, and I wanted mine to be first. John was full of joy, he danced
excitedly round the bend, over another hurdle or two, as camera
men chased him. For an instant I thought I wasn't going to catch
him up as he leaped foward to go down the back straight again.
The man was astonishingly full of running. Camera men called

him back and with a wide smile he waved at the ecstatic crowd. When I reached him, it was as if I brought him back to reality a little. His mind took a few seconds, then he beamed in recognition. I shook his hand and put my other arm on his shoulders telling him how well he'd run and congratulating him for not only winning but also beating the world record.

As I headed back across the high jump area, where Mary Peters was later to stun and charm the crowd in her world-beating pentathlon, I watched the scoreboard and saw confirmation. Ralph Mann second 48·51, David Hemery third 48·52, my second fastest time ever. We were all taken for dope tests, then proceeded to the medal ceremony area. A note arrived from my brother saying 'well done' and that my family sent their congratulations and wondered if I wanted to go out for a meal that night. That sounded good. At the medal ceremony I again met the Marquess of Exeter. As he presented me with my bronze I apologized saying that it wasn't quite what I had hoped for. He was hearteningly sympathetic saying, 'Jolly well done, better than me – I was fourth.' I had not recalled that he also had attempted to retain his Olympic title in 1932.

My feelings were mixed. I was sorry although not desperately disappointed by not winning but I felt awful for all the people who were with me, in person and in spirit, particularly those who were close to me. During the evening I reached Coach Smith by phone. He was superb. I repeatedly apologized to him for not making it. I had so badly wanted to run an unlimited race. He told me that he didn't want to hear any more apologies and summed it up with, 'If you can't accept a bronze medal, then what's the Olympics all about?' 'Thank you coach.' I was so glad he understood. I felt very close to him and sad that this was the end of our time together. Later that night I tried writing Billy a letter. My eyes were glistening and my throat hurt. How do you say thank you and good-bye to someone who has gone through everything with you.

I ran over the race a number of times later, and just as I looked for reasons how on earth I'd won an Olympics, I was now looking for reasons why I lost. One obvious flaw was that at no point in the race did I consciously try to relax. I haven't misjudged many races in my life, why was one of them an Olympic Final? Some people compared my 48·5 to 48·1 at altitude. All I knew was that at the outset of 1971 my 'impossible dream' was aimed at 46·8. A time of

ANALYSIS OF THE 1972 MUNICH OLYMPIC 400 METRES HURDLES FINAL
Taken from B.B.C.-T.V. Video Tapes

Strides to 1st hurdle and leading leg	Lane 1 Akii-Bua (Uganda) 21 (r)		Lane 2 Gavrilenko (U.S.S.R.) 21 (l)		Lane 3 Zorin (U.S.S.R.) 20 (l)		Lane 4 Seymour (U.S.A.) 21 (l)		Lane 5 Hemery (G.B.) 21 (l)		Lane 6 Mann (U.S.A.) 22 (l)		Lane 7 Schubert (U.S.A.) 21 (l)		Lane 8 Tziortzis (Greece) 22 (r)	
Hurdle	Secs.	Place	Secs.	Place	Secs.	Place	Secs.	Place	Secs.	Place	Secs.	Place	Secs.	Place	Secs.	Place
1	6·1	4	5·9	1	6·0	1	6·1	6	6·1	3	6·0	1	6·1	4	6·2	8
2	9·8 (3·7)	3	9·8 (3·9)	4	9·7 (3·7)	1	9·9 (3·8)	6	9·8 (3·7)	3	9·7 (3·7)	1	9·9 (3·8)	6	9·9 (3·7)	6
3	13·6 (3·8)	3	13·7 (3·9)	5	13·5 (3·8)	2	13·8 (3·9)	7	13·4 (3·6)	1	13·6 (3·9)	3	13·7 (3·8)	5	13·8 (3·9)	7
4	17·4 (3·8)	2	17·6 (3·9)	4	17·4 (3·9)	2	17·7 (3·9)	7	17·2 (3·8)	1	17·6 (4·0)	4	17·6 (3·9)	4	17·7 (3·9)	7
5	21·3 (3·9)	2	21·5 (3·9)	5	21·4 (4·0)	4	21·7 (4·0)	7	21·1 (3·9)	1	21·3 (3·7)	2	21·6 (4·0)	6	21·8 (4·1)	8
1st 200	23·0	2	23·2	4	23·1	4	23·4	7	22·8	1	23·0		23·3	6	23·5	8
6	25·4 (4·1)	2	25·9 (4·4)	6	25·6 (4·2)	4	25·9 (4·2)	6	25·1 (4·0)	1	25·4 (4·1)	2	25·8 (4·2)	5	26·1 (4·3)	8
7	29·5 (4·1)	2	30·3 (4·4)	7	30·0 (4·4)	4	30·2 (4·3)	5	29·3 (4·2)	1	29·7 (4·3)	3	30·2 (4·4)	5	30·3 (4·2)	8
8	33·7 (4·2)	1	34·7 (4·4)	7	34·5 (4·5)	4	34·5 (4·3)	4	33·6 (4·3)	2	33·9 (4·2)	3	34·6 (4·4)	6	34·8 (4·5)	8
9	38·1 (4·4)	1	39·3 (4·6)	5	39·4 (4·9)	7	39·1 (4·6)	4	38·2 (4·6)	2	38·4 (4·5)	3	39·3 (4·7)	5	39·4 (4·6)	7
10	42·6 (4·5)	1	44·0 (4·7)	5	44·4 (5·0)	8	43·5 (4·4)	4	43·0 (4·8)	2	43·1 (4·7)	3	44·2 (4·9)	6	44·2 (4·8)	7
Run in	5·2		5·7		5·9		5·1		5·5		5·4		5·5		5·5	
Finish	47·82	1	49·66	6	50·25	8	48·64	4	48·52	3	48·51	2	49·65	5	49·66	7
2nd 200	24·8		26·5		27·2		25·2		25·7		25·5		26·3		26·2	
Difference between 1st and 2nd 200	1·8		3·3		4·1		1·8		2·9		2·5		3·0		2·7	

48·52 was not a true reflection of what I felt I was capable of running, after the work of that year.

Others asked me if I hated Akii for taking *my* gold medal. No, I didn't hate Akii but I did feel bad for my parents and family, my coaches and all the people who helped and hoped, and were running with me, whose hopes rested briefly in my legs and lungs. I had mixed feelings. I had not won, but this didn't sink in any more than winning had four years before. I was tired, a little sad but also almost relieved that it was over. At least I knew I'd tried. God, I had tried; through the whole year and into the race. I'd tried to leave the other seven finalists early on, I'd given my everything and was left standing at the finish. No excuses, Akii ran well. Akii harnessed nature, a good mind, a strong body, a willing spirit, a burning desire to prove himself and his country and a lot of hard work.

Soon after Munich I received a letter from Tom Beatty, a Boston University student with whom I had trained and who had made his own way to the Games. At 21 he had a mature and understanding head on his shoulders. It read as follows:

'I had hoped to see you after everything in Munich was over. But, simply, what I wanted to say was congratulations. To some, it may not seem appropriate to congratulate a person after he has not totally attained his projected aspiration. But I think that to look at your success or failure in terms of a gold medal exclusively would be wrong. Everybody who runs must realize how personal the sport they call track is and must be. Everyone who runs knows when he has run his best and only he actually knows this. Each has his own 'Gold Medal' he aims to reach. Sometimes it takes retrospect to realize that he has actually achieved his personal 'Gold Medal'. An individual's first commitment is to himself. In 10–20 years the important thing won't be what place you finished in that race but rather if you gave yourself totally to the effort. As an outsider, there is no question that you did.

'Track is only a microcosm of the real world into which we all plunge sooner or later and because of this, I think any discussion of whether or not you should have come back after Mexico is unfounded, if its conclusion is based on the aspect of the gold medal. The dedication, the sacrifice, the time, the pain, and the

regurgitation at the track were joined, in pursuit of your internal
commitment. All indicate what it takes to succeed in the outside
world. I've always felt that track should only be used to help
one prepare for his future and when one loses this perspective
I think he has lost the point.'

It is possible to accept any situation, in time. But while still in
Munich I held a burning feeling that I wanted to make amends
and we still had the 4 × 400 metres relay to come. Each in his own
way, the British quartet wanted to make this a good effort. Martin
Reynolds had had trouble achieving an Olympic qualifying time
for 200 metres and had finally made it in the 400 metres. Alan
Pascoe had not qualified for the semi-final of the 110 metres
hurdles and Dave Jenkins, European 400 metres champion had not
reached the Final in his speciality. We started spending some time
together, building up a feeling of unity and resolve. We also discussed the fact that the key to running well would be to keep an
element of relaxation down the back straight, so that we could
finish strongly.

The race lost some of its flavour with the sad news from the
International Olympic Committee that two of the American
sprinters were not to be allowed to run, owing to their casual
conduct at their 400 metres medal ceremony. Is the Games for
individuals or politicians? With John Smith injured, the U.S. were
not able to field a team!

Relays hold an added excitement not generated in other races.
Perhaps it has to do with the build-up of anticipation and hope.
Knowing that a fresh man with a new chance is on the line, waiting
to take over. For some reason Britain has always done well in the
4 × 400 metres relay. Adding up their individual times beforehand
would never put them in with a chance of a medal, but time and
again they've held with the best and come away with medals.

We won our qualifying heat with a time of 3 minutes 01·3
seconds, only 0·1 outside the U.K. record. This put our tails up.
Could we be in with a chance? The Final on the following day
would be close. Kenya, West Germany, Poland, France, Sweden,
Finland, and Trinidad, all had capable teams through to the final.
On paper Kenya and West Germany were the best, the rest was
anyone's guess.

On the morning of the Final, nerves began to build. Would we be good enough for a medal? Would we run up to expectations? The relay teams were the only athletes on the warm-up track. Tension increased within each of us. Reporting time came and thirty-two men, all avoiding each other's eyes, moved down the tunnel towards the arena opening. We were held from going on to the track, and I could feel the shaky weak feeling which nerves produced in me. Each of us knew the extent to which the others on their teams relied on them. The pressure was on and I was glad to feel the adrenalin there again. I was scared. I didn't want to let anyone down. Our team knew that Dave Jenkins was one of the best relay runners in the world. We had to put him in with a chance. This is all he asked for and it was what we had talked of together. We had to stay in contact with the field. Finally the officials lifted the rope and allowed us to release some of our pent-up nerves in last minute warm-up strides. A yell and some shoving started in the stands above us and as we turned Jenkins snapped, 'Don't look. Ignore it.' The pressure was on him and he knew the single-minded concentration required for the task we had at hand.

Martin was on lead-off, perhaps the most difficult position of all, as it is cold, a straight 400 from blocks. From the gun, the runners to follow watched in suspense – seeing if their hopes were being kept alive. Was Martin moving too slowly down the back straight? No maybe not. Oh, come on Martin! Please hold in there. Martin gave it everything he had, passed the baton to Alan, got off the track and passed out cold. Split times in relays are difficult to take, but Martin had run about 46·2 or 46·3. His best for the year and a good start for us, as we were still in contact, although in sixth place. Kenya was away, five yards ahead of the field. Second came West Germany who were about two yards clear of Poland and Sweden. Then came France and Britain and we had three yards on Finland and Trinidad. Pascoe had trained mainly for 110 metres hurdles but showed he had the strength for the longer hurdle event. Matched with some of the best quarter-milers in the world, he held beautiful control down the back straight. I couldn't believe my eyes as he moved wide coming into the home straight, and started to gain ground. Up front, Schloeske of West Germany was running an amazing leg, pulling back the Kenyan's lead and taking West Germany three yards ahead. Poland and France handed off in third and fourth but Alan's scintillating 45·1 brought us past Sweden into fifth place.

When I took the baton Germany were about nine yards ahead of me; but Alan's run had not only kept us in contact, the chance of a medal was high in my thoughts. I went out hard for the first 100 metres, then reminded myself to relax. The speed which I had built up seemed almost easy to hold and I was rapidly coming up on the Frenchman in fourth place. I decided to hang on to my speed and go by him down the back straight. By 200 metres at the end of the back straight I was on the heels of the leaders and one of them moved out to run wide. I held stride and moved out into lane three round the bend. It might add extra yardage, but I wasn't going to break my momentum at this point. My mind started questioning, 'Could I hold on to this or was I going to fade?' Briefly in the home straight I levelled with Kenya and Poland in second and third, but with sixty metres to go I could feel that there wasn't much left in me. For half-a-yard my stride faltered and I thought that they were going to pull away, but they were as tired as I was. We held in echelon to the exchange. West Germany led, two yards clear. Then came Poland, Kenya and ourselves, with France close outside us in fifth.

Because I was wide on the track at the exchange Dave Jenkins was still back in fourth place and Germany's Karl Honz had four yards on him. This distance was more than doubled as Honz raced the fastest 200 metres of his life. Some timed his first half in close to 20 seconds. Kenya's Julius Sang overtook his Polish rival, Andrzej Badenski, just before the second bend and headed after Honz. Karl had run so much lactic acid into his system from his incredible early speed that with forty yards to go he became a nightmare vision of lead legs that just wouldn't move. David Jenkins had pulled close to the leading group and coming into the home straight moved wide. He accelerated past Badenski and sprinted for home in Kenya's wake. He caught Honz five yards from the finish line. The fast-finishing Frenchman, Jacque Carrette, completed the disaster for Honz by edging him out of third place. Sang had run the second fastest relay leg ever recorded, to bring Kenya the gold and David had brought Britain from fourth to silver with the fastest relay leg ever by a European. We were delighted as a team and I felt good to have helped earn part of that silver. Times on the splits varied; however the official result gave me 44·9, Jenkins, 44·2, and Sang 43·6.

This was to be my last Olympics and I was happy to retire with a complete set – gold, silver, and bronze. The only other Briton to have achieved this was Mary Rand-Toomey.

My last run as an amateur in Britain was at the Crystal Palace in the I.A.C./Coca Cola meeting. Before the Games I had stated that we probably wouldn't want to see another 400 metres hurdles race again, so a 300 metres hurdles was scheduled. Akii-Bua decided not to stay around for this, but good competition came from Ralph Mann and Alan Pascoe. The world best for 330 yards stood at 35·7 by Geoff Vanderstock worth about 35·5 for 300 metres. It was a cool, calm mid-September evening and I wanted this last run to be a good one. I hoped to hold thirteen strides for the full distance, so during the race I relaxed between hurdles two and three, then really opened up with full power and effort round the bend and down the home straight. I caught Alan by the fourth hurdle and he caught Ralph by the fifth. I held my stride to the seventh and last hurdle and felt superbly strong accelerating to the finish. There was no feeling of fatigue and I really believed that I could have run on to the 400 metres mark with little difficulty. Alan finished second with Ralph third. Alan had come within 0·1 of the previous world best, with 35·6.

My winning time was 34·6, bettering the previous best mark by almost a second. That time for 300 metres is 46·1 pace for 400 metres. Obviously I wouldn't have held that speed and pace all the way to the finish of 400 metres but it confirmed my belief that 48·5 was not a true representation of my year's training. I harboured a faint wish that I could be on the start line again in Munich. I'm not saying that I knew I could beat Akii given the race over, but there's always a question mark.

Coach had said after Munich, 'Time now for you to find a wife, settle down, have a family and forget about track.' I wrote him from England with my wonderings, saying that it is probably the nature of man never to be satisfied for long, that there is always the belief that there's still a chance to improve, to do even better next time. Browning's line is so accurate, 'A man's reach should exceed his grasp, or what's a heaven for?'

CHAPTER 10

Superstars

For months after Munich I felt free of the requirement to train. Following his gold-medal-winning orgy, Mark Spitz didn't go near the water. He didn't find it recreation just to swim for fun. I was going through the same mental process. When I did take exercise, it was playing basketball with some of the Millfield students.

Six months after my last race I was invited to the Esso Young Athletes Course at Lilleshall in Staffordshire. This is where the first three finishers in the All England Schools Intermediate age group boys and girls have a week-long training camp. I was asked to coach hurdles and give a lecture. I was able to come for two days and on my first night there I joined the staff and some of the athletes in the coffee shop. I noticed an attractive girl sitting with the coaching party and I asked George Tymms, a fellow hurdling coach, who she was. I wasn't sure if she was on the course. George laughed at that, as she was actually a 24-year-old teacher, with a first class honours degree in Maths. As I was in teaching, I went and sat next to her at someone else's lecture the next day and started talking to her about the world of education and her involvement in athletics. Gloria turned out to be an 800 metres runner, up for a few days' training under her coach Harry Wilson. She was intelligent and interesting. I talked her into accepting a dinner date when I was next in London when I could pass on a book of mutual interest, a résumé of the work of psychologist Abraham Maslow, to whom I shall refer later. The book came to London with me but I obviously found Gloria more interesting as it wasn't passed on at that time. A mild romance developed and one weekend she came to visit Millfield. She had to do a training session of thirty minutes steady running. All of a sudden my thoughts of the distastefulness of training disappeared. I joined her for an easy run on the country roads of Somerset.

To my discomfort, I found out that you can't take six months off and then run non-stop at a *good* stride for half an hour. The area isn't without its hills and within ten minutes I was trying to conceal my dramatically heavy breathing. Five minutes later, I wasn't concealing anything. I was confessing how terribly far out shape I was and by this time the blood pressure in my head was causing a few stars and my stomach wasn't sure if it wanted to carry my lunch much farther. To my eternal gratitude we looped past the car at the twenty-minute mark and I told Gloria I'd jog on and intersect her running course again on her way back. At that moment I made a few vows to myself about staying in shape!

Getting back into shape is not easy at any age and it's pretty depressing when it takes so little to let yourself fall out of shape. I worked hard for a few weeks so never again had to face the ignominy of being dropped in a distance session with my wife-to-be. On Boxing Day, December 26th, 1973, Gloria Mary Anna O'Leary and David Peter Hemery negotiated the required portions of the marriage service and made our personally written and chosen pledges to each other at the Harvard University chapel in Cambridge, Mass.

Having been shocked, if not shamed, back into training and pretty good condition by mid-1973, I felt somewhat frustrated not to have any significant athletic aim. To my surprise and delight the event known as Sporting Superstars was just being organized. It had been difficult to train very consistently with just the aim of keeping fit. This is perhaps only a problem for those who have become superbly fit through training for the goal of international representation in their chosen sport. Now the fact that I could train for a specific purpose lifted my spirits immensely.

Superstars is a sports concept primarily geared for television. Stars in individual sports often become household names through repeated television appearances. The idea is to bring together the individual stars from various sports. The individual is not eligible for the sport in which he is a champion unless handicapped.

I really enjoy playing almost all sports and here was an opportunity to channel my competitive instinct for fun and possibly some economic reward. I was always strict with myself as an amateur athlete. It may have been naïve not to run for money where it was available but I felt lifted and strengthened by staying clean within my own mind. I would strongly campaign to have the rules altered if I believed they were unfair or outdated but while they existed I chose to remain within them. As my retirement from international competition meant no more Olympics for me, competing for a prize of £4,000 seemed an interesting and worthwhile venture.

The event was to be held at or near to Crystal Palace depending on the sport. The contestants in that summer of 1973 really were among the best known of Britain's sporting heroes. Joe Bugner, European Heavyweight Boxing Champion; Barry John, Wales and Lions rugby football star; Bobby Moore, England's soccer captain, capped over 100 times and a most brilliant reader of the game; Tony Jacklin, winner of the British and American Golf Championships; Roger Taylor, multi-tournament winner and Britain's top tennis player; Jackie Stewart, World Motor Racing Champion and some say the best driver of all time; and myself.

The organizers, Trans World International, chose ten sports. Each individual had to select eight out of ten events, dropping his own speciality. In my case there was a problem as two running events were scheduled; 100 metres and a 600 metres steeplechase. Rather than ban me from both running events it was decided to handicap me in the steeplechase which was the final event on the second day.

During my years in athletics I had met great track and field athletes from around the world but here was an opportunity to spend some time with people who were tops in various sports. This group turned out to be delightful. Because they had each reached the top of their field they didn't appear to need to prove themselves to each other. They accepted each other as individuals, knowing that each had achieved his position through years of dedication to developing his skill. Each event was taken seriously during competition; however, between events there was tremendous wisecracking and banter.

One of the early events was pistol shooting. Joe Bugner proved to be 'dead eye dick' which caused Jackie Stewart to line Bugner up between himself and the target. Jackie is a crack clay pigeon shot. We were lined up ten yards from five white discs only two inches in diameter. We had twenty shots to break all five discs.

Tony Jacklin found this event a problem. His first five shots didn't touch anything, so he lowered his gun, turned to us and said, 'well at least I've got them surrounded'. As he raised his gun again, the wind caught one of the discs and it fell to the ground. Tony elatedly turned to the crowd and asked if they had heard him fire. Then he mumbled, as if to himself, 'at least someone's on my side'. Tony maintained his good humour throughout. Half-way through the competition he was asked which event was his strong one and he half-laughed and half-cried, 'I don't have one. I don't think I'm going to win a single point.' Points were awarded for the first five finishers in each event; 10 for the first, then 7, 4, 2 and 1.

As was predictable, Barry John won the 100 metres. Unused to wearing spikes, he caught them in the track soon after the finish and we saw his rugby action as he executed a perfect forward roll. Barry and I shared a number of meal times at the hotel and I found him to be a warm and personable man. He and I were the two amateurs among the professionals. For both of us, this was our first step outside our amateur competitive sport days. When he finished a close runner-up to me in this contest, I suggested that perhaps we established our finishing order according to our economic need.

Jackie Stewart and Tony Jacklin were old friends and the same high level of humour came from Jackie. He asked if he could wear flippers for the 50 metres swim and, on discovering that this was not on, decided to forgo that event. Tony wasn't at all sure he'd complete the race and started pleading with the officials to let him swim in the outside lane, so that if he started sinking he could hang on to the side. Tony, in fact, swam quite well, although one reporter likened his style to a man swimming away from the 'Titanic'.

Most of the sports called into play muscles that we rarely used with the result that we were all fairly stiff and tired at the beginning of the second day. Joe Bugner still wasn't around at Crystal Palace by mid-morning and Jackie Stewart started to play act Joe's manager. 'Come on big Joe – you can do it. Get up Joe. 7, 8, 9, Joe, you've got to get up.' This was accompanied by much towel-flapping over the imaginary prostrate carcass of Joe. Actually Joe was probably the fittest man there, something he proved in the gym exercises by shifting the long legs of his 6 feet 4 inch frame from a press-up position to a squat and back again sixty-eight times in 60 seconds. I think that all of us will attest to the fact that this is the most demanding of all the exercises we had to undertake. The fact that Tony reached fifty-two for seventh place really showed that the overall standard of fitness was extremely high.

Bobby Moore was under a distinct disadvantage as he was not released from morning football training during these two days. He proved a competent swimmer and golfer. Many youngsters felt he should have been placed higher than he did in the 100 metres dash. To me, the fact that he did not, showed the brilliance of his positioning on the soccer field. He gave so many of us and his team mates confidence having him in the England defence for so many years.

Roger Taylor surprised us all by chasing Barry John down to the wire in the 100 metres and proved he has stamina as well, by placing high in the steeplechase. His downfall came in the soccer penalties where the balls came from his feet like shooting stars but unfortunately none towards the back of the net.

Wives, girlfriends, and children accompanied most of the competitors and it was good to see another side to these men's lives. Television tends to leave viewers with a single dimension of sportsmen as 'the runner' or 'the tennis player' as if that is all there is to that person and his life.

For me, Jackie Stewart epitomized mind over matter. He channelled all his mental energy and determination into getting everything out of himself. In the parallel-bar-dips, he brought himself up three extra times like a dolphin swimming, in order to top the previous best. I am a firm believer in the huge extent to which the mind determines one's physical potential. I once read an article in which Jackie was explaining that most racing drivers take a few minutes to adapt themselves to the phenomenal speed at which they race. Jackie told how he usually managed to get the jump on the other drivers at the start by being mentally tuned to the speed by the time the flag dropped. Ron Pickering, B.B.C. commentator and adviser on the Superstar event, was singularly impressed with Jackie. His stature is small but he combined will-power with his basic fitness to achieve an extraordinary level of performance throughout.

Two events stand out in my recollection of my own performance, the cycle race and the steeplechase. The cycle race was a 400 metres time-trial. Most kids have bikes and I was no exception, but mine didn't have such sophisticated accoutrements as gears. The Raleigh bikes were brand new and we had explicit instruction on how to change gear. Terrific. The start was fine and seventy metres out I started trying to change gear. The wheel wobbled and I'd changed the wrong way. My legs caught up with the rapidly flying wheels and I tried again. This time my right foot flipped forward on the pedal as I was heading into the back straight with a racing left foot and a hesitant right. By this time I was in the lowest possible gear but decided, to hell with it, put my head down and pedalled like a maniac. Down the back straight and round the second bend someone clocked my pedals at 3,000 r.p.m.!

With my head down and eyes closed I entered the home straight at what felt like 60 m.p.h. Unfortunately, one foot again slipped forward and a flying toe burnt into the track. The next thing I knew, both my legs had spun off the pedal, so with sixty yards to go I started free-wheeling, legs either side of the pedals. Cries of 'Cocky bastard' filled my head but there was no way of getting my feet back on the pedals. I shot across the line, unbelievably, clocking the fastest time. Jacklin said, 'There's no way he can win doing it like that.'

Cycling was the penultimate event and Barry John still held a half-point lead over me. Barry had scored well in the ball games, winning the tennis, soccer penalties, and placing well in the golf. In order to win, I had to finish ahead of him in the final event, the steeplechase. Barry joined Bobby Moore, Joe Bugner, and Roger Taylor on the starting line. Jackie and Tony had decided to opt out of this one. The four had to run 600 metres, that's a lap-and-a-half – going over the water jump twice and five hurdles. Ron Pickering decided that I should be handicapped 100 metres which also meant an extra hurdle. If the group ran at a good stride there was really no way I could make up that distance, perhaps 50 metres but never 100 metres. Unbelievably, the group trotted off after the gun, as if the race was 60 miles rather than 600 metres. In fact Joe was going so slowly he didn't have enough momentum to take the water jump, and 'refused'. Approaching the barrier, I couldn't believe my eyes – Bugner was coming towards me as he circled back for another try! He took off at greater speed this time, but his frame wasn't built to hurdle. The ensuing splash in the twelve-foot span of water was substantial. I caught him with 300 metres to go but was still not sure about catching all the others who had increased their tempo.

Bobby Moore I overhauled with 200 metres to go and then I set my sights hard on the figures of Roger Taylor and Barry John. Barry was looking over his shoulder and almost appeared to be waiting for me. I was approaching fast, clearing the water completely on the final jump, and started sprinting for home. In the last 100 metres Barry pulled back the 15 metres deficit he had on Roger Taylor, I passed them both with about 60 metres to go and, after the final barrier, lifted my knees as much as I could, to make certain of not being caught. Kids from the 10,000 crowd swarmed on to the track to congratulate me. I had become the winner of Britain's first-ever Superstar event. Following Barry John, Jackie Stewart and Joe Bugner tied for overall third place.

I was pleased to reflect that although the financial reward may have been a stimulant for all to take part, once the competition had started, taking part and trying to do one's best was the most important element and this held true for everyone. (Of course, the prize was an added and very welcome bonus.)

An inevitable by-product of being well known is the heavy round of invitations to compete, talk, fund raise, open buildings, or attend functions. Often at charity affairs top sportsmen meet again. The sportsmen's own charity is SPARKS – the Sportsmen Pledged to Aid Research into Crippling. For the last couple of years the organizers of this charity have brought a dozen or more of Britain's top sportsmen and women to motor-racing tracks. The first of these was at Brand's Hatch in the winter of 1972. Ford supplied brand-new Granadas, big, powerful, standard production, family cars. One requirement for taking part in the ten-lap race was to have a practice session. I fixed a day, drove the 200 miles from Somerset and arrived just in time for a thunderstorm. Regardless of this, I was taken through a demonstration drive with Gillian Fortescue-Thomas. She talked of an 'easy lap' to give me some idea of the course. I heard about half of her comments as I was praying the rest of the time! At each turn, I was thrown hard against my double-harness seat belt and then into the car door. We approached the famous Paddock Bend at about 100 m.p.h. The road curves right, then drops steeply farther right over a crest. I just hoped that the wheels were going to be the first part of the car to touch the ground.

When my feelings had abated to mere fear, Gillian stopped the car and left me behind the wheel. Following a cautious look at the bends and some face-saving acceleration between them, I progressed, in the space of fifty minutes, to taking the bends as fast as I possibly could. I was sure there would be better clip points, driving angles, and turning points than I was using, so I asked Tony Dron, another test driver, if he'd mind acting as co-pilot in my car.

The rain had stopped; the drive path was drying out, and all was going fine. Tony even went as far as to say I was driving fast and well, and then it happened – at the notorious Paddock Bend. The speed was 90 plus and Tony's command 'turn now'. The difference between the call and my turn was probably only a few 100ths of a second, but it was sufficient to put the wheels on the left side into the wet and the car started to turn. Twice going down the hill at 85–90 m.p.h., I marginally corrected the skid, but nearing the bottom there was no response and I over corrected. The two front wheels were now on the dry and the back two on the wet, came round fast. In the space of a fifteen-yard grass verge the car completed its 180 degree turn and slammed to a dead halt against the sleepers. My only thought was an expletive for not controlling the car properly. Tony moved from the crash position and said his only thought was, 'I wonder what it's going to feel like crashing at Paddock – having tried to avoid doing exactly that over the past years of driving.' Fortunately the car had come to rest exactly parallel with the sleepers and therefore was not badly damaged and we were both fine. Less fortunate was golfer Mike Bonallack in his practice run, again with Tony Dron on board. At the same turn, Mike took away ten feet of sleepers and rolled his car over three times. Hard to believe, but Tony came back to instruct the following year's drivers.

The race itself was much less spectacular but far more fun. Graham Hill was there to wish everyone good luck and asked if I was going to put running spikes on my wheels. Cricketer Rachael Heyhoe-Flint and Henry Cooper were asking themselves before the race what on earth they were taking part for and then drove just like that: Rachael was given a front row starting position and we funnelled back by turn in alphabetical order. Rachael joined ranks with cricketing colleague Colin Cowdrey and 'our 'enry', to cause a sportsmen's traffic jam on the first bend. This gave Chay

Blyth, the round-the-world yachtsman, a great get-away. From the back Tom Percival, powerboat champion, and Richard Meade, equestrian gold medallist, saw what was going on and made up a dozen places on the inside grass verge. Chay drove aggressively and narrowly held off Tom Percival for first place with Richard Meade third. During the race, I moved up about half a dozen places to finish seventh.

Following this experience, it doesn't surprise me one bit that the pulse rates of racing drivers can reach 180 before the start of a race, due to concentration and anticipation, or that Jackie Stewart lost 5 or 6 pounds during a Grand Prix!

The second year of Superstars saw Chay as a competitor. No one still knows how he talked his way into the rowing event, since he rowed the Atlantic single-handedly, but I believe he claimed that his first sport was yachting where he twice sailed single handed round the world. Rowing was a new event to the competition and Southampton's football star, Mick Channon, was nearly arrested for trespassing, as he rowed his boat through someone's back garden.

The rowing final was a close-run affair. Only in the last ten yards was it settled. Colin Bell, another of England's brilliant footballers, started pulling back my lead. Unfortunately he rowed his stern into my side so that I could not use my right oar. We coasted across the line while Chay, on the far side, obtained a 0·2 seconds winning margin.

Three weeks of 'flu prior to the 1974 competition saw my stamina sadly lacking and this left the door wide open for the super-fit John Conteh. John tackled the event as a true professional. His trainer, George Francis, a super guy himself, found John top coaches for each event and John worked hard. As Colin Bell had once scored 160 in an innings for his club Conteh surprised even himself by winning the cricket, getting the most runs off six balls from an automatic bowling machine.

For some reason, the 1974 contest didn't quite hold the same level of humour and good feeling as did the previous year. Perhaps some individuals were too apprehensive of not doing too well and it was taken too seriously between events. Certainly one contributing factor was bad health. Mike Channon was covered with German measles spots. I was recovering from 'flu. Squash Champion Jonah Barrington had sprained his ankle and could not take part, and Phil Read was involved in a minor accident on his 500 c.c motor cycle in a Grand Prix the day before and was also out. Cricketer Tony Greig was healthy and felt increasingly confident about the contest as he won the 50 metres swim and then astonished everyone by scoring six penalties out of six against England goalkeeper Peter Shilton. Another boxer, John Stracey, stepped in at the last minute and for his state of fitness did very well.

The running events were won by the footballers each time, split by Conteh. The duel in the 100 metres between Channon and Bell was settled in Channon's favour but unsatisfactorily, as Colin stumbled badly coming out of the blocks and just failed to catch John Conteh for second place. Colin however, got his own back in the 600 metres steeplechase and this year there was no way I was going to catch them. John, Colin, and Mick all set off at a hot pace and I again started with a 100 metres handicap. The two others in the field were Tony Greig and John Stracey who had a solid respect for the barriers and the distance. I passed both of them with 200 metres to go but still was 60 metres down on the other three. I could see that the distance and early pace was telling on Mick and that Colin was now getting the better of John. If Mick really faded, I might just catch him. But after he shakily cleared the last barrier he took a look over his shoulder and put in a final spurt. We crossed the line virtually together, with him retaining third place. I'd run 5 seconds faster than the previous year but these guys had run it as it should have been run, hard and fast all the way.

Colin Bell proved to be a strong competitor throughout and he finished only five-sixths of a point behind my second place total. Colin was staying at the same hotel and again it was enjoyable to meet a genuinely nice person. I thoroughly enjoy talking with sportsmen, finding out what they feel about their sport, how they see it and what it's done for them. I believe that an individual learns a great deal about himself and life through striving for excellence in a sport.

The man of this Superstars contest, however, was John Conteh. John knows where he is going, has a tough, determined, and dedicated attitude towards competition, but also has a very charming and human demeanour. In spite of his success he has kept his feet on the ground. John and I had a tussle in the weight lifting. Admittedly, I don't look like a lifter and John does; but looks don't always tell the story. Any athlete may bulk up, when he does press-ups and lifts weights or he may just gain tensile strength, i.e. the muscles become stronger but not necessarily much larger. By the time we'd reached our body weights most of the other competitors had been eliminated. Ten pounds at a time we lifted and passed each other's best. John finally won the contest with a lift of 210 pounds, I went out at 200.

John is conscious of the image that the general public has of boxers. He has gone a long way to prove that a boxer can be intelligent, articulate, and a gentleman. The boxing fraternity can be proud of its representatives in the Superstar events so far, Bugner, Conteh and Stracey.

In my opinion the concept of the Superstars event is excellent. Apart from its merit as the televised National event for professional sportsmen, the idea of the good all-rounder can be fostered for amateurs and in particular for youngsters. I believe that kids should not be forced to specialize in one sport when very young. If it were possible to run a widespread series of superstar competitions at various school age-levels, perhaps youngsters would be introduced to a wider variety of sports. The Walls Five-Star Award Scheme in athletics currently allows this type of experimentation and is already proving a great success. It would take considerable organization to achieve it on a multi-sport basis but I believe the benefits would be worth the effort.

Plans for a 1977 World Superstar competition took major strides forward in 1975. While contests were being organized in Australia and Japan, the first European Superstar event was held. Six preliminary rounds preceded the Final.

John Conteh would no doubt have been one of Britain's top representatives, but unfortunately he broke his right hand in his fight with Willie Taylor only a few months before the European heats. I was chosen as one of Britain's representatives and competed in August in the first heat held at Aldershot. The contest turned into a two-man battle between myself and the Dutch hockey centre-forward, Tiese Kruize. The events see-sawed. He won the tennis; I won the weight-lifting. He won the swimming, I won the rowing. He won the 100 metres, which I was not allowed to enter; I won the gym event which he had opted out of. Both of us dropped the pistol shooting. He won the soccer penalties; I won the cycling.

We were almost even going into the final event the 600 metres steeplechase. I held only a one-and-a-half points lead, so I had to finish ahead of him to win. Unfortunately, the handicapping was still as it had been for the less fierce competition of 1973. I was again to start 100 metres behind the rest of the field. Tiese took off hard from the start. Perhaps my eagerness to catch up diminished the attention one must pay to a steeplechase barrier, but whatever it was, I ran at it as if I was going to hurdle over it into the water. Only at the last second did my mind jump into focus so that I had to take off my other foot and step on to the barrier. I hopped forward awkwardly, swung my right foot to the top of the barrier – but luck wasn't with me. My spikes didn't grip and my foot started sliding away along the barrier to my right. My forward momentum was so great that I couldn't check myself and I flipped over the barrier . . . into the deep end of the water jump! I felt as though I was carrying 10 pounds of water inside my shirt, which I probably was, as I tried to get going again, and by now the leaders were 120 metres ahead. I picked up my pace and managed to catch the last two men at the finish line, to gain fourth place – but Tiese was second and the overall winner.

The camera crew from the Netherlands were very upset. They said it was a hollow victory which left a bad taste, that the handicap was unfair. They kindly said they would petition for me to be in the Final. As it happened I qualified in any case as the highest point-scoring non-winner. Then only a few weeks before the Final, Tiese was involved in a serious car crash and broke his thigh. It was, of course, a great disappointment for him. I was sorry about his injury and also disappointed, as I had hoped for the opportunity to turn the tables on him in the Final, and had been practising the events where he had beaten me.

Handicapping had to be reviewed for the Final as five of the nine finalists were from track and field athletics. The field was as follows: from Belgium, sprinter Alfons Brijdenbach; from France, Guy Drut, who had just set a new world record in the high hurdles of 13·0 seconds. The man I most respected apart from Drut was the Swedish representative Kjell Isaksson, former pole vault world record holder at 18 feet 4 inches (5·59 metres). The Netherlands had two representatives, triple Olympic gold medallist Ard Schenke, and his speed skating successor Harm Kuipers. Germany was represented by motor racing star Jochen Mass, and Spain by distance runner Mariano Haro. For Britain, Malcolm MacDonald, Newcastle's football star, who had qualified well by winning the heat in Sweden and myself.

The Final took place in Rotterdam in November. Both competitors and organizers recognized the more serious atmosphere. Although competitors did enjoy some social interchange, the tension of a new international sports competition was apparent.

The first day of competition lasted about twelve hours and was quite a strain on one's reserves. The character of each competitor showed up clearly during the contest. In contrast to the once-for-all performance of an athlete flashing before an audience, possibly followed by a few minutes close-up talk, this event keeps the competitors continuously together, in their sustained and varied applications of skill, concentration, and effort. As Super Mac pointed out, 'competing is fun for the sportsman'; but at the same time the effort involved is deadly serious.

It was the first time I had met Malcolm MacDonald. He has a quick mind, a good sense of humour, and I enjoyed getting to know him. My first encounter with him in a competitive situation was the 100 metres. With the new system of handicaps I started 4 metres behind him. At the finish I'd caught all the others, but was $4\frac{1}{2}$ metres behind Mac. I was never an international sprinter, but I should be able to hold my own against non-track athletes. It was generally agreed that Mac must be one of the fastest footballers around. His heat clocking of 10·9 seconds is worth 5–8 metres faster than those recorded by Mick Channon, Colin Bell, and Barry John in their Crystal Palace runs. Mac also showed his power in the overarm medicine ball throw and in the weight-lifting event but this was not what impressed me most. Behind the cool and tough exterior was a genuine and considerate individual. By the time of the weight-lifting event it was clear that I was in with a good chance of finishing in the first three, in the overall competition. I had already lifted a personal best of $203\frac{1}{2}$ pounds and was attempting 209 pounds (95 kilogrammes). After my first failure, Mac jumped up and asked to lift that weight, in order to give me a pause, saying under his breath as he passed me, 'Go on, sit down and take a rest.'

Again, going into the final event he asked me if there was any way that he could run which would help me to catch up the 40 metres deficit on the field. I had to finish ahead of Ard Schenke in order to move into second place overall. I told him that I really appreciated his asking but that I'd just be running hard from the start and that he should run his own race. Throughout the competition Mac was solid and controlled. When we were warming-up together, jogging before the cycle race, I asked him if he was at all nervous. He said, 'No, not when I'm competing for myself, but I do get nervous in a team where I don't want to let the others down.' Mac showed that he can be as concerned for others as for himself. Super Mac is a super guy. He finished in seventh place with $18\frac{1}{2}$ points.

At 5 feet 5 inches Mariano Haro was dwarfed in the company of the other competitors. His lined weather-beaten face makes him look all of his 35 years. He had great difficulty getting into the scoring at all, but his radiant smile remained throughout, which soon made him a favourite with the crowd. His soccer penalties underlined his poor luck as well as his questionable skill. His series of five shots finished up as follows: just outside to the left, just outside to the right, just over the top, into the crossbar, and into the goalie! Mariano kept plugging away, giving it every effort but he only managed to score in three events to finish ninth. One must wish him well in his quest for a medal in the Montreal marathon, He finished fourth in the 10,000 metres in the Munich Olympics race and has finished the runner-up to different people in four successive International Cross-Country Championships.

Guy Drut is also a man who could win Olympic honours in Montreal. He has an excellent chance of the gold medal in the high hurdles. His mind was certainly focused many months ahead. Several times during the competition, talk returned to the coming Olympic Games. He reminded me that I was the last European to have beaten him in the high hurdles and that was six years ago. For Guy, Superstars proved to be a frustrating competition. We were drawn together in the tennis preliminaries. He played over-cautiously and was well below his normal game. He lost 15–10.

I was particularly embarrassed and sorry for our collision in the rowing heats. Guy and I were drawn next to each other. The boats were practice sculls, requiring considerable skill. It was my first time in a boat with a sliding seat and I had great difficulty maintaining the necessary flow, without tipping and turning the boat, as one or other of the oars were drawn back for the next stroke. Near the finish I had pulled so close to Guy that neither of us could stroke across the line. The Dutch judges ruled that I had not impeded him until after the prows of our boats were across the finish line, but I felt bad that there was still a question in Guy's mind.

Guy felt very unwell after the cycle sprint and although he came back to lift well and take third in the soccer penalties, he still only finished eighth with 16 points.

In sixth place a point-and-a-half ahead of Super Mac was Harm Kuipers. He will soon be finishing his medical studies and unfortunately that workload was too great for him to train for the 1976 winter Olympics. During 1973 Harm had spent the year cycle training, to condition himself for skating. His cycling had to be seen to be believed. His thighs were immense and that was all one saw on the bike. He and his speed skating rival, Ard Schenke, went to the line for the cycling Final. Harm, the younger by five years, proved the better, winning in just over the minute for 800 metres. Harm was softly spoken but his direct piercing eyes showed the keen and fierce resolution which is necessary to take any individual to the top.

Harm finished only one point behind Belgium's Alfons Brijdenbach. Alfons at 21 years was by far the youngest of the contestants. He scored in four events, fourth in the pistol shooting and the 600 metres steeplechase, second in the soccer penalties, and he won the tennis. His great speed and natural rhythm were put to good use behind the football, but his greatest area of success was his deceptive and frustrating mode of tennis. His speed allowed him to get to any ball and he didn't make any mistakes on his return. A better player than I would probably have been able to put the ball away, but my visits to the net were greeted with a couple of excellent lobs. I lost to him in the semi-final and he put away Kjell Isaksson in the Final.

Fourth place went to Germany's Jochen Mass. Jochen again showed how tough and talented are motor racers. Great all-round athletic skill and solid determination have been portrayed by Jackie Stewart, James Hunt, Jackie Ickx, as well as Jochen. He flew direct from winning a Grand Prix in South Africa, to arrive at six o'clock on the morning of the competition. His first and most successful event was the swimming which he won in fine style, clocking 30·2 seconds for the 50 metres. He came second in pistol shooting, third in rowing and the gym event, fourth in tennis and football, and fifth in weight-lifting. Only by one place did he fail to score by coming sixth in cycling; an excellent showing.

Often this sort of sportsman is classed as a playboy, in an exciting jet set life. This may be so, but Jochen was first to the doctor's room after I fell at the last steeplechase barrier. He told me to get my wet shirt off and gave me his shirt and track suit top before he left the room. He also phoned the next morning just to see that my ankle wasn't broken and to say good-bye. Like the other drivers, Jochen is genuinely personable and I enjoyed meeting him.

Ard Schenke is the archetypal Adonis, 6 feet 3½ inches tall, blond haired and good looking, all on a 220 pounds frame. He would have won a fourth gold medal in the last winter Olympics had he not fallen in that event. Ard had only just married and his wife was with him. She said that this would probably be his last competition and that he was not very fit. They had been working on renovating a big old country home. On little training he did very well. He won the soccer penalties and the pistol shooting; placed second in rowing and cycling and was fourth in the 100 metres. Ard hadn't expected to place in the first three, and seemed pleased to have done so. He and his wife made a point of coming to say goodbye as Gloria and I left the hotel. It's possible to get to know some people quite rapidly. Gloria and I liked them both and hope that their life together works out well.

One man, Sweden's Kjell Isaksson, had prepared one step more than me and it paid off for him as he became the first winner of the European Superstars. He had totally dominated his heat and he wasn't far off doing the same in the Final. For two events I stayed ahead of him. I finished second in the 100 metres dash and the 50 metres swim. In both of these events he placed third, but when we moved to the rowing area he told me that he'd been practising in a single scull . . . and it showed. He rowed smoothly and powerfully to a clear win, whereas I had my lowest finish in any event, fourth place. In the tennis we didn't meet each other but I met Brijden-bach before he did; Kjell was second to my third.

The final event of the long first day was the gym test. I couldn't get off a good throw with the medicine ball and finished seventh to Kjell's third. We moved on to the parallel bar dips, where he set a formidable standard of thirty-six. It took a lot of concentrated effort but I managed to press out thirty-seven for a first to his second. The same order pertained in the squat thrusts, he was second to me,

However because of my lower placing in the throw, he placed first
and I was second in the overall gym result. So Kjell ended the first
day with a 7-point lead. On the second day he had opted for pistol
shooting and finished fifth. I pulled back 3 points by finishing third
in the 800 metres cycle, which he had dropped. The weight-lifting
would be decisive. Kjell had brought his own lifting belt and had
obviously had expert instruction. He won the whole event. I
thought that I was reasonably strong for my weight. I lifted a personal best of 203$\frac{1}{2}$ pounds, 40 pounds more than my body weight.
Three times I cleaned 209 pounds (95 kilogrammes) but just
couldn't jerk it. Kjell then attempted and managed 214 pounds,
60 pounds more than his body weight. This may not be exceptional for weight-lifters but it is a challenging target for sportsmen
other than weight-lifters. Guy Drut took second place only 0·7
kilogrammes ahead of me.

I wanted to redeem my reputation in the 600 metres steeplechase, the final event. It was held indoors at the Ahoy Stadium
and a water jump had been ingeniously built into an infield stair-
well especially for this event. The system of handicapping brought
me to this jump just as the main pack were all taking it. In fact it
was Ard Schenke who pulled wide into my line of running just before
the barrier, making a clear jump impossible. I took a step up and
made a two-footed landing into the water behind him. I picked up
my pace and passed the main group as the gun sounded for 200
metres to go. Harm Kuipers and Kjell were still ahead. I caught
Harm over the hurdle in the back straight and sprinted after Kjell.
I came alongside him just before the last water jump and he took a
look across at me. This time I can't tell you what happened. I
pushed off from the top of the barrier and I think that the angle at
which my left foot landed on the incline just rolled my ankle over.
Whatever it was, my ankle collapsed and for the second time in as
many steeplechases, I was soaked. My mind didn't wait to ask
about injury, all I could think of was getting to the finish line 50
metres farther on, before Ard could come by. I tried to regain a
sprint but found it difficult. Harm had passed me while I was in
the water but I held on to third, Kjell had won.

I sat down to take the weight off my left foot and then discovered
that my aching left ankle had swollen to double its normal size. The
young P.E. students who had been assigned to help us each day
wouldn't let me walk. They lifted me from the ground and literally

ran me to the medical room. The sports doctor wouldn't allow me to return to the presentation ceremony; it was a rapid trip to the Rotterdam Hospital for X-rays. There was no break but badly torn ligaments were diagnosed and a half cast put on so that I wouldn't use the ankle. Athletes are always too impatient to get back to training after an injury, but I was to find it somewhat frustrating to be off the foot for six weeks.

Kjell had waited at the hotel entrance for my return from the hospital, which wasn't until 1 a.m. He said that he hoped nothing was broken and that he hadn't been the cause of the accident. I assured him that it wasn't his fault. I don't think we touched in the air, and if we did it was only in the course of running.

Kjell's form illustrated the more serious approach at the Final. Good spirits still prevailed among the competitors but, as in most international sports contests, the atmosphere was intense during each event.

Like every second-place in sport, I was stuck with the inevitable frustration of being so near and yet so far. I reflected on what might have been – if only I'd won the rowing, as I did in my heat, and had not fallen in the steeplechase, then I'd have won. But that's what makes this event so intriguing. The combinations of scores and possible finishing positions of each man provides endless speculation. As in the track and field decathlon, every event counts, every point makes a difference. I'm sure that it will become an established event on a world-wide basis, as it has great appeal and enjoyment for the participants as well as the viewers. I have enjoyed taking part and will enjoy watching when I no longer compete.

CHAPTER 11

Sport's Troubled Scene

We are living in a time when many aspects of society are becoming too large and complex to be controlled. The Western world is experiencing the unique and unsettling time of an inflationary depression. No one knows for sure what to do. Prices rise and money becomes more scarce. Magazine articles in the U.S. suggest growing your own vegetables, and young people talk of trying a simpler life style, where they're not compelled to join the rat race for money and promotion.

Over the last few years a great deal has been said and written about 'doing your own thing'. Many people have started looking at their treadmill existences and are realizing that they only have a certain amount of time on this earth and why should that be spent in blinkered unawareness. They are just as capable, as anyone else, of finding out and doing what they really want to do. This has been evident in Black consciousness, Women's Liberation, and the Gay Revolution. Perhaps Western Society had become so techno-logy-orientated, so bureaucratic, and so dehumanized that man has had to re-assert himself, to re-establish his own identity and to say to his fellow men – *Man* and *his self-development* is really what's important.

Sport has been one area which for several years held the illusion of purity. Men and women trained and struggled mainly with the elements and within themselves, then occasionally laid themselves on the line, in public, in open competition with others. It was all about challenge. Man, working, willing his body and spirit to new heights in an area where there is always a new frontier; the chal-lenge to mould and develop the mind and body to move faster, more smoothly, more gracefully, more powerfully than anyone has ever before. For most of these individuals, this was the most exciting element of their lives. They were being creative.

As technology improved and the globe shrank, people from various areas, then countries, challenged each other. Public and press became interested and organizations developed to control, standardize, and oversee the competitions. The Olympics have only become as significant as they are through the media of television. After Harold Abrahams won the 100 metres in 1924 in Paris, he was mailed his gold medal! Today the organizers of the 1976 Olympics initially asked Europe to pay $30,000,000 for the rights to televise the summer Games. America agreed to pay $23,000,000. This is big business and with it has come all the trappings of the modern world. The number of nations brought into the Munich games swelled to 126 and the number of competitors to over 9,000. With this size has come not only an increased opportunity for contact and communication between nations in peaceful endeavour but also the worst of politics, graft, bribery, drugs, and even the violence of today's world. Nations use their representatives as political pawns; shoe manufacturers induce athletes to switch to their brand, so that *their* style of shoe will be seen on television; at Munich two U.S. 400 metre medallists were banned from future Olympic competitions because they appeared to be acting too casually during the medal ceremony. Is this not equating nationalism with an Olympic ideal?

For me, the Olympics are in sad danger of collapse if they continue to grow in size and move away from the most important ingredient – youth expressing its hopes and talents in individual display.

The Olympics have become the venue for political and social comment. Prior to the opening of the Games in Mexico, students planned a rally, while the world's free press were present. The Mexican authorities issued a ban on all rallies. Mexicans were in fear of their police and militia. The rally went ahead, anyway, in the huge Plaza of the Three Cultures. Thousands of men, women, and children gathered in the early evening to hear speeches. Two British correspondents present were Chris Brasher of the *Observer* and John Rodda of the *Guardian*. Their eye-witness reports were frightening and sickening. Tanks moved in to block the exit roads from the square – and from a helicopter overhead came intermittent bursts of machine-gun fire aimed indiscriminately at the crowd. Small-arms fire continued for some time. John was held at gun-point with some other journalists and told it was for his own protection. Plaster was shot away above the balcony where John was lying. Over 200 people died. Later reports put the figure much higher. I met one of the student leaders at the village. He had come to assure us that the disturbance was not aimed at the Games or the participants – but that they had to make their voices heard.

Mexico is a country of 'haves' and 'have nots'. Housing is one visual proof of this. Gorgeous villas surrounded by high walls sharply contrast with corrugated iron shanty-town huts. Too many of the students who have become educated also become corrupted by the opportunities open to them. They lose their untainted record and spirit and are then caught as ineffectual 'haves'. The student told me of a recent demonstration on their Mexico City campus, where tanks drove straight over some of his fellow students. He said that when parents went to the police to ask where their son or daughter was, they were asked to produce the documents to prove they had such. When produced, these were taken and the stunned parents were left with the statement, 'you have no son or daughter'.

When I was young, I held a dream about the Olympic Games. Perhaps naïvely I saw them as a time when, just for a few days, in addition to business as usual, the world paused to observe and briefly absorb, the elevated spirit of hope in youth's quest for fitness, excellence, and self-mastery. I was aware that life and death struggles took place daily around the world, be it for political or economic gain, for religious fervour, or to overcome injustice. But this dream died in Munich. The world and I were forced to watch the macabre acts of kidnapping, terror, and death within the confines of the Games. The Olympics with its 600 million spectators was too large a stage to be passed by. Eleven Israeli athletes were shot to death and with them died much of the hopes for future Games.

The Games in Berlin were used for political ends in 1936. In Munich in 1972 the Germans went out of their way to portray a non-militaristic front. However, this evaporated when I.R.A. bomb threats brought armed guards to patrol outside our British dormitories and the Israeli massacre forced the authorities to seal off the village.

In Mexico the Games became a forum for social comment and political pressure even from individual competitors. Perhaps the most poignant was the head bowed, black power salute by black American 200 metres specialists, Tommy Smith and John Carlos. Regardless of whether they were right or wrong to use that time to demonstrate, *it was their time*. On top of the world, with all eyes watching, they made everyone aware of their feelings and beliefs on the treatment of blacks in America.

In Munich, black opinion was united against the inclusion of Rhodesian athletes. This issue was complex. Rhodesia had been banned by the International Olympic Committee. Some late compromise was made by the I.O.C. to bring them back in, under the British flag, the flag they had so recently abandoned. The team had blacks and whites. The African countries, threatened withdrawal if these Rhodesians were included; then members of the U.S. team joined the threatened boycott. For the Africans, a political leader took the decision and regardless of any individual's attitude, all athletes had to go along with it. If one again sets aside the rightness or wrongness of the action both of the I.O.C. and the black boycott threats, the underlying problem which bothers me is that the decisions are based on national ideologies rather than individual beliefs. If individuals wish to withdraw from a competition on grounds of conscience, that's up to them. What appears to be unjust is that talented individuals, who may not hold any strong political views, are banned from competition because they happened to be born in North Korea, Formosa, Rhodesia, China, or South Africa. This gives rise to the ridiculous situation where outstanding performers such as Sin Kim Dan (1 min. 58·0 seconds women's 800 metres in 1965) or Ni Chih-chin (7 feet 6 inches high jumper in 1970) are barred from competing in the Olympics and their world records are not recognized because their countries do not belong to the organization which runs the World Championships, the Olympic Games. Maybe there is no solution for these people. National subsidy and recognized standards are a prerequisite for allowing individuals to compete. In our diverse world certain norms and standards must be adhered to in order to allow an event such as the Olympics to take place. However, I still lament the absence of such talented participants and hope that somehow, someday, a compromise can be reached which would allow the best individuals, regardless of their race, creed, colour, birthplace, sex, profession, or nationality to take part.

Most people have recognized that the size of the Games is one reason for concern. They are too big. In a token effort to reduce, one walking event was cut out. This was useless except as discrimination against the walkers. In terms of reducing numbers the move is a farce. Developing countries are rapidly producing more coaches and increasingly competent athletes. Add to this the emergence of women in sport in many countries and the number of participants could very easily be doubled. In fact a full quota in every sport, from every country, would bring the total number of participants to over 30,000!

There are a number of proposed solutions. One is to drop all the sports which already hold their own world championships, such as soccer, yachting, or weight-lifting. Another suggestion came from U.S. decathlete, Bill Toomey, to combine some of the predominantly winter sports such as basketball, weight-lifting, boxing, wrestling, with the winter Olympics. A further suggestion which I believe has great merit, was made by the Duke of Edinburgh. His idea was to split the Games into smaller sections. The expense of staging a modern Olympics precludes the majority of countries including, of course, Britain. Splitting the Games would allow smaller countries to develop their facilities, encourage domestic sport, promote tourism, and perhaps foster again a simple national pride in the act of hosting a section of the Olympic Games. Prince Philip's suggestion was to have venues in four different countries, one for team sports, one water sports, another the basic sports of athletics, swimming, and gymnastics, and one for the remaining sports of archery, fencing, and equestrian events, etc. These could be run in the same or different years.

By dramatically reducing the number of persons at any one Games area, the control, cost, and co-ordination could all be improved. Gigantism, which has so dominated current thinking, could give way to the thought that, in this case, small is beautiful. It might be too much to hope that the horrors thrust on to Munich would not be repeated in a setting of reduced magnitude. However, where single sport championships take place, the problems have so far remained internal, as at Wimbledon, the Grand Prix and World Cup soccer.

An element within the Games which is increasingly distressing to many people is the use of drugs. For some time certain stimulants and depressants have been banned. A stimulant would be used by someone undertaking an explosive event such as a 100 metres runner. Caffeine, found in coffee, is a stimulant not specified on the list and therefore used by some. Depressants would be used by distance runners to suppress the pain of an endurance event or to calm down and steady the nerves of pistol shooters and archers. To a large extent these aids were under control.

However, during the last decade a new disturbing group of drugs has become widely used and these are anabolic steroids. Steroids have been used under medical supervision for years to assist old persons to recover from operations. One physician told me that we normally absorb about 10 per cent of the protein from eating a piece of meat or drinking a glass of milk. With steroids, up to 90 per cent of the protein is used by the body. For athletes such as weight-lifters or throwers, the muscles that they are working grow larger and more powerful and their competitive performances improve. It is not unusual for a big man to gain fifty pounds in body weight. Methods of detecting these drugs are becoming more sophisticated but if the athlete stops taking the drug at least two weeks before the test, there should be no trace in his or her system.

The trouble is that steroids may cause any of the following: acne, headaches, jaundice, gastro-intestinal haemorrhage, increased or decreased libido, urethretis, hepatitis, testicular atrophy, or ulcers. Tampering with one's basic hormonal make up or metabolism may sound like an extreme sacrifice for an individual to make. I have mentioned some illustrations of what can and in many cases, has happened with these drugs, but weight men today face a hideous dilemma. I'm sure that the majority would like a clear-cut test so that it would be impossible ever to use such drugs without detection. However, this is not yet possible. The extent of usage is so widespread that the records in heavy events have been dramatically re-written. I don't envy the youngster in this field. If he or she wants to reach world class there is at present no choice but to join the chase for size.

And the problem does not end there. World-wide experiments are going on with runners and jumpers. It has been accepted that the jumps and sprints are power events and therefore athletes in these events also benefit from the build-up of muscle power. Now further research and experiment is going on involving all distances, not to build-up bulk, but to aid daily recovery and therefore to allow the runner to sustain higher quality training sessions and competitive performances. In the running events drug usage is becoming more widespread but there will never be a substitute for natural talent, hard work, and the athlete who believes in himself. However, drugs are a fast-growing fact of life for athletes on the track and in the field in Britain and elsewhere.

Some doctors are convinced that there will be no ill effects if drug taking is under medical supervision. Sir Roger Bannister is strongly opposed to any and all drug usage in sport. His distinction between the taking of drugs and the taking of, for example, multi-vitamins, is the fact that the latter can be found in natural foods, the former not. It has yet to be ascertained whether heavy dosage users or their offspring suffer any permanent physiological damage. I and many others hope that this drug usage is curtailed through, the development of a clear-cut detection process.

Such clarity was established for the women's sex tests. From scrutiny of a single hair it is possible to establish sex identity, regardless of the female sexual organs of a competitor.

Women's emancipation has been a long time in coming to all countries. Women have only just become aware of their freedom, rights, and role in sport. This can only be a positive move. Sport has so much to offer in terms of health and self-development. Through my involvement in sport at all levels, I have become convinced that sport can be a unique tool for self-growth. At any level of participation an individual can learn about self-expression, self-control, and commitment. The fitter one becomes and the more involved in improvement, the more vivid life can become. On the physical side, life involves body-awareness, feeling health, strength and fitness. In emotional development one faces challenge, fear, sorrow, elation, and satisfaction. Mentally and spiritually life can become more real. At times, mind and body may join in dramatic pursuit or merely relax and enjoy running for fun.

It is because of all these things and more, that we must not let the Olympics crumble. The Olympics is the show case, the top of the pyramid, the meeting place of all nations in a sharing of one of the quality products of our world – ourselves, engaged in a non-destructive endeavour. In spite of politicians making nationalistic capital out of success, our eyes must be kept focused on the important aspect – men and women trained to make movement look at once powerful, graceful, and effortless.

Despite the crime in Munich personalities did shine through. The pert, petulant, and precocious little Olga Korbut stole the hearts of the world on the gymnastic floor. Mark Spitz performed exceptional aquatic feats to capture no less than seven gold medals, and John Akii-Bua showed his uninhibited delight and glee to have fulfilled his hopes and dreams after his hurdle win.

The Games hold a mixed bag of athletes ranging from the casual to the intense, the pre-teenager to the middle-aged, the metal badge collector to the hippie, the Don Juan to the recluse. This is as good a place as any to put one myth into perspective. Many people have asked me whether the Olympic village is a hot house of sexual orgies. Well, in spite of the women's quarters being off limits to men, the men's are not off limits to the women and it is not a difficult task to get together in the village or outside. However, there is no obsession. Most athletes proceed with life as they normally live it. Less sex takes place at an Olympics than at a comparably sized University campus.

I find it rather nonsensical that, at the Olympic Games, the females' quarters have been caged off. Not even married couples were permitted each other's company during the silent hours of darkness. Inevitably, a test of the security had to be made! In the village in Mexico, the British men's block faced the high-fenced women's quarters. On one evening a couple of our walking fraternity decided to stage their 'break-in'. With John Webb dressed ready for entry, his walking mate escorted 'her' to the path where the female guards stood sentry duty. With his arm still round 'her' shoulder, he gave 'her' a delicate peck good-night and let John slide towards the forbidden quarters. Great cheers and whistles erupted from the U.K. athletes watching from the windows of their quarters. The game was up and heavy-booted ladies raced to catch our fleet-footed friend at the door.

I hope that the Olympics will always exist in some form and perhaps the ultimate would be an international situation such as Wentworth or Wimbledon, where the best of amateur and professionals take part together in open competition.

Many people have asked me whether the professional athletics which is underway with the I.T.A. (International Track Association) will catch on. Many Olympic Champions and other top athletes have joined this group, who tour to cities around the world. I.T.A. competitors are gaining world records and with them greater renown and credibility. I believe that following the 1976 Olympics a number of new competitors will join the I.T.A. whose competitors see themselves as the group who will help to bring about 'open' athletics.

In a sense open athletics already exists. A large number of top amateur athletes are already competing as individuals on the open market. The quip from I.T.A. shot-putter, Brian Oldfield, was not far off the mark: he referred to the current athletes as the 'pros' and the 'cons'. There are many outstanding invitational athletic meetings outside the traditional two-sided international meetings or the major Games. Invitational meetings are potentially great crowd pleasers, as each event can bring together good individuals. Top athletes also prefer this, as good competition provides the stimulus for better performances. However, often the same individuals, usually in the middle distances but not restricted to them, are in demand by every meeting director or promoter. Quite a number of these world-class competitors are offered inflated expenses to encourage them to attend one meeting or another. It has not taken long for athletes to establish a going rate for their presence in a meeting. In the early 1970s this was anything from £50 to £1,000 depending on how big a crowd puller was involved. However, less than 10 per cent of the participants in the greatest invitational meeting can command *any* appearance money. The ones who get it are those who ask for it and, more importantly, those whose presence will almost certainly affect the size of the crowd.

For one minute, ignore the current amateur rules and consider the following. Athletics followers like to watch a match between the best, Ryun versus Keino; Bayi versus Walker; Pascoe versus Bolding, versus Akii-Bua; Foster versus Bedford versus Stewart. Meeting promoters can make a few thousand pounds from the crowds at such matchings. Athletes can be the performing monkeys, training their hearts out, travelling thousands of miles, and too often paying to take part. Should those who bring in the crowd be denied some compensation? To an extent, payment to top individuals has been going on since the 1930s and increasing since the early 1950s. Very few countries in the Western world have no athletes and/or meetings involved in this practice. It now runs from promoters of inter-club league level, to national officials, in some countries. Individuals taking part are from all countries and both sides of the Iron Curtain.

If, in addition to this, one considers the fact that there are thousands of state and privately supported athletes, plus those in the armed services or police corps, and thousands of students with full athletic scholarships, all of whom are able to train and compete to the extent that they desire, I can only deduce that there is a requirement for an *up-to-date* and *honest* re-evaluation and re-writing of our amateur rules. Committees of the I.A.A.F. (International Amateur Athletic Federation) and the I.O.C. (International Olympic Committee) should seriously question the validity and necessity of retaining some of the amateur parts of their laws. I am not saying that there should be no rules, no guidelines, no standards – they are essential. However, there needs to be a re-vamping and re-writing of the codes based on open competition, anyone from any background being eligible to enter, even those currently in the I.T.A. and other professional groups. Athletes run because they want to. If they wish to make athletics their full-time aim for a year or two they should not be penalized for that decision. Other people are paid for working on their talents such as painters, writers, computer programmers, golfers, and tennis players, so why not athletes? Amateur athletes at International level currently train as hard and dedicate themselves, to just as great an extent, as any paid professional; in some cases they probably train even more.

Some top amateur administrators have put forward the argument that not more than ten athletes from any one country can command appearance money. Why change anything for them? I have two objections to that argument. Firstly they are ignoring the aforementioned thousands of paid state, business, university, police, or service supported athletes. Secondly, the ten or so individual stars from each country are the ones that the crowds come to see and the ones that television producers *pay* the governing bodies to record. Television and press coverage establish some athletes as household names. The public comes to know these individuals, just a little. They enter their lives and run with them. The crowds come to see them, as people, almost as friends who are to compete against their top rivals or struggle in their aim to break a record. Like it or not, the few at the top are the shop window who bring paying people in to watch. Of course, athletics is far more than just the shop window, and those in the window are made by those who strive to replace them.

British spectators will often root for the underdog, but people like a winner. Perhaps life has too few winning moments for most people and here is a chance to live with and feel the excitement, joy, and pleasure of success. It is a fabulous feeling to have one's sensations and whole being lifted by watching a great race. From the stands, I ran with our 4 × 400 metres relay team at the European Championships in Rome. I warmed up with Cohen, Hartley, Pascoe, and Jenkins. My breathing and pulse rate went up as the time of the start neared. I could feel the flow and strain of their every stride and I was literally lifted from my seat with the anticipation, excitement and final fulfilment of their combined winning effort.

People want to see the best. The I.T.A. should survive, as it has a large number of current and recent-past greats. They virtually have a travelling Olympics. Most people would like the opportunity of seeing this group on their home ground. But I believe that there is limited scope for having professional league matches – except at a top level. Track and field has much less element of chance than a sport such as soccer. For example, a second or third division team can lift itself into a Wembley Cup Final and win. This degree of flexibility of performance is not there in athletics. With a few yards' difference, David Jenkins would beat a club 400 metres runner in 100 races out of 100. The element of suspense comes in when David is matched with the best from Africa, America, or Europe. I would like to see 400 metres competitors such as John Smith, Lee Evans and Vince Matthews, all of whom run with the I.T.A. compete with David in Montreal. I'm sure that all of them would agree with me that nothing can ever replace the set date, the fixed day of trial, the day of an Olympic final.

This is one more reason why I want to see the Games retained and if some people wish to earn their living for a few years travelling with a pro track tour, that should be their choice, and I can see nothing wrong with it. If someone can make a living by doing something he both enjoys and does well then this should not bar him from an Olympics. Some athletes might like to make guest appearances in these meetings and remain independent as I have done. Still others might aim solely for Internationals or for the Olympic Games themselves. It is my hope that in a few years' time within new rules, all will be free and eligible to run when and where they choose and be eligible for the Games – not for profit, nor for any other reason but that they are the Olympics: the time when any top athlete should have the chance to take part with the very best in the world.

CHAPTER 12

Working Towards a Peak

Following the Mexico Olympics, I was asked, on more than one occasion, what I had had for breakfast on the morning of the Final – as if *that* had made all the difference. Humans are complex. Mental, physical, and emotional factors each play a part in any competition. It is therefore extremely difficult to assess how we can bring the best out of ourselves. Each of us is different, so there is no right way to become great. However, there are a number of guidelines or ways of looking at sport and life which may help one to improve.

In a later chapter, I shall look at some of the influences which one's mind and attitudes can have on performance. However, in this chapter, I want to share some of my thoughts on the work required to get into top shape. For me, each element of training held its own particular fascination.

For anyone starting from scratch, it should be understood that *running* is the best fitness conditioner. There is no substitute, but it is not easy. When starting again, I used to feel that I had never run in my life. I would rapidly feel sick and be almost unable to keep going. Huge question-marks filled my mind. 'What has happened to me?' 'How can I be so bad?' 'Will I ever get back into shape again?' It was always the same. It was tough overcoming that initial period of starting back. However, within two or three weeks, this feeling of complete debility passed and the background conditioning could begin. The aim was to have a peak date in mind and gradually work towards that date. The two most important peak dates for me were the times of the Olympic Games, in 1968 and 1972. My year was roughly divided into five phases. If it can be worked, the best way of reaching a peak is to spread the preparation over a number of months. The initial phase is arguably the most important, as it establishes the base on which the athlete can build. This is the time when strength and stamina are acquired. The running can take place on the road or over the country, at a steady pace. In the early part of this phase, the body should be given time to adapt to the workload. Everything is being asked to change at once. But aching muscles and blisters gradually clear up and it becomes possible to begin to absorb more external stimuli on the runs and simply to enjoy them for their own sake. My running venues have varied greatly from Somerset roads, where the pervading odours were of the fields and farmyards, to the London North Circular Road where inescapable exhaust fumes clog the air. The latter makes one appreciate the country. During February 1974, my wife and I attended a coaching course in Finland. The contrast in the air was dramatic and frightening. The cold, crisp Finnish air was so unpolluted that it seemed scented. Gloria and I drank it in, in great big mouthfuls. I believe that a change of environment every once in a while can do wonders for both morale and perspective.

Apart from distance running, the background should include strengthening sessions using both natural terrain and weights. Coach Smith was a firm believer in hills and sand dunes. The hills varied from many repetitions on fifty-yard hills, to a few times up a half-mile ski-slope before the snow came. The short hill was run at full leg-speed. This enabled me to maintain *some* rapid leg cadence throughout the winter. Even though I ran these in spikes in the cold, there was little or no chance of any muscle tear injury, because the hill held back any thoughts of dramatic speed.

One of the hill sessions I thought related quite well to a 400 metres hurdles race. We found a hill which was approximately 300 metres up – but it had a gentle slope, almost immediately over the top and 50 metres down the other side. I ran up and felt the full fatigue of the climb, but then continued over and down the hill. This forced my momentum to increase, so I concentrated on accelerating my leg speed, as if I was heading from the last hurdle to the tape.

I have always enjoyed running hills and dunes. The latter are, in my experience, unique. I have never been able to reproduce the

total state of *rigor mortis* of the thighs quite like that produced by
the dunes. I'm not sure if it has to do with the slipping sand, but
fifteen to twenty seconds was sufficient to bring so much blood and
lactic acid into my thighs that they felt as if they could explode.
This happened after a few repetitions. Every muscle seems to be
brought into play. My lungs would heave and my legs virtually
come to a standstill, but strangely enough, recovery afterwards was
very rapid. I enjoyed feelings of tremendous good health following
the dune sessions. The height of the two sand hill areas was approximately 90 feet and 120 feet. The most I would ever do on a longer
one would be fifteen to eighteen times and twenty-five to thirty-
two on the shorter one. I liked the feeling of being able to put out
everything I had, in every step of the dune sessions.

It wouldn't be right for everyone, but for me, the hardest way
was the best. During the winter of 1971–72, while I was a graduate
student at Harvard University, many athletes were using the
indoor board track under an inflated, heated dome. Outside on the
football pitch, I was bounding through the snow. Perhaps it was
the psychological edge I felt, by thinking that no one else would be
doing the same – given the opportunities I had. It is the same
approach as that of an American friend of mine, Dick Farley, who
for a time played U.S. professional football. During the summer
he would run, as do many others, but at 90 degrees he would
still be in his track suit, making it that much harder for himself.
U.S. football is a tough, contact sport and Dick told me that
he'd sometimes practise tackling by running into trees! This
may sound extreme but it's not if you know the size and structure
of some of the pro football players. When Jim Ryun was running
so well in the mid 1960s, he said he believed it was because of the
Kansas winters. He had to work that much harder than anyone in
a good climate. How apt is Albert Camus's statement: 'Man's
greatness lies in *his decision* to be stronger than his conditions.'

Perhaps it needs to be stated here that youngsters can be easily
stimulated to do too much. Far better that they should be introduced and encouraged to enjoy a variety of sports than be driven
at too young an age to strive for early success in one area. I have
seen parents at Little League Baseball games or mothers at the
side of swimming pools, literally screaming at their children to
produce. The role of parents and coaches is a very delicate balance
between showing sufficient interest and encouragement and push-

ing the child, perhaps even trying to live through them. Interest and encouragement are needed by the child for positive growth. However, undue pressure to do well may cause the child to revolt. Consciously or unconsciously, the child will decide to quit, to relieve the pressure or to assert himself. The most important aspect is that the child is understood and unconditionally accepted, allowing the decision to do well to come from inside him.

For child and champion it is important that the whole body is worked into good condition. During the first phase, while covering distance and working on hills and dunes, it is easy to forget about doing exercises. There is little thought of muscle injury so flexibility is too often neglected. Stretching exercises should be continued all the year round. I also believe that weight training and circuit training can be valuable adjuncts to running training. There is no need for an athlete to become bulky or tight-muscled through using weights. I found them invaluable in that specific sets of muscles could be worked on and developed.

One exercise from which I gained great benefit was step-ups. My starting speed improved dramatically from the results of one winter's work. I used about my own body-weight on a bar which I put on my shoulders. Dumb-bells would be equally effective. The ball of one foot was placed on the edge of an 18-inch bench and I stepped up on the bench ten times leaving that foot in place all the time, then switched to the other leg. The work was almost all done by the raised thigh. I was told not to push off from my foot on the floor and also that the most important aspect was to perform the exercise with *fluid speed*. If I was slowed down by the weights, I should reduce the poundage to begin with and gradually increase it over the weeks – but always maintaining speed of movement. I usually did three sets.

When one is working hard in training, as well as at work or study, it is essential to have sufficient rest in order to allow the body to recover and rebuild stronger tissues. Some athletes are afraid to take a day off in case they lose their form. In my opinion, rest days are valuable for physical and mental rejuvenation especially if training is intense.

Between the slower Phase One and track work in Phase Two, I used a couple of types of transition sessions. On the Franklin Park Golf Course near Boston, one of the hills is about 200 metres long. It was smooth enough in its incline to allow me to sprint both up

and down. The uphill run was a good gradual resistance run but
the aid to speed came in the downhill run. My legs were forced to
move faster than usual, and certainly faster than I could have
moved them on the flat at that time.

The other transition work was fartlek running. This can be done
at any time of the season as it is speed play. It can be completely
free expression, running hard, striding, sprinting, or jogging
whenever you feel like it during the run. It can be far more controlled, as in Coach Billy Smith's method of having the athlete run
tee to green around a golf course, jogging only between the green
and the next tee.

Phase Two had a change of emphasis towards the track to about
three days of volume work each week. This is the time when concentration is on rhythm, cadence, flow, and just adaptation to
running on a track again. Sessions for me usually totalled 3,000
metres, e.g. 15 × 200 metres strides or 10 × 300 metres. Sometimes under that total with 6 × 400 metres and at other times over
with 5 × 800 metres. An equal distance walk or jog was taken as
recovery between each run. The pace was usually a good stride,
intense enough to feel like stopping before the full quota was
reached. Billy Smith usually held me to the pre-established number which he and I agreed on before the start of the session. Perhaps
I am basically lazy, but I used to feel like calling it a day a few
before the end, and often used to offer the Coach one or two at a
faster pace, rather than the final three or four. He never bought
my sales pitches. He knew what was needed. He also knew that as
you train, so will you race. If you constantly quit on sessions, the
same will happen when you want to ease off in a race. Also during
the race you have to call on all-out effort. If you have never
done that in training, how can you expect it just to happen in a
race.

This second phase would begin in April, once the snow in
Boston had cleared to make track work possible. It was also the
time to re-introduce hurdle work. All under-distance repeat work
over the hurdles was run at end-of-season race pace. For example
during 1968, 5 × 200 metres hurdles or 3 × 7 hurdles were run at
sub-50-seconds pace to help me get used to running over hurdles
at my target pace for the full race. Unfortunately, the adductor
muscle injury prevented me from hurdling during this phase in
1972, but if it is possible *hurdlers should practise over the barriers*

almost every time they are on the track. If it is not the main part of the session, then it should at least constitute part of the warm-up. Hurdling requires specific muscle endurance. Part of it is a question of technique practice but it is important to condition the body to the event. I was running on the flat better in 1972 than in 1968 but did not have specific hurdling endurance. The same applies to many technical events. Throwers and jumpers may become very strong through weight training but have difficulty converting this added power into better distances or height. This emphasizes how important it is in weight training to simulate movements which correlate most closely with your event movements.

Gradually, during this second phase, the number of repetitions is reduced and the quality increased. This provides the transition into Phase Three, in which the athlete will begin the competitive season. The emphasis moves even more fully on to the track, up to five days every week. Training in the country would only be thrown in as light relief from the intensity of track training. In my case distances on the track were under and over my competitive distance. Under-distance work helped me to gain speed; over-distance tried to incorporate the stamina work by maintaining sustained momentum. I practised relaxing and 'floating'.

During track work, I valued having a coach tell me the time of each repetition. This not only gave me an accurate assessment of my progress but also aided my sense of pace-judgement. Once I was in top condition, I would usually estimate the times I had run in practice to within a tenth-of-a-second, or could run within a tenth or two of the times asked of me. This is something which just came with practice – over a period of years – and it was really useful when running controlled qualifying rounds where inaccurate pace-judgment can put one out of contention by running either too fast or too slow. Of course, this is only applicable for those who run 400 metres or more as all shorter events would be run at full effort.

Another valuable tool is the training diary. I recommend that anyone who trains reasonably consistently should maintain a detailed training diary. Each day should record the place; weather (including the temperature); your own condition (e.g. good, very tired) and the work-out details (e.g. 3 × 800 metres, in 2 minutes 0·8 seconds, 2 minutes 01·4 seconds, 2 minutes 0·2 seconds). Also anything special about it, if you trained with someone else, or had to stop because of a cramp. This not only gives you the opportunity of charting your progress but it is an extremely valuable reference on which to base future training.

Phase Three was the early season peak time. Most of the endurance work had been completed so that only one or two sessions every couple of weeks were all that was required to keep me in touch with my background stamina. Competition was frequent through school and undergraduate days. During the 1968 season, I raced almost every weekend. For several weeks during May and June, each week had its own mini-phase. Following competition on a Saturday, I would either jog lightly or take Sunday off. Monday's session was moderately hard; Tuesday very hard; Wednesday moderately hard; Thursday light, sometimes an extended warm-up of thirty to forty-five minutes; Friday was a rest day before the Saturday competition.

The competitive days were quite strenuous not only from the psychological point of view. I usually ran a couple of individual events and anchored the 4 × 440 relay. The three most hectic days are burned into my memory. One was the last day of my Freshman Season against Tufts University. I competed in ten events on one day – winning six firsts, a second, third, fourth, and fifth place. The most demanding indoor competition was against Boston College in my final year at Boston University. I won the 600 yards and the 1,000 yards and the next event after the 1,000 was the 4 × 440 relay. We won it but I couldn't walk without being sick for about half an hour afterwards. Finally, the best overall day of my 1968 University season was at the New England Championships, with morning heats of 14·4 seconds in the 120 yards high hurdles and 52·8 seconds in the 440 yards intermediate hurdles; and after lunch a high hurdle semi-final of 14·1, final of 13·9, and 440 yards hurdles final of 50·5 and then an anchor leg in the 4 × 400 yard relay in 47·7. During the 1972 Season, I really missed the opportunity of competition within a University. As a graduate student in the U.S. I was ineligible for the University team.

The emphasis in Phase Three was on speed and in 1968 this phase was completed by mid-July when I had gained a place on the British Olympic Team for Mexico. As the Games were to be held in October, Phase Four was a return to a similar type of work as in Phase Two. Less days were spent on the track and I moved back on to hills in Richmond Park. West German research has shown that this Fourth Phase is essential for producing a higher second peak in the later season competition.

Phase Five was similar to Phase Three. Following over fifty weeks' training, the only thing left to do, once I had reached Mexico, was to couple the essential ingredient of speed with hurdling technique. There was no need to do a great deal of volume in the four weeks before the Games. The aim was to become faster and looser, to run relaxed at speed.

Getting to the most important meeting of the year in top condition is a long process and one that should not be thrown away by last-minute carelessness. Each athlete finds his/her own particular way of dealing with pre-race nerves. The feeling can begin days and even weeks before the event. Sometimes I felt my pulse-rate increasing, then I became aware that my subconscious had been working on the race. More often it was my conscious thoughts which produced the butterflies. I would run my race over and over in my mind, trying to go through every possible variation in weather conditions, or other competitors' actions during the race. In this way, I felt I became more prepared as, in a sense, I had gone through it all before. The most important mental run-through was how I planned to run *my* race, regardless of others. It had to be grooved in, so that under the intense pressure of competition it would be second nature. Perhaps too often we forget to schedule dream time in our lives. After all, dreams are what reality is made from. As Shaw said, 'Some dream of things that are and ask: "Why?" I dream of things that never were and ask: "Why not?"'

Pre-event nerves are a common experience from child to champion; from actor to athlete. Before performing in public, committing yourself to trying to do well, there is often self-doubt, sometimes even fear, that you will not do well enough. This is a time for great self-control; not allowing yourself to become fearful. You can consciously slow down your breathing to a slower, deeper rhythm and produce a certain degree of calm and relaxation.

Fear can also be produced through an overwhelming feeling of all the top athletes being present at once. This is especially true of the Olympics, While I was on the plane flying into Mexico City, I told myself, well, after all this is only another track meet, and instead of dealing with all the competitors at once I thought about each one separately. I mentally raced the ones I regarded more highly. Each time, on a one-to-one basis, I thought I could win. The belief in that possibility was essential to do well.

Under extreme stress many humans pray. Often those who claim to hold no religious beliefs find themselves praying, almost as if it's the natural thing to do. I was no exception, and having been brought up in a Christian home, it was not an unusual thing for me. I shall have more to say on this subject in a later chapter.

On the day of a race nerves often affect my appetite, making it difficult to eat much. It's essential to have sufficient food so that the body doesn't become weak but there's no need to eat anything you don't feel like. We rarely listen to our bodies carefully. I found that by running a few possibilities through my mind I could usually find out what my system was saying it needed. Although I couldn't eat much on the day of a big competition, I also didn't like to run feeling hungry. My pre-race diet was almost always Cadbury's chocolate and a Coke! It's an interesting phenomenon how a carbonated drink will settle a stomach.

As I have mentioned earlier, the day before and the day of the race consisted of what might be termed planned trivia. Nothing was done to excess, a short walk, some reading, a lie down. Nothing was undertaken that was out of the ordinary and that included my warm-up. This had become a routine before every track session and really only needed to be adapted if there was a significant temperature change in either direction. The warm-up before a race was a time for concentration. It was a mental as well as a physical preparation time for running as fast as possible over a set distance. Distractions had to be avoided. It was a time when I had to put off those who, innocently or otherwise, tried to interrupt me. It took me years to learn to say no to autograph hunters. 'After the race, please.' Most people are unaware of the distraction they cause athletes by stopping them just before a race, to sign just one more.

Once the race was under way the tension disappeared. Then it was a matter of concentration and commitment. I had to go as and when I'd planned to go. Win or lose I'd planted my stamp, my training, and my full efforts into the race. If I did that there was no need for personal regret. I could learn from an error of judgment or become aware of a weakness, but at least I'd know that I'd tried. This way, no matter where I finished, I could face myself, my coach and the public. Those with regret are those who've never made the commitment.

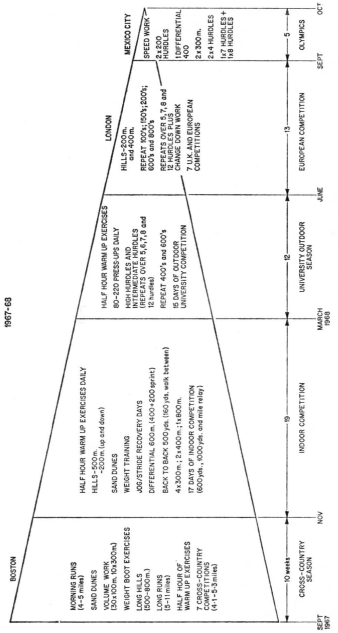

How my training programme in the two important years of my career progressed from greater volume to greater intensity.

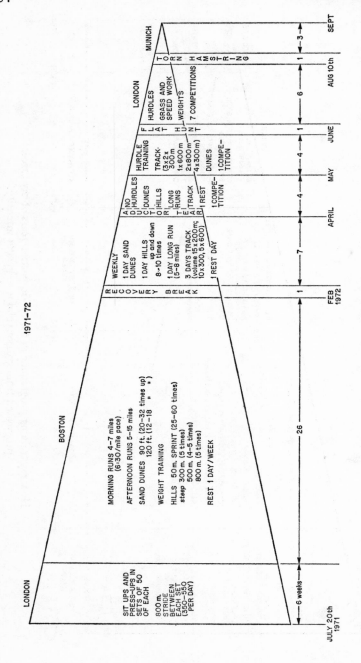

The shape of the diagram is intended to illustrate my gradual progression from doing a great deal of work at a very moderate pace through to doing less and less volume but increasing the intensity in effort, i.e. from a *large base* to a *peak*. During my first winter at Boston University, Billy Smith presented me with a list of exercises which he had compiled from his own reading and experience together with information from the leading hurdle coaches, Wilbur Ross and Dr LeRoy Walker. I had to follow this routine prior to every work-out.

(1) Jog a minimum 800–1,200 metres.
(2) 30 to 50 side-straddle hops, commonly known as jumping jacks. (These were later deleted.)
(3) 30 side bends.
(4) 30 wide, vertical arm circles, forward and back.
(5) 30 bends forward and back strengthen legs holding feet.
(6) 30 trunk circles.
(7) Resistance while sitting for quadricep development.
(8) Straddle position, fingers interlocked behind head, touch elbows to ground repeatedly.
(9) Straddle position, touch ground between legs as far behind as possible, repeat 20 to 30 times.
(10) Lie on back, elevate legs and hips; do 30 bicycle or running steps in the air.
(11) Bounce stretching leg scissor movements from same position as previous exercise, alternately touch the ground behind shoulders with one foot at a time.
(12) Leg abductors, lie on back; start with legs apart, slowly and against resistance provided by a team-mate (on the inside of ankles) close legs together.
(13) 15 sit-ups, followed by 10 cross over, followed by 10 v-types.
(14) Lower back – lie on stomach, interlacing fingers behind head, arch back and return to starting position, repeat 30 times.
(15) Hamstrings – lie on stomach, raise lower legs to verticle position and return; resistance on legs applied by team-mate.
(16) 30 push-ups.
(17) Quadriceps – lie on back with legs elevated in bent position

and with team-mate applying resistance against feet, straighten legs out, repeat 20 times.

(18) Running on the spot; standing on one spot, begin by making jogging movements but remain on the same spot; next, begin to run, on the same spot, pulling the knees up to the chest, body at an approximate running angle and arms moving just as in running; do not stamp hard on the ground, aim for speed and fluency of movement but also tread as lightly as possible; continue the high-knee running on the spot for a slow count of 25, then jog on the spot for a similar count; next, repeat the jogging for the 25 count; gradually work up to 150, adding 25 after each jogging period.

(19) High-knee bounds; this is a most difficult but useful exercise to master. The object here can best be described as running with a full-stride high-knee lift and well off the ground all in slow motion. The movement is an exaggerated, high-bounding stride. Begin by running slowly, then spring off right foot gracefully and well off the ground. On springing the left knee is brought well up so that the thigh is parallel to the ground, while the right leg trails backwards as straight as possible. On landing, extend the left leg to take the weight and with another high bound bring the right knee high up and let the left leg trail; continue in unbroken sequence for at least 100 yards. Although this is done in slower, more deliberate action than actual sprinting, the length of stride in each bound should be within an inch or two of full running strides. The main thing about this exercise is that it necessitates full control while reaching forward as far as one does while running; it assists in knee lift as well as leg-trail control while running.

(20) Alternate high-knee bounding; begin by hopping lightly on both feet, taking the weight on the balls of the feet; next, spring off one leg as high as possible while bringing the other knee up towards the chest; on landing, bounce lightly on both feet again then spring off other leg bringing the opposite one up towards the chest. Continue in unbroken sequence trying to go higher and higher with each spring Do this until the knees have been brought up to the chest

25 times. Try to keep more or less on the same spot while jumping.

(21) 2 × 120 yards high hurdles in 16·0 to 17·0 seconds. Walk 120 yards back to start between;

(22) Run past the left side of 5 or 6 hurdles at competitive speed and snap the trail leg over each hurdle; walk back to start – between six to eight repetitions; and

(23) 5 × 5 high hurdles, concentrating on body lean at take-off, snapping down lead leg after crossing the hurdle and pull through on trail leg; use 5 steps between hurdles, walk back after each.

(24) Build-up strides, 3–4 × 100 metres.

1967–68 DIARY

SEPTEMBER   WEEKS 1–4

Because of the hamstring tear, I did the following exercises with 17 lb. boots:

Three sets of ten on each leg. (*a*) leg extensions while sitting; (*b*) hamstring curl while standing; (*c*) knee lift while standing.

During the first two weeks, these exercises were done daily, the second two weeks, every other day. In the first three weeks of September, I ran 4 miles before breakfast almost every morning. During the fourth week, this was stepped up to 5 miles.

Volume work on alternate days:

7–12 × 300 metres (45 secs. average) or 25 × 100 metres or 4 × 1,200 metres.

Two visits to sand dunes, 25 × up and down a 60 ft. dune.

OCTOBER   WEEKS 5–9

12 × 5 mile morning runs.

Cross-country meetings every week over 4·8 mile course (average mile time reduced from 5 mins. 31 to 5 mins. 07).

Sporadic weight boot exercises.

8–10 mile run once a week (10 mile time 59 mins. 30).

Three hill sessions – five to eight times up and down Big Blue half-mile ski run.

Other sessions

4 × 1 mile on country road (5 mins. 10 average).
3 × 1¾ miles (9 mins. 10 average).
10 × 330 (42·5 secs. average).
Two sessions 5 miles (45 secs. hard run, 3 mins. jog – repeated to end).

NOVEMBER   WEEKS 9–13

8 × 5 mile morning runs (approx. 5 mins. 30 per mile).
3 days 8–11 mile steady runs.
4 × ½-mile on road (average 2 mins. 06).
1 × 5 mile steady run; 45 secs. hard; 3 min. jog – repeat.
10 × 500 yards uphill in forest.
Last cross-country meeting Nov. 13th.
30 × 100 metres moderately hard run.
8 × 200 metres (26 secs. average).
6 × 300 metres (42 secs. average).
10 × 200 yards up and down grass slope.
First Indoor Meeting – Nov. 25th. 600 yards 75·0 secs.
2 × 500 yards 68·0, 67·1 secs.

DECEMBER   WEEKS 13–17

7 × 5 miles steady run.
3 days: 4 × 500 yards uphill in forest, 83·0, 82·0, 81·0 secs.
2 Indoor competitions: 600 yards in 82·7 and 82·9 secs.
2 days: 4 × 300 yards standing start (average 33·4).
1 day: 30 times up sand dunes, 10 seconds sprinting.

JANUARY 1968   WEEKS 18–22

Alternate days: 20–30 mins. jog stride.
A rest day before and after each competition.
2 × 500 yards, 160 yards between (62·2 and 68·7 secs).
440 yards 50·6; 220 yards 24·0 secs.
2 days: 2 × 660 yards aiming for 62 at 440 yards then kick 88·4, 88·8, 88·4, 87·3 secs.
2 × 220 yards, 23·8, 23·5 secs.
2 × 300 yards, 35·0, 34·8 secs.

4 Competitions: 3 × 600 yards: 71·8, 74·9, 72·5 secs.
4 × 440 yards relay leg, 49·5, 50·0, 49·0, 49·0 secs.

FEBRUARY   WEEKS 22–26

One week ill.
6 days Competition:
600 yards 74·6, 72·5, 74·3 and 2 mins. 20·3 for 1,000 yards, 70·2
secs. and 2 mins. 14·5 for 1,000 yards.
Relay legs, 48·8, 50·8, 48·2, 48·8 secs.
Tracks varied.
2 × 440 yards 51·2, 49·6 secs.
3 × 5 intermediate hurdles plus 880 yards stride in 2 mins. 07.

MARCH   WEEKS 26–30

1 week off – injury.
3 × 600 yards, 72·4, 70·8, 72·1 secs.
2 × 2 × 440 (160 yards walk between) 56·2, 57·0, 58·2, 55·3 secs.
1 week off end of Indoor Season.

APRIL   WEEKS 31–35

3 × 3 mile morning runs.
10 × 200 yards up and down grass slope.
Hurdle sessions:
2 × 660 yards, 89·0, 87·5; or
1 × 660, 87·8, 88·2, 86·7, 84·7 secs.
4 days, 5 × 6 high hurdles, plus
1 × 7 intermediate hurdles 33·8, 33·5, 31·9 32·5 secs.
7 days competition:
120 yards high hurdles: 14·0, 14·4, 14·7, 13·7 secs. (wind assisted).
440 yards hurdles: 51·8, 52·6, 50·7, 52·7 (heat).
440 yards relay lead off, 46·9.

MAY   WEEKS 35–39

4 × 220 yards intermediate hurdles (24·0 average).
6 × 440 yards (52·6 average).
2 × 500 yards hurdles, 63·5, 63·6.

3 × 660 yards, aim 85 secs: 84·3, 83·6, 81·3.
1 × 660 yards, 78·5.
May 1st. Competition. 120 yards hurdles, 13·9 (head wind).
440 yards hurdles, 50·6.
May 25th. New England Championships.
120 yards hurdles heats, 14·43.
440 yards hurdles heats, 52·8.
120 yards hurdles semi-final, 14·1.
120 yards hurdles final, 13·9.
440 yards hurdles final, 50·5.
Relay leg, 47·7.
Day off before and after each meeting.
Last 2 weeks: 6 days press-ups started in sets of 30–50; 110 to 120
per day.

JUNE   WEEKS 40–43

June 1st. I.C.A.A.A.A. Meeting, 400 metres hurdles, 50·4.
2 × 660 yards, 85·0, 81·8.
Intermediate hurdles, 3 × 220 yards (24·3 average).
1 × 8 hurdles, 35·6.
2 × 500 yards hurdles, 63·5, 62·4.

N.C.A.A. Championships – 3 days:
400 metres hurdles, 50·9, 50·2, 49·8 secs.
June 18th. Back to U.K.
10 days × 100 press-ups.
1 × 8 intermediate hurdles plus 660 yards, 85·0.
2 × 660 after hurdles, 88·0, 84·0.
2 × 7 int. hurdles, 30·8, 30·3.
June 25th.
400 metres hurdles, 50·4.
2 × 800 metres, 2 mins. 01·4, 1 min. 59·0.
1 × 500 yards hurdle, 63·0.
1 × 660 yards, 82·0.

JULY   WEEKS 44–48

2 days bend hurdling, chop down work:
2 × 600 metres, 87·4, 84·5, 81·7, 79·2.

2 × 500 metres hurdles, 61·2, 60·4.
2 × 8 hurdles, 36·5, 35·8.
3 × 6 hurdles, 27·6, 26·0, 26·0.
2 × 7 hurdles, 31·2, 30·3.
2 days hill running: 4 × 300 yards, 4 × 200 yards.
July 12th–13th. A.A.A. Championships.
440 yards hurdles heat 51·6 (30·5 at 7th hurdle coasted in).
Final, 50·2 (30·8 at 7th hurdle) 49·8 at 400 metres.
July 28th Romania:
52·9 heat: 50·4 final. 46·5 relay.

AUGUST   WEEKS 48–52

1 week off with 'flu.
5 days hill running, 200 to 400 yards.
4 days relay practice.
4 days half-hour jog, stride, and exercises.
2 days Fosbury flop jumping.
10 × 100 metres.
3 × 220 yards.
2 × 150 yards.
1 × 600 metres, 85·9.
Aug. 24th. 400 metres hurdles, 49·6 secs.
Relay, lead off-leg, 46·6/47·2.

SEPTEMBER   WEEKS 53–56

Sept. 2nd. Relay 46·5 (tactical).
2 × 7 hurdles, 30·8, 30·7.
1 day, 6 × up and down 220 yards grass slope.
12 × up 110 yards steep slope.
4 × 220 yards intermediate hurdles (22·9 average).
1 × 500 hurdles, 58·3 (400 metres time 49·8).
Sept. 14th: 325½ yards hurdles (!) 35·2.
Sept. 15th. To Mexico City.
1 week walk, jog warm-up.
2 × 300 metres stride, 36·0, 33·3.
1 × 600 metres, 83·8.
2 × 6 hurdles, 24·3, 25·5.
1 × 600 metres 78·3 (400 metres time 53·5).

October 1968
2 × 200 metres intermediate hurdles, 22·2 hard effort, 22·8 relaxed.
1 × 8 hurdles, 34·3.
1 × 7 hurdles, 29·7.
1 × 400 metres (second half over intermediate hurdles) 49·0 (24·0
– 25·0).
Oct. 13th. Heat of Olympic 400 metres hurdles, 50·3.
Oct. 14th. Semi-final, 49·3.
Oct. 15th. Final, 48·1, World record.
Oct. 19th. 4 × 400 metres relay heat, 45·1.
Oct. 20th. 4 × 400 metres relay final, 44·6.

1971–72 DIARY

JANUARY–APRIL

Road running, 5–12 miles and weight training.

MAY–JUNE

Some wrong leg hurdle work. A little general track work. 100
metre strides.

JULY–AUGUST

Sit-ups and press-ups in sets of 50 of each.
800 metres strides between each set, total 350–550 per day.

SEPTEMBER   WEEKS 1 AND 2

September 14th, to Boston.
2 sand dune sprint sessions. 10 × 120 ft. up.
1 day rest per week: 8 road runs – 83 miles total.
10 mile runs (63 mins., 64 mins., 60 mins. 30, 64 mins. 65 mins.).
1 rest day per week.

OCTOBER   WEEKS 3–7

17 days double sessions.
Morning runs 3–7 miles (6 mins. 30 per mile).

3 dune sessions, 12, 18, 15 × 120 ft. dune.
1–3 hour hill climb.
3 sprint hill sessions – flat-out up trail in 25 strides (7 secs.) 25, 50, 40 repeats.
Road work: week 3: 7 runs – total distance 62¼ miles.
week 4: 6 runs – total distance 50 miles.
week 5: 5 runs – total distance 42 miles.
week 6: 9 runs – total distance 72½ miles.
week 7: 9 runs – total distance 78 miles.
1 rest day per week.

NOVEMBER WEEKS 8–11

13 days double sessions.
Morning runs 4–7 miles (6 mins. 30 per mile).
4 dune sessions: 16, 20, 15, 16 × 120 ft. dune.
3 hill sessions (2 on sprint hill 40 and 50 repeats 5 × 300 metre hill).
2 weight training sessions.
Road runs: week 8: 8 runs 64 miles (up over and down Heart Break Hill on Boston Marathon course (10 miles, 55·34).
week: 9: 5 runs 49 miles (10 miles, 56·50).
week 10: 8 runs 66 miles (10 miles, 55·25).
week 11: 7 runs 53 miles.

DECEMBER WEEKS 12–16

1 day rest per week.
10 days double sessions.
Morning runs 4–10 miles (6 mins. 30 per mile).
3 dune sessions 18 × 120 ft. dune, 30 × 30 × 90 ft. dune.
4 sprint hill sessions, 40, 41, 44, 50 repeats.
6 weight training sessions.
Road runs: week 12: 7 runs total 52½ miles.
week 13: 6 runs total 51 miles.
week 14: 6 runs total 55 miles.
week 15: 5 runs total 51 miles.
week 16: 6 runs total 55 miles.
Average mile pace just under 6 mins.

JANUARY 1972   WEEKS 17–20

1 day rest per week. 2 days off ill.
2 sand dune sessions 25 × 90 ft. dune, 15 × 120 ft. dune.
3 sprint hill sessions, 50, 40, 50, repeats.
4 weight training sessions.
Road runs: week 17: 6 runs total 62 miles.
           week 18: 3 runs total 33 miles.
           week 19: 4 runs total 24 miles.
           week 20: 5 runs total 38 miles.

FEBRUARY   WEEKS 21–24

1 day rest per week.
3 dune sessions. 30, 32, 30 × 90 ft. dune.
2 sprint hill sessions. 50, 60 repeats.
4 long hill sessions: 5 × 300 metres hill, 4, 4, and 5 × 500 metres hill.
Road runs: week 21: 2 runs 20 miles.
           week 22: 7 runs 50 miles.
           week 23: 4 runs 24 miles.
           week 24: 4 runs 18 miles.
           Move towards fast sessions.

MARCH   WEEKS 25–29

Week 25, 4 days recovery break.
1 day per week rest.
1 day per week dunes, 20–30 repeats.
1 day per week hills, 5 × 800 metres or 8 × 200 metres up and down grass slope.
1 day per week long run 8–10 (6 mins. per mile).
3 days per week track work: when track out of use due to snow, bounding 25 × 100 metres.
Track work, always standing start:
March 8th. 15 × 220 yards, average 25·9, 220 yards walk between
March 10th. 10 × 330 yards, average 39·9, 330 yards walk between.
March 13th. 8 × 440 yards, average 56·8, 440 yards walk between.
March 17th. 3 × 660 yards, average 89·5 (aimed for 6, chest cold).
March 20th. 6 × 440 yards, average 55·2, 1 lap walk first 3, 2 laps next 2.

March 24th. 5 × 660 yards, average 89·2, 1½ lap walk first 2–2½ laps next 2.

March 27th. 5 × 660 yards, average 88·6, similar intervals.

March 29th. 6 × 440 yards, average 53·4, 2 laps walk between.

March 31st. 2 × 880 yards, 1 min. 58·5, 1 min. 56·0.

APRIL   WEEKS 30–33

1 day per week rest.

1 day per week long run, 6–8 miles.

1 day per week hills, 8 × 200 metres up and down; 4 × 350 metres up and over hill (35 secs. up, 7 secs. down) 20 × 100 metres on hill.

1 day per week dunes, 15–25 repeats.

3 days track.

April 3rd. 10 × 220 yards, average 25 secs.

April 5th, 15 × 150 metres.

April 6th, hurdles + 2 × 300 metres, 35·4, 37·8.

April 10th, 4 × 660 yards (average 83·8).

April 12th, 2 × 500 yards hurdles (54·6 440), 62·3; (52·8 440), 61·2.

April 14th. 2 × 220 yards hurdles, 23·9, 23·6

April 17th. 3 × 7 intermediate hurdles, 30·8, 30·1, 29·6.

April 21st. 2 × differential hurdles (2nd 220 with hurdles) 23·7 + 26·1 = 49·8; 23·7 + 25·9 = 49·6.

April 24th, 'flu! Adductor tear (another month away from hurdle training).

April 28th, Penn Relays, finished 2nd in 400 metres hurdles, 54·6 after hitting 10th hurdle and falling (30·3 at 7th).

MAY   WEEKS 34–37

1 day per week rest.

1 day per week long run (5–7 miles).

1 day per week Hills (8 × 200 metres up and down).

1 day per week dunes (12–15 × 120 ft. dune or 20–25 × 90 ft. dune).

3 days per week track or grass run.

May 5th. 5 × 660 yards, average 85·2.

May 8th. 5 × 880 yards, average 2 mins. 01·3 (heavy, cold, rain).

May 10th. 3 × 500 yards, aim at 440 in 51 secs., times at 440 yards shown first 49·8, 56·6, 49·3, 56·0, 48·8, 55·8.

May 12th. 3 sets 2 × 330, 110 yards between 37·5, 37·5, 37·6, 36·1, 36·8, 36·4.

May 15th. 2 × 660 yards, aim at 79·0, 440 time shown first, 51·5, 78·5, 51·3, 77·8.

May 17th. 4 × 440 yards aim at 50 secs. 50·8, 49·9, 50·5, 49·6.

May 19th. 8 × 150 yards, aim at 12 × 150 at 9/10ths effort.

May 22nd. 1 × 660 yards, 440 time shown first, 51·0, 77·6.

May 24th. 440 hurdles, 50·3 secs. (time trial).

May 25th. 4 × 500 yards hurdles, 440 time shown first, 55·0, 63·0; 55·1, 63·1; 55·0, 63·0.

May 29th. 3 × 440 yards with hurdles 8, 9, and 10 in place; 49·6 50·9, 50·2.

May 31st. 3 × 7 hurdles, 31·1, 33·3, 32·0.

JUNE   WEEKS 38–41

1 day per week rest.
1 day of hills.
2 days of dunes.
4 days off ill.

June 2nd. 3 × 7 hurdles, 30·5, 30·5, 29·9.

June 5th. 6 × 150 metres hard.

June 7th. 3 sets 2 × 330 yards with 110 yards walk between 36·2, 36·2; 36·6, 37·0; 37·2, 37·2.

June 11th, N.E.A.A.U. Championships. 440 yards hurdles, first in 50·2.

June 13th. 1 × 660 yards, 440 time shown first, 49·6, 76·4.

June 14th. 1 × 12 high hurdles, wrong lead leg. 3 × 120 yards high hurdles, wrong lead leg, 15·3, 15·2, 15·8. (11 hurdles in place.)

June 16th. 2 × 880 yards (aim 1·56·0, 1·54·0) 58·5–57·5–1·56·0 (1·55–800m) 56·1–56·7–1·52·8 (1·52·1–800metres).

June 19th. Cold.

June 20th. 2 × 440 (aim 5 × 440–52·0) 51·2, 50·8.

June 21st. 4 × 330 (aim 6 × 330–36 point) 37·0, 35·6, 35·6, 35·8.

June 23rd. To London.

June 27th. 2 × 330 yards, 35·0, 34·7.

JULY WEEKS 42–45

July 1st. National League 400m 47·1 (1) relay 46·3.
July 3rd. 4 × 120, 10 × 80 sprint.
July 4th. 12th Hurdle and grass fartlek work.
July 14th. A.A.A. Championships. Heat 400 metres hurdles, 50·8, Final 49·7.
July 17th–22nd. Grass fartlek and hurdles most days.
July 19th. 500 yards hurdles, 62·3 passing 440 in 53·5; 1 × 8 hurdles 37·7.
July 25th–26th. G.B. v Finland, 400 metres hurdles in 49·3; relay 47·4/48·2 including dropped baton!
July 29th. National League, 400 metres flat 47·5.
July 31st. 2 × 8 hurdles, 35·5, 35·1.

AUGUST WEEKS 46–50

Aug. 1st–5th. 400 metres hurdles 49·9, relay 47·0/47·2.
Aug. 6th. 12 × 100 metres.
Aug. 7th. weights and acceleration sprints of 100 metres (50 metres hard, plus 50 metres leg speed).
Aug. 8th. 10 × 120 yards.
Aug. 9th. Weights, 2 × differential 440 yards hurdles, 25·2 + 25·1 = 50·3; 24·3 + 25·0 = 49·3.
Aug. 10th. 6th 100 metres fast striding. Pull in right hamstring!
Aug. 11th. 2 cortisone shots.
Aug. 13th. Jogging.
Aug. 14th. Jog, exercises, running in water, physiotherapy.
Aug. 15th. As yesterday.
Aug. 16th. Jogging, exercises, strides, and physiotherapy.
Aug. 17th. Fartlek.
Aug. 18th. 6 × 4 hurdles (only 15 strides).
Aug. 19th. To Munich.
Aug. 24th. 8 hurdles, 24·3; 7 hurdles, 29·9.
Aug. 27th. 1 × 400 metres hurdles differential, 22·8 in flat – 24·7 with hurdle = 47·5.
Aug. 28th. 300 metres stride 33·8.
Aug. 31st. Olympic 400 metres hurdles heat 49·72.
Sept. 1st. Semi-final 49·66.
Sept. 2nd. Final 48·52.
Sept. 8th. Relay leg, 45·2.

Sept. 9th. Relay leg, 44·9.

Sept. 15th. Crystal Palace, 300 metres hurdles, 34·6, world best (46·1 400 metres pace).

Oct. 1st. G.B. *v.* France 49·3 (400 metres hurdles) (13 strides to 7th hurdle).

CHAPTER 13

Hurdling – A Precise Skill

As with running training so it is with hurdling, there is no one perfect way. Each individual's structure and movement is different. However, there are many helpful tips and thoughts on how to cross a barrier at speed. Much of my knowledge has come from my coach, Fred Housden, but I have also gained insight from Italy's Professor Calvesi, America's Wilbur Ross, through *The Hurdlers' Bible*, and many other individuals. And in my teens I devoured any publication which made reference to how to hurdle.

I loved hurdling and the action fascinated me. However in the early days I could feel myself wasting time by floating through the air over the hurdles. In this technical event just trying harder wasn't the answer. Hurdling became a form of self-expression and I searched for ways to improve.

The greatest compliment to my hurdling came when I heard comments like, 'You made it look as if there wasn't a hurdle there – you just ran over it.' That is really what the hurdler is trying to achieve, an action which will let him deviate as little as possible from normal running. However, anyone who has tried to jump any high object while running at full speed will understand that this is easier said than done. In the high hurdles, the stride has to be over a height of 3 feet 6 inches and to negotiate it well the distance from take-off to landing is not far short of 12 feet.

The most obvious requirement for hurdling is flexibility, but this is closely followed by the need for speed and specific muscle strength. Regardless of whether I was running or hurdling for the work-out, my warm-up was quite a demanding part of the session and worked on all three of the aspects just mentioned.

Two specific hurdling motion exercises were shown me by Fred Housden and before every session I would repeat them many times. They isolate the basic movement of each leg in clearing a hurdle efficiently.

The two exercises should be done where there is access to a fixed bar at a height of about three feet, preferably a metal rail which may be gripped with the hands. For the first exercise, the lead leg kick, stand with your side at the rail, with the leg you will put over the hurdle first, next to the rail. Rise up on the toe of the leg farthest from the rail, i.e. the take-off foot, and, at the same time, lift the knee of the leg nearest the rail as high as possible. The knee of the leg on the ground should never be bent. The hips should always be kept as high as is possible. While the knee is being drawn up, the heel of the lead leg must remain close to the thigh. Shoulders should be kept square but they are brought slightly forward while the knee is being raised. It is most important not to allow the hips to sink while the knee is being raised. Throughout keep the toes of the lead leg cocked back towards the shin. When the knee reaches its high point, kick the heel as hard as possible, at the height of the hurdle 3 feet or 3 feet 6 inches. While doing this, the body from toe to head must remain slightly forward, as if driving over a hurdle. Common errors by the novice are throwing their shoulders back as they kick, pointing their toe down, allowing the lower leg to sail high, or performing the exercise in separate, jerky movements rather than flowing. It is, therefore, extremely important that the motion of knee up, heel out, is performed as if moving in a forward direction. The arm not holding the rail can be used to balance this vicious kick. The arm action is as follows: at the same time as the lead leg knee is raised, the opposite arm, bent at 90 degrees, is raised to shoulder height. While the knee is coming up, the forearm will briefly be parallel with the shoulders and while the heel is being kicked out, the elbow should come back still at shoulder height, keeping the arm bent. The main point of this exercise is to develop a fast-rising lead leg which will help the hurdler not to float over the hurdles.

One way of practising this motion without a rail is to imagine holding a piece of wood in both hands with arms out-stretched in front at a height of 3 feet to 3 feet 6 inches above ground. Walk forward, and, as before, raise up on the take-off foot, keeping that leg straight, hips high, and body angled forward. Lift the lead leg knee as high as possible and then with the heel try to break the imaginary piece of wood between the hands. Remember to keep the body in the same forward driving position throughout.

The object of the second exercise is to practise the motion of the trail leg (i.e. the leg of the take-off foot). A hurdle should be placed not less than three feet from the rail with the cross bar parallel to the rail. For a high hurdler, the height may be 3 feet 6 inches, although, to begin with, a lesser height is advisable. The athlete should get into a position in which his hips are just behind the hurdle when he is holding the rail. At the start of the exercise, the upper body will be almost parallel with the ground with the arms outstretched either side of the head and hands shoulder-width apart, holding the rail. The leading leg, which corresponds of course, to the landing foot, should be placed six to eight inches in front of the hurdle (on the rail side of the hurdle). The athlete should remain on the toes of this foot as in landing over the hurdle. The hips and shoulders should be kept as square as possible throughout.

It is the *knee* which has to be raised to the side, to go over the hurdle. At the start of the exercise, the trail leg should be extended directly behind the athlete in mid-air. The arms should pull the body towards the rail, to simulate the forward momentum and allow the leg to move over the hurdle naturally. The trail foot should be turned outwards, the toes cocked up towards the shin as far as possible. The knee should be rising away from the lead leg and the *heel of the trail leg brought in close to the seat.* In this way, the motion of the trail foot approximates to a more direct path from immediately behind the athlete over the hurdle to in front of him. The knee, which is being lifted to the side to come over the hurdle, must continue to rise, almost as if it is being brought under the athlete's armpit, *until it is directly in front of the chest. Only,* when the knee is right in front should the heel be brought away from the thigh and extended forward towards the ground below the rail. Throughout the exercise, the lead leg *must* be kept straight, the knee *never* bending, and the hips kept as high as possible. At the 1969 Conference of European hurdle coaches Professor Calvesi stressed the importance of keeping on the toes with the hips as high as possible *throughout a hurdle race.*

This means that the landing leg acts as a pivot, to maintain constant forward hip movement on each landing. The heel should never touch the ground and the knee should not be bent at all on landing.

Professor Calvesi also showed the good continuity of upper body angle of Eddie Ottoz, the 1966 and 1969 European Champion, *into, over* and *away* from each hurdle. This continuity of lean will also assist the hurdler to maintain his momentum. The athlete must have in his mind the fact that the short hurdles race is a sprint over hurdles. It is very natural to allow the hurdling difficulties to interrupt the concentration on just *sprinting fast* from the block to the tape.

In order to run fast over hurdles there has to be a minimum of deviation from a direct path. In this sense it resembles tightrope walking, in that foot placing, arm movements, and balance are critical. Fred Housden used his knowledge of mechanics to explain to me the relevance and importance of the axiom 'for every action, there is an equal and opposite reaction'.

Even a minor movement out of the line of running can cause a hurdler to swerve out of his lane or at least to fight his way back on to balance before taking the next hurdle. One aspect of direct-line running when approaching the hurdle is bringing the lead leg knee up high in the line of running, with the heel kicking straight out at the hurdle top. If the knee is not lifted sufficiently high, the whole leg may be swung in an indirect circular motion over the hurdle.

Apart from the kicking exercise there are a couple of other ways of improving the speed and strength of the lead leg lift. One is to take a walking step or two towards a steeplechase barrier and then rapidly bring the lead leg knee up high enough to allow the ball of the foot to step on top of the barrier. This knee lift action should be very vigorous. Another useful exercise involves weight boots. The weight boots are strapped to the user's shoe. Three exercises proved very helpful for me. The first two, the standing high-knee lifts and the seated leg extensions were valuable quadricep strengtheners. The third weight exercise was a standing hamstring curl. I went through three sets of each exercise ten times for each leg. These three exercises constituted the mini weight session I used to recondition my legs after the bad tear in 1967.

It is advisable for a hurdler to learn how to hurdle off either leg. Therefore all exercises and hurdle practice should be repeated for both legs. It is worth noting that when aiming the lead leg at the hurdle top, the direct leg line will be a few inches off centre, to whichever side is the lead leg, e.g. two inches right of centre if the right leg is the lead leg.

Another aspect of direct line running is the arm and shoulder movement. The shoulders should be kept square to the hurdles at all times. They should be held forward to help the athlete not to sail over the hurdles, i.e., they counter-balance the vigorous, upward knee motion.

Too often hurdlers swing their arms so wildly that they cause their whole upper body to rotate as they come over the hurdle and this movement continues on landing, with the result that energy and time are wasted as the athlete fights for balance and counter-rotation for the next step or two. The arm on the lead leg side of the body should be kept as close in to the athlete's side as possible, bent at the elbow, with the hand almost at the level of a trouser pocket. The opposite arm which moves forward with the lead leg usually causes the most damage when swung wildly. If possible, just as in sprinting, this arm should never be fully extended. As the hurdler takes off, the elbow is extended to the front with the forearm moving up to chin level parallel with the shoulders. The hurdler doesn't have to think about bringing the elbow back – it should be held forward as long as possible and will, automatically, move round behind him. The elbow still bent should be kept high as it comes back. The return position of the arm is much better for sprinting than if it has been straightened.

Moving both elbows vigorously on landing, will help the athlete to get away from the hurdle fast. In order to help the new hurdler to develop a good forward lean and square shoulders, it can be beneficial to have them extend both arms forward, while going over the hurdle. Only the elbow of the arm on the trail leg side should come back on landing. The other arm should return straight back to the side of the body.

One tip from *The Hurdlers' Bible* which I found helpful in getting down over the hurdle, rather than floating was that the hurdler's high point should be two inches *before* the hurdle. In this way, the athlete literally steps *down* over the hurdle. It's not a high jump – it's more a diving, running action. From the ground, the action is a drive over the hurdle. A take-off point approximately seven feet from the hurdle will enable a full leg and ankle extension from the driving take-off leg. The action over the hurdle is determined at this take-off point. Getting too near the hurdle on take-off can cause a floating, time-wasting clearance. In the high hurdle, the landing foot should be about four feet beyond the hurdle. In the high hurdles I had to accentuate my forward body lean over the first hurdle to make sure that I didn't carry too far over the hurdle following the first rapid fifteen yards. If I did travel too far over this hurdle I came too close to the second hurdle. Apart from the exaggerated lean, Fred brought hurdle two about four inches nearer to the first hurdle in training. This forced my legs to move faster to approach hurdle two a little quicker.

Moving the position of the hurdles during practice can also help if the athlete is having difficulty reaching the hurdle, i.e., the hurdle is brought in a few feet and very *gradually* moved farther away. Another aid is temporarily to lower the hurdle height.

All these points are geared towards a continuity of speed over and between the hurdles. The action over the hurdle should always be practised at speed. Therefore, even when jogging between the hurdles, the athlete should always accelerate on the last couple of strides going into the hurdle.

The running exercise for isolating the trail and lead legs are performed by running down the line *beside* the hurdle and bringing either one or other of the legs over the hurdle depending on which side of the lane the athlete is running. For the sprint hurdle race, it can be helpful to run at full speed bringing only one leg over the hurdle. This will give the runner a greater feeling of the action being that of a sprint race.

A useful alternate leg practice is to place the hurdles at normal markings, but in two lanes alternating either side of the athlete's running line. The athlete takes one extra stride between hurdles and brings alternate legs over the hurdle.

It is important that the athlete hurdles frequently in order to develop good *visual awareness*. It will become possible to 'eye in' the hurdle from quite long distances. The worst possible loss of speed occurs if he is forced to stutter-step in front of the hurdle. He should practise enough to overcome any inhibition about the height of the barrier or the distance of the race. I recommend youths, juniors, and intermediate hurdlers all to practise part of the time over the senior 3 feet 6 inches high hurdles. The hurdles seem to become higher towards the end of a race anyway and good

technical skill over the higher hurdles will help to ensure main-
tenance of good quality and fast hurdling throughout all other
hurdle races.

On the stamina side, it's quite a shock to discover how much
stamina is involved even in a sprint hurdle race. Try putting up
twelve hurdles in practising the highs and intermediate hurdles.
Form over hurdles eleven and twelve will let the athlete know his
true stamina condition. The athlete will find that he will have to be
in shape to run well on the flat for between one-and-a-half and two
times the hurdle race distance, in order to be in condition to run
his hurdles event well. One work-out I did to help my specific
hurdling stamina was thirty minutes non-stop sprint work from
blocks, over five high hurdles, with just a walk back between each
run. All runs were at maximum effort. Once after twenty-nine
minutes of this session, my spikes caught the ground after the last
hurdle. I fell and grazed my knee and elbow rather nastily. Billy
Smith looked at the damage and then said, 'You have a minute
more to go.' He knew that after a fall a horse may shy away from
a barrier. I was damned if he thought I had any inhibition about
falling so I ran another repetition hard before heading in to be
patched up.

The start, from blocks to the first hurdle, is the most critical
part of the race and should be practised frequently. Although
synthetic tracks are a fabulous asset for training in all weathers, the
cinder track has one distinct advantage. The track may be swept
before each run making it possible to see where the spikes have
made their impression. This helps to check the stride length at each
point and that the foot placement does not deviate too greatly
from the direct running line. On Tartan, flour can be used (not
self-raising flour, or watch out for the rain!)

At the start of the sprint hurdles most beginners have a tendency
to stand up when coming out of the blocks. You don't have many
strides before you must rise for the hurdle but at least during the
first few, the shoulders should be kept low, as in a normal sprint
start.

Another factor to be checked by the coach is that the head level
of the athlete shouldn't rise or fall between or over the hurdles.
Many athletes tend to sink on to their heels between hurdles and
rise up over the hurdles.

I would like to stress the fact that Fred Housden was incredibly patient in correcting my hurdling faults. If all aspects had been thrown at me at once I'm sure I'd have become quite confused and if not that, at least felt terribly pressured. During any practice run the hurdler should only be asked to think about *one* thing at a time and *not too many* in any one session. The aim is to improve the hurdler's style of action to the point that it becomes second nature and even under the pressure of a full-effort run all that has to be thought about is speed, moving the arms and legs as fast as possible.

There are many descriptive phrases I have heard for the strong hurdling action: smooth violence; controlled fury; channelled aggression; deliberate and fluid motion. The athlete must learn to slow down the action in his mind, to relax and develop self-control even while in the excitement of competition. Perhaps the duck provides a good moral – be calm and placid on the surface but paddle like the devil underneath.

CHAPTER 14

Each Person Has His Own Gold Medal

Within each of us is the capacity for self-awareness. This has evolved in man, but is at different stages in each individual. Awareness is gained by becoming sensitive to our reactions, to the world and to others, and by seeing how our actions affect others. A significant reason for increasing our self-awareness is that each of us can discover more about ourselves as we are now and more importantly, to gain insight into what we can become. I find this an exciting prospect, as it means that to a large extent, we have it within our power to change and develop our lives. Linking self-awareness with the desire to change and progress, each of us has his future in his own hands.

Sport is one avenue through which an individual can develop a greater awareness of being, and his relationship to our world. Strengths and weaknesses are soon discovered but more than that is to be learned and absorbed. To increase our own awareness, requires conscious thought, sensitivity, a willingness and openness to receive cues, and an attempt at honest detached objectivity. We have to be tough with ourselves.

Perhaps the most difficult aspect of positive change is our self-doubt, and the negative feelings of not quite being able to make the grade. Too often we listen to the negative side of our conversation with ourselves and opt out. Also others are often eager to put us down; perhaps to help their own need for survival. By pushing us down, they feel that much higher up. If we listened to all the abuse and 'put downs' we receive through our lives we'd rarely be off the floor. However, in each of us there is the innate desire to survive, which somehow keeps our spirits alive. This personal life force should be latched on to. Whatever the essence that makes you unique as an individual, this is your mainspring. Self-awareness; self-knowledge; self-acceptance; we have to begin with ourselves and are the only people who can do it.

During one course at Boston University I had to answer the following questions in depth. 'Who am I?' 'What am I?' 'Where have I come from?' and 'Where am I going?' Being forced to answer these questions helped me to gain insight into where I was coming from, who I was and what I wanted to become. I recommend the task to everyone. In fact, they are questions which should be re-answered periodically. The last question is the most difficult for me to answer as it is so open ended. It is in this question of where we are going in our lives, that the dare to be alive and experiment comes in. Too often, I feel, people play it safe. 'The important thing is this: to be able at any moment to sacrifice what we are for what we could become' – Charles du Bois. Usually our self-image is pitched too low. Doubting our capabilities is the first fatal step towards failure.

In a speech during 1968 I heard the first heart transplant surgeon, Dr Christian Barnard, make a remarkable statement. He said that he believed that man could achieve anything within the scope of his imagination. I applied this to what man was currently achieving. Because man believed that he could walk on the moon, all it took was a tremendous amount of work and applied knowledge to achieve that feat. If Roger Bannister had not believed that he could break four minutes for a mile, he would not have been the first to do it.

It will probably amuse Sir Roger Bannister to hear that when he broke the four minute mile barrier, I, at the grand old age of 10 felt a slight disappointment that the opportunity had now been lost to me.

I've often wondered what drives a person to achieve something. Why is it that some people with great talent don't believe in themselves and others with mediocre ability, hang in there, to achieve something great. Perhaps it has something to do with the fact that those with great talent don't have to work so hard to achieve something. Whereas the less gifted realize that they have to work and may force themselves to become the best. Part of our drive to achieve has to do with our image of ourselves – our ego ideal. Part of it has to do with motivation.

During childhood a large part of our character development

depends on identity. When I was young I can remember identifying with certain characters. Perhaps the nearest to home was actually in my home, and that was my Dad. He played sport with us as children and was good at it. But he had many other attributes which I still admire. He, like my mother, seems to be remarkably 'other' oriented. That is, he'd do anything for anyone that would ease their way along in life. My parents established a very consistent, encouraging and secure environment in our home. Their concern and love for us as youngsters gave us a great base from which to start our own building.

A second element of identity came through childhood teachings. Again, mostly from my parents I learned to value the system of Christianity: to treat others as you would want them to treat you, etc. *Pilgrims Progress* was read and I remember admiring the picture and story attached to the Knight – Great Heart.

Later in life I did a good deal of reading about Christianity and other religions. The most striking features, to me, were their similarities; especially related to philosophies of living. For me religion gives a person a value system on which to base moral and social behaviour, one's attitudes towards others and life in general. The individual who continues to be exceptional in my understanding is Christ. I suppose that that could classify me as a Christian, however, I dislike such 'label placing'.

I am also disenchanted by organized religion's requirement for exclusivity – 'Ours is the only way'. Peter Ustinov's statement that 'man is united by doubt and divided by conviction' holds considerable truth. I have enjoyed the search through various writings. Recently I read a helpful phrase of theologian Paul Tillich. He wrote that God is being itself, not a being. I am still formulating my thoughts but two aspects seem clear to me. The first is that the way you act in your dealings with others, does portray yourself and your value system. One Dutch philosopher says that 'your religion is your attitude towards life'. Another expression I have heard is that 'each day is a video tape of your value system'. Taking a look back on a day can be quite a shock. What have I done? With whom have I come into contact? How did I relate to them? Did I really put sufficient effort into what I did? Once or twice I've asked myself what I would do if I knew that I only had a day or two to live. How would I spend that time? Whom would I contact and to say what? Sometimes I wanted to say 'I'm sorry' to someone or to say 'I really love you' to another. I believe strongly in honesty and openness in our communication and relationships with others. So often we hold back, we don't bring something out and we may harbour hatred or guilt, frustration or pity, distrust or hope, concern or love. Man is so complex, so easily hurt and can so easily hurt others, without thinking. We are in control of most of our actions. Taking time to think about what we're doing and saying will make more than a little difference to ourselves and others. My early identity with Christ, and his strongly humane social actions, helped me to form my own ideals.

The second aspect of religion and a search for God which still absorbs me is that of a meaning and purpose to life. What is life if it has no basic value, no worthwhileness, or no direction?

In spite of my direction not being quite so clear to me now, it is only right to say that prior to Mexico in 1968 I gained a considerable peace of mind and inner strength and resolve through praying. At that time I felt a clear and direct attunement with God. I didn't pray to win races, I prayed that I should be enabled to do my best and that my life should be used to help others, regardless of the outcome of my Olympic race. Although this may have been a scared plea for shared responsibility, I didn't see this as deferring responsibility for my race, but rather, putting it into a more meaningful, overall context.

Apart from family and religion, my other area of 'ideal' was on the track. For my 10th birthday one present was a book about the great Czech distance runner Emil Zatopek. At about the same time I thrilled to the excitement of Chris Chataway beating Vladimir Kuts at the White City in a world record 5,000 metres race, the same year as Bannister's first sub-four minute mile. I can remember wanting to become one of the best and was delighted when someone told me that I ran like Bannister.

Years later during a university course I read of a challenge that American psychologist Abraham Maslow used to leave with his students. He ended a lecture with the query – 'Which of you is going to become great?' After a long pause, while his students looked at each other, Maslow concluded – 'If not you, who then?' As one who by all physiological rights should not have become exceptional in athletics, I know how amazingly accurate is Maslow's challenge. Too few people recognize that they can become exceptional, in any number of ways. It is my belief that just about everyone can become an exceptional individual, if he or she wants to, and is prepared to work. I shall return to Maslow later, but first to continue this theme. I have already quoted the phrase written in a letter to me 'Each person has their own gold medal'. To me that says it all. You have to aim high and you have to bring out of yourself the best you have. If you do this, you will have reached your own gold medal. The disabled person who learns to shoot an arrow straight may have reached just as high a personal standard as an Olympic medallist. The important aspect is the level of application and dedication to master yourself in mind, body, and spirit. I believe we all have talents and it is our duty to develop them to the best of our ability.

Of course there are many incredible stories, such as youngsters with polio working their limbs back to health and strength and going on to become Olympic Champions. Bob Richards' book, *Heart of a Champion* had many such inspirational stories. I used to feel inspired to push myself harder when I read such tales. I also found some sayings and poems that had an element of toughness, or inspiration. The ones which readily come to my mind now are 'If' by Rudyard Kipling; Michael Quoist's prayer 'Time' and the book *Jonathan Livingston Seagull* by Richard Bach. I read the last just prior to the Munich Olympics. The thought that our limits often centre in our minds, appealed to me. In the years prior to Mexico I had asked – why couldn't the 400 metres hurdles be run faster? and set about looking for ways to do it. Too often I feel that the attempt to find a way is not there or there is an excuse as to why it is not possible. Flexible thinking, lateral thinking, openness to new ideas and a willingness to experiment; should be in all our minds. Change seems to be the only constant in life, so we ought to try to make ourselves and the things with which we come into contact, change for the better.

I have always wanted to improve on my previous best in almost anything I do. I mentioned earlier that part of the desire to achieve and improve is tied in with motivation. Purely in the sports area I can see how my own motivation has changed over the years. Obviously there will have been several factors of which I am not aware. However, it is interesting to see the continuation of an activity in spite of changing motivation.

In childhood the major influence was the sheer enjoyment of physical movement and play. I enjoyed trying to master each new physical activity. My first athletics competition was at the age of 8, a 50 metres dash which I won, but even at that age I was just as interested in pushing myself to new personal levels of endurance records, as I was in competing with others. I used to keep personal records, e.g. how many times I could cover the length of the outdoor veranda on a pogo-stick, daily trying to achieve a greater number. I can remember going to tell my parents of my new records and them being duly impressed and displaying sufficient interest in my achievements to help sustain my enthusiasm. At that time I enjoyed keeping many records but particularly of world best athletic performances. Perhaps subconsciously I hoped to be one of those people one day.

Before the age of 10 I also used to have races with my brother, John, who is a couple of years younger. In retrospect I feel bad about what I was probably doing to his competitive psyche. He might have been on a bike or running but I would give him a start that was of sufficient distance to make it a challenge and close – but also put me 'in with a chance' of winning. Some of the races were desperately close but I seem to remember usually digging down sufficiently deeply just to come by before the finish line. Competition seems to be good for those who experience winning, but not necessarily so for those who never do. Although my brother is more physically gifted than I, he disliked athletic training in later years – I truly wonder whether this was as a direct result of his early experience.

Both of us enjoyed team sports and made most school teams. Parental expectation was another motivating influence here. Both our parents had competed in sport. They enjoyed it and helped us to find the fun and self-enhancement which can come through it. They often came to watch our games. Encouragement came from them to do well, but I can never remember feeling pressurized. Often I heard Dad say – 'Just try and do your best', 'We'll never feel badly if you don't win', 'Please don't feel you have to win for us', 'Best wishes, we're with you in spirit'. My parents' support for my endeavours was certainly one of the most influential features in my sport success.

By the time I reached America, at 12, I was reasonably competent at a number of sports. This helped me immensely in maintaining my self-esteem, i.e. being able to think 'I'm okay' – esteem being the basis of worth and self-respect. Looking back at the photograph taken in my first year at Thayer Academy I wonder how any but lowly esteem was held. I was younger than the rest; very undersized; my voice hadn't broken; I had a 'strange' – to them – accent; and was rather odd looking, but I could run: through athletics, more than anything else I could justify myself to myself and to my peers. At that time I didn't have Olympic gold medal hopes looping in my head, although I never counted out the possibility of one day running on the National team. All I wanted then, was the chance to show that there was more to me than could be seen on the surface.

Sport is one area where recognition is clearly possible. Track competition is perhaps the most demonstrably clear and measurable representation of oneself at a point in time. The athlete is alone – in full view of all – with two clear measures, the time taken to complete the event and his position at the finish. Simply meeting the challenge of taking part will give an individual a sense of accomplishment and a genuine self-regard.

Once a reasonable level had been achieved in school, what then was the motivation to continue in university? I did want to see how far I could go when putting all my energies into one sport. The upward spiral has been mentioned before. Under the guidance and encouragement of two great coaches, work produced an improved performance, which in turn gave me awareness of greater capabilities. Gradually I gained the capacity to accept more work which resulted in new improvement. My self-confidence increased through the knowledge that greater work was improving my times. Belief in my coaches and their training ideas and their belief in me helped to develop new confidence. Over the four years from 1964– 68 my sights were continually lifted; from 'making' the Olympic team in the high hurdles, to doing well in the 400 metres hurdles, to making the Olympic final and finally, during the build-up year to Mexico, realizing tht I had the potential to win and break the world record. I had to be continually changing and lifting my level of realistic self expectation.

It might not have worked that way. I could have been injured. Would it still have been worth all the training? The answer is still 'yes'. Each day was worthwhile in itself. I enjoyed pushing to new levels in training. I enjoyed the empathy between the coach and myself, in the mutual struggle and the shared friendship and humour among the training athletes. And I learned a great deal about myself and life.

Meeting new people and other national representatives was an added excitement and experience. However, some of the draw-backs came after the ultimate performance of breaking a world record and winning an Olympics. Then, public expectation was that I should set a personal best or break a record every time out. This I tried to do in the high hurdles until I had had enough of the pressure that this caused. I had to step back and ask myself why I was running. Some of the 'fun' or basic enjoyment was missing. I recalled a story told by Australia's great distance runner, Ron Clarke. Following the A.A.A.'s Championships in 1966, Ron spoke at a dinner about a changed attitude which had influenced his running. He had been struggling to break the world record for 10,000 metres and on a number of occasions had been frustrated by coming close without succeeding. He'd worked excessively hard and it was getting him down that he was not getting the returns. During one run his personal dissatisfaction brought him to a standstill on top of a sand dune. As he gazed towards the sea his attention was caught by some creatures flopping about on the edge of the water. He heard some squealing, then saw a ball. As he thought they were porpoises he went closer to investigate, but nearer the water he discovered that it was a group of paraplegic children playing volleyball. The water was supporting their bodies and they were laughing and screaming with delight. Ron said that he had a look at himself, one of the greatest runners of all time, in perfect health but carrying a burden of depression at not being able to run a few tenths of a second faster. Then he looked at the kids, enjoying their sport, delighting in the water, the weather, and what health and strength they had, even with paralysed legs. He said that this incident had changed his whole attitude towards his running. He relaxed and enjoyed his running – working hard but from a new perspective. He told us this at the end of his most successful season, having broken several world records – including the 10,000 metres. The story spoke clearly to me, of appreciating and being happy with my health, strength, and talent. Each for a time, Ron and I had lost sight of some of the inherent joy of running.

I have sometimes found that running was an outlet for extremes of high or low feelings. In the spring of 1974 I watched a very intense television film called *Brian's Song*. It portrayed the life and death through cancer of Brian Piccolo, the room-mate of a great American football player, Gail Sayers. It came at the same time as the death of two close friends of mine, my hurdles coach Fred Housden, and Mexico Olympic team mate John Cooper. After the programme I had no choice but to go out and run. As my legs pounded the road, my mind also ran, asking what life was all about. A love bond had been severed by death. Life is so ephemeral. No one knows how much time they have; so our time should be used well. Strive, while we have the chance.

The desire to strive seems to be at different levels in each person. Man's progress indicates that there is something innate which drives him to push back boundaries, and conquer new frontiers, on the globe, in space and within himself. It seems, however, that only a few men and women move man forward. Surviving appears to be all-consuming for most, with the result that too many people never achieve their potential. Barry John and I talked during our time together in the Superstar contest. He referred to the value he placed on a balanced life. For him, there had to be time for his sport, his work, his family and himself. Man has many sides and I believe that none should be neglected. Education is necessary for the spiritual/moral, the aesthetic/emotional, the intellectual and the physical sides of man. In order to appreciate and use what is learned one must be teachable. This means being open and receptive to new ideas and suggestions and being able to put them into practice. Being teachable is a key to positive change and growth, all one's life.

I believe that sport in general, and athletics in particular, can be a unique learning tool. For example, we all have experienced the difficulty of overcoming apathy and inertia, in ourselves and in others. A well-known Chinese proverb states that, 'each 1,000 mile journey begins with a single step.' On the track the athlete practises taking that first step; to launch 'the next repetition'. Often this is when he is tired, but he learns to hold on, to make a personal commitment to the session and to his progress.

Perhaps one of the finest elements to be learned through sport is the building of a conscience; one which brings a personal question, 'What *ought* I to be doing?' That question requires all types of decisions. A coach may be able to help with advice and guide lines, but the final decisions are the athletes' choices.

One may well ask why an athlete chooses to undergo discomfort
and even agony? Much of the answer is tied up in the desire
to improve. There must be many enjoyable aspects; however, it
remains true that most things which are worth having are not too
easy to acquire. I think it will always remain true that athletic
success is *earned*. Progress is slow and never unbroken. Patience
and perseverance are a requirement. Strength and weakness have
to be understood, accepted, and worked on.

In the course of any season, the athlete will face all of the
following: defeat and victory; sickness and health; tension and
relaxation; degrees of pain, doubt, disappointment and despair, as
well as satisfaction and even ecstasy. The spectrum and intensity
of experience is delightfully varied. When all is going well the sense
of achievement is great. When 'downs' come it is necessary to
maintain self-control, which in this case means the mind and will
are resolved to keep a clear focus on the final aim.

Training and preparation are becoming progressively more
scientific and technical. This is a trend which will continue.
Therefore it is all the more important to bear in mind the phrase
'Keep it simple'. Franz Stampfl used it before Ian Thompson ran
the European Marathon in Rome in 1974. Soon after the start, Ian
found himself in the lead and thought: 'I guess I'll keep it simple
and stay here!' which he did – all the way to his fourth consecutive
victory. Sometimes it's easy to lose sight of the fact that what you
really have to do is run and run hard. With all the scientific,
economic, and personal backing in the world, it still comes down
to the individual's effort in the end.

Success in sport receives perhaps a disproportionate amount of
acclaim in the news. This may be because it is so easy to identify
with human movement. Also it can be lifting to 'identify' with
success, be it a team or an individual. However, regardless of the
reasons it provides a considerable avenue for the successful parti-
cipant's progress in the 'hierarchy of human needs'. Abraham
Maslow established a theory of man's growth towards 'self-
actualization' – that is, becoming the person you are capable of
becoming – as a fully functioning human being. Maslow was an
optimistic psychologist, believing that man is basically good and
that given the opportunity, he will strive to improve himself.
Maslow's hierarchy of human need is briefly as follows. He maintained that there are five levels, like rungs of a ladder. Each level

must, in some way, be satisfied before progression may take place to the next highest level. We will always be returning to our basic lower level needs. However, the overall progression is one of ascent. The two lowest levels are physiological. The lowest rung is the need for food, sleep, sex, shelter, water and air. The next level up is the need for safety and security. The third stage is seeking love and belongingness. (To an extent a sense of belonging can be formed within a sports group.) The fourth rung is the desire for self-esteem and the esteem of others. It is at this level where I believe success in sport has an exceptional role. Self-mastery, self-control, and reaching towards your own gold-medal-level will certainly accomplish this.

Sport may or may not be a part of the top step, self-actualization (becoming what you are capable of being). It depends on the individual and his capabilities. Also it need not be limited to an athlete's sporting achievements.

Athletics is not everything to me, but it is part of me. For me, it *is* an area of self expression. At times I felt as though I was actualizing my full potential on the track. Just a couple of times, my body ran as my mind thought. I wasn't forcing my running. I felt I was expressing my inner movement self in a sprinting, powerful flow, on the flat and over the hurdles. One of those times was in Mexico. I felt truly in tune, in harmony with life and clear in my direction.

Direction outside of athletics is never quite so clear. Following an Olympic win and a world record, the avenues to pursue in life are generously open. The search for direction is as difficult as it is exciting and challenging. Everyone suffers the problem of 'what to do'. The uncertainty during the time of search should not be off-putting; it is a necessary element.

Maslow stated that we will feel guilty and dissatisfied with ourselves if we are not on the path to self-actualization, using our talents well and growing. I feel as though I've been on the path and off the path. The sense of purpose and excitement in knowing I was on the right path and the personal dissatisfaction when I was not in tune with the direction for me, leads me to believe in Maslow's statement.

Whether or not one prays to God, or meditates or just takes time to be alone and think, I believe that each of us can find a direction, a purpose in life, which will be right for us at a particular time. It will change as we change; however, as I am also an optimist in

terms of my belief in man's basic good, I believe that each of us
can find a way to use our talent and personality to make life positive, creative, and useful. I believe that it is our duty to try to bring
the most we can out of ourselves. We each have a contribution to
make. By aiming high and working hard we each can attain our
own gold medal.

APPENDIX I.

Athletics Administration

Britain can claim to have originated many of today's worldwide sports. The rules were established not only for the games but also for player eligibility. Predominantly, sport was for the leisured class. Under the guise of the purity of amateurism, 'gentlemen' who didn't have to earn a living could afford to participate in sport.

I am thankful to say that since that time attitudes towards sports participation have changed dramatically. Also the structure of society in Britain and around the world has altered. Britain has a Minister for Sport and a Sports Council advocating 'Sport for All'.

Kenya's great distance runner, Kip Keino, once told me that he never felt bad about not winning nor would he ever look down on someone who came fourth or fifth, because he knew how hard each person in the competition had worked, even to get into the race. In his own words Kip had summarized the Olympic ideal that the most important aspect is to take part.

Throughout Britain local authorities are now concerned with the development of sports centres. For eighteen months I was director of one of Britain's newest and largest indoor multi-sport centres, the Michael Sobell Sports Centre. This is based in Islington, a densely populated urban area, with few sports facilities. One of the best features of the Centre is the co-operation with local schools. Coaching is given in sports such as badminton, squash, fencing, archery, ice skating, judo, trampoline, table tennis, volleyball, and basketball. At least the first couple of sports have typically been associated with exclusive middle-class clubs. This is where a community sports centre can provide an invaluable socializing service. At the Michael Sobell Sports Centre, time and space is allocated to the Inner London Education Authority for 6,000 youngsters from forty local schools to have their physical education classes there. It may take years to educate everyone to the benefit of physical health through regular sport but the opportunity to participate is the first requirement.

Local authorities have a great responsibility as well as an exciting chance to plan for the future. Consideration should be given to the following: most people will use a facility if it is close to them, their 'local'. Also, how many existing facilities, local football grounds, local schools, and other educational establishments, could be brought into multi-purpose use? With building costs escalating so rapidly, neighbouring local authorities could combine in the development of jointly sponsored, larger facilities. Various small sports 'locals' could be scattered around each borough. Within each 'local' there should be basic fitness training areas but also some different sports focus. Urban sports centres must consider including 'springboard' activities, for example skills such as climbing, canoe building and rolling, and ski training, taught as activities, which can later be pursued in rural areas. This should build in the flexibility for spectator accommodation in the larger centres. Seeing the best play can stimulate youngsters to take part. The clientele will range from beginners to internationals, each having his or her own requirement. Social meeting areas are important but first it should be clarified whether the centre is for sports, community activities, or whatever. When big business is seeking planning permission for high-rise offices, or living quarters (if such projects must be pursued), one stipulation should be the provision of at least one floor for sporting recreational facilities.

It is good to see so many people in the United States now using local school playing fields and outdoor courts in the evenings and at weekends. One can only hope that similar action is soon taken in Britain.

Changes are not only slow to take place but also at times slow to be recognized. At international level the days are long gone when one could turn up and have a go, having decided to stay off the beer and smokes for two weeks. Over the last few decades standards have risen to the point where dedication is almost obsessive. An individual may make national representation the top aim of his mind and body. For several years he will practise, learn, and work to become one of the best. Through television coverage, increased sponsorship, technological and medical advances, plus the athletes' own desires to improve, the spiral of rapid progress at the top almost defies belief. Air travel now facilitates regular international competition and the stresses on these young competitors are intense to say the least.

At the top, sport, players and administrators have, by and large, become professional. However, the Olympic movement still ties the hands of the predominantly amateur sports, athletics, swimming, gymnastics, and some of the winter sports. The rise in standards and the resulting demands on the individual participants has been just as great in these Olympic sports. However, recognition of the need for specialized assistance and care for these international representatives has been slow in coming.

The Olympics still hold great appeal and they will not disappear overnight. The rules for participation are in the process of being modified. This is necessary for the survival of the Games. 'Professional–amateur' athletes are already so commonplace that the crack is there to break down the Games unless some rapid alterations are made.

Allowing subsidy and broken time payments to amateuhavei s been one step in modernizing the rules. However, this only brought to light that our current administration is inadequately staffed and at present not structured to cope.

A move in amateur athletics to meet the specialized needs of the international was made when the British Amateur Athletic Board was set up in 1937 to oversee and co-ordinate the *International* side of track and field athletics. However, it has become the parent body for all administration and coaching for men and women throughout Britain – overseeing competition and development for schools, clubs, university, inter-services, tug of war, road walking, cross-country, and internationals at junior and senior level. Quite a handful for part-time officials.

Many could foresee and others have felt the inadequacies of our present administrative set-up. Support for the idea of full-time paid professional administration is growing fast. The names involved reads like an athletics *Who's Who*: Douglas Lowe, Godfrey Brown, and Donald Finlay, all athletes of pre-war vintage, had serious confrontations with the international team administrators. The latter two supported the move for professional administration as far back as the early 1950s. In Melbourne in 1956 it was

John Disley who took up the torch. In 1958 the International Athletes' Club was formed and the crusade for reform was taken up by Peter Hildreth and Derek Johnson. Also in 1958 an A.A.A. Sub-Committee made a recommendation to appoint a well-paid professional administrator. In the early 1960s some of Britain's greatest-ever coaches were allowed to walk out and we lost Geoff Dyson, Lionel Pugh, and Jim Alford. In 1964 at Timsbury Manor before the Tokyo Olympic Games, Robbie Brightwell, Mike Lindsay, and Adrian Metcalfe led a campaign cry for reform. 1967 brought Eric Kennel's A.A.A. Committee of Enquiry. This was followed by the report from Lord Byers and his Committee. Then in 1968 came the Farrell Report.

All recommended reforms. The need for full-time paid professional staff was still being stressed. Alan Pascoe tried again in Helsinki in 1970. In 1971 the I.A.C. proposals went through John Boulter, the athletes' representative to the Board. And I made my major comments in an open letter in September 1972. This received support from the Sports Council, all international athletes, press, and virtually everyone who read it. Yet it was not taken as constructive comment.

The desire or need for reform has been expressed in various forms ranging from informal, passionate pleas, to the detailed document of the 1967 Report of the Committee of Enquiry into the Development of Athletics under the direction of the A.A.A. and the B.A.A.B. The Rt Hon. Lord Byers, O.B.E. chaired this distinguished body. Meetings took place throughout Britain and evidence was taken from many individuals and organizations. The A.A.A. and B.A.A.B. found the report unsatisfactory as it 'included statements of such a general nature'. So they decided to concern themselves 'solely with a thorough examination of the recommendations'.

The A.A.A. therefore established a sub-committee to report on the 'policy for future development of athletics'. This was known as the Farrell Report. After several meetings the Farrell Committee produced their report, which carried the Byers Report a stage or two further in specific recommendations. The report did not meet with the approval of the B.A.A.B. and A.A.A.'s officers. So two years' work by some eminent and busy individuals was virtually thrown out of the window.

The frustration resulting from such inaction has many first-hand parallels. A good illustration was the request in a press statement in September 1971, that the B.A.A.B. select the Team Manager for the 1972 Munich Olympics early. It was stressed that such an important post should not be combined with the no less important post of Honorary Secretary of the B.A.A.B. The athletes also asked to elect their captain to be able to work with the Team Manager, to ensure a happy and well-prepared Olympic team.

At the request of the I.A.C. Committee in June 1972, a copy of the September 1971 document was sent by the club secretary, then Derek Boosey, to Arthur Gold, Honorary Secretary of the B.A.A.B. It was requested that urgent consideration be given at the July 1972 meeting of the Board to this document. At the July 16th meeting it was agreed that the document be returned to Mr Boosey and that the Honorary Secretary of the I.A.C. be informed that the Board could not deal with representations direct from a club and that if the I.A.C. wished the document re-introduced they should submit it either (*a*) through the elected representative of the current international athletes on the Board, or (*b*) via the Southern Counties A.A.A. to which area they were affiliated to the A.A.A. The next meeting of the Board did not take place until November 18th–19th 1972 *following* the Olympic games.

During the summer of 1971 I was the Meeting Director of the Coca-Cola/I.A.C. meeting and was based at Crystal Palace. Various sports organizers, coaches, managers, athletes, and officials came to or through the centre and I talked with hundreds. It was a time of growing personal awareness for me. One of my discoveries was that athletics is by no means alone in its administrative problems. Politics, pettiness, and inertia involve themselves in varying degrees in most amateur sports administrations. Very few sportsmen or coaches were satisfied with those running their sport. In our supposedly democratically elected and administered amateur sports, frustration at ineffectual administration is rife.

I wondered whether I was in a position to do anything. I was on reasonably cordial terms with the Board officers and had no reason to bear any malice towards them. They had always been fair in their dealings with me. I had had personal experience with the international team, had also spent months talking and listening to a wide cross-section of persons involved with the sport. My first attempt was a personal approach to Harold Abrahams, Chairman of the Board. In a long letter I outlined the modern management principle that *individuals should be involved in decisions which per-sonally affect them.* My letter requested that the athletes have *some* say in who their team manager should be. I received a cordial reply to my letter but found that it had fallen on stony ground. Harold believed that the principle was a good one but that its application would present real problems. While he agreed that people should feel involved in decisions which affected them, he just wondered where it would stop. For example, would the next request be for athletes to choose directly the Selection Committee, or even the team?

As the 1972 Olympics were coming up fast I didn't think it would be constructive to draw the attentions of the team away from doing their best in the Games. However, during and following the Games I continued to accumulate the opinions, experiences, and reflections of athletes, coaches, and officials. The thought of an open letter was germinating. The first requirement, before there can be any constructive change, is the recognition that there is a problem.

So with masses of notes and some assistance, I drafted an open letter to the Sports Council, B.A.A.B., and all those interested in the future of British Athletics. The initial part of the letter sum-marized the main problems with the administrative system as I and others saw it in 1972. Power appeared to be almost entirely in the hands of Harold Abrahams, Arthur Gold, and Marea Hartman. Decision-making appeared virtually to start and stop with them. The latter two held several different positions in athletics adminis-tration but were still fulfilling responsible positions in the business world. Jealously guarded administrative autonomy within the 'Areas', is carried on by individuals in Scotland, Wales, Northern Ireland, and the Northern, Midland and Southern Counties of Britain. Also the determined separation of the women from men's administration in all Areas except Northern Ireland causes con-siderable disunity and administrative difficulties.

Communication was grossly lacking both in terms of essential information and in terms of human relations. It is my belief that the core of the problems lay here. Many athletes, coaches, and officials felt uninvolved and ill-informed. Too often they seemed to be taken for granted. Some athletes' demands for attention led to public statements that they could not get any satisfaction from the Board. The hard-pressed, over-worked officers resented the criticism and a mutual hostility was established. This has been going on for so long that *clear* communication is difficult.

A couple of personal experiences may help to illustrate this. In Munich over lunch one day I discovered that the women's 4 × 400 metres relay team were getting quite upset about the designated running order. A similar problem was experienced by the men's 4 × 400 metres team before the Mexico Olympics. As the girls were reluctant to talk to Marea or the coaches, rather than see them suffer in silence and perhaps detract from top performance, I told them that I would at least let Arthur know of their disquiet. I arranged to see Arthur but at the appointed time he was involved in another meeting. He did absent himself to listen to my request that the girls' own views be taken into consideration. A friend of mine happened to be in the meeting and he said that Arthur's first words as he returned to the meeting room were, 'David Hemery's joined the rebels'.

It's strange but even when the Board officers make a thoughtful move they seem to lack something in the handling. Before I left for Boston in 1971 Arthur had told me that I was to captain the 1972 Olympic team. I was pleased and honoured and prepared letters to go to the prospective candidates. No word came, and during the summer of 1972 long after I returned to the U.K., I saw Lynn Davies being interviewed on television about his appointment as team captain. Lynn was an experienced competitor and I was happy for him, but it was not until I was standing around at the airport waiting for the flight to the final pre-Olympic meeting that Arthur Gold came over and said he'd like to explain why the selection of captain had been changed. It was felt that I had sufficient pressure on me in trying to retain my title not to be additionally worried by the duties of captaincy. The reason was considerate, however I do wonder why it was not possible either to ask me if I thought I would feel pressurized by the role or at least notify me of their change of mind prior to it becoming public knowledge.

Another problem was the lack of attention being given to the requirements of current internationals. No consultation would then take place concerning the athletes' potential needs in terms of equipment, medical care, training facilities, coaching requirements, or planning for the season to come, for example for training at altitude or competing in a warm climate. In fact the experimental camp prior to the Mexico Olympics was forced into being by the

I.A.C. Unfortunately the altitude research findings were insufficient, as many endurance competitors discovered four years later.
Most of our distance athletes were brought down from altitude too
late for proper body adjustment prior to the Munich Olympics.

Another illustration of the lack of attention to athletes' problems
is provided by an incident at the Rome European Championships
in 1974. The rooms for our representatives were very crowded. To
me it seems ridiculous that an athlete may train for a year to prepare himself mentally and physically to do his best at a major
championship and lose it all by lack of sleep in the village. Many
people saw it as the role of Arthur Gold, as team leader, to com-
plain about the terribly over-crowded conditions for competitors.
Dave Black, Brendan Foster, Dave Jenkins, Steve Ovett, and
Coach Harry Wilson, went to see Arthur Gold to obtain permission
to sleep in the almost empty hotel opposite on the night before
each of their competitions. Some anonymous, generous sponsors
had agreed to pay for the expense, so that neither athletes nor
Board would have to find the extra cost. This offer, however, was
not accepted by the B.A.A.B. Officers who decided to take the
responsibility upon themselves to allow the athletes who requested
it to stay in the 'Board sponsored room' for the night before their
Finals. However, I was told by one member of the delegation that
this was not granted without a warning that their action could have
resulted in all being sent home!

Another area of concern was the lack of advertising and there
was little or no attempt to engender enthusiasm before some international competitions. Small crowds reflected the situation, and
many people wondered what the sponsors were getting for their
money. One sponsor's gift was, in fact, abandoned. In Mexico the
Ford Motor Company had courtesy cars for the use of the British
Team. Many athletes were there for acclimatization four weeks
before the Games, yet they were refused permission to pick up the
cars at the border and no other arrangements were made. It is well
understood that the costs involved in running the sport are
immense and that inflation has been making things worse. However, some items of further expenditure deserve consideration; for
example, it should be *automatic* that officials who give their time to
officiate at international meetings are at least reimbursed their
travelling expenses.

The B.A.A.B. rather than the I.A.C. should be the sponsors of the physiotherapy scheme for internationals. Several years ago the Board agreed in principle to take it over but have not yet done so. The I.A.C. weekend is the one annual occasion when the internationals get together to train, find out about the season's plans, hear lectures, see films and have a social interchange. The Board has agreed to contribute financially but never actually did so until 1975 when the B.B.C. channelled some assistance through the Board. Until then it came from club funds and from Coca Cola.

The final problem area concerned selection. This subject has caused dissension for years. It has been felt that no consistent criteria for selection was being used; that some members of the full selection committee had no international athletics experience, either as competitors or even travelling with a team; that some overseas invitations never come through to athletes, the B.A.A.B. deciding for them that they will not want to, or will not be able to compete; that Arthur Gold should send back the names of interested talented athletes who are available if they are wanted, when a star athlete has turned down a foreign invitation; that as the vast majority of overseas invitations are for middle distance runners, the B.A.A.B. should do what is done in other countries where if a middle distance star accepts an invitation the foreign meeting promoter takes another athlete of his choosing from a less popular area, a field event or a woman athlete.

The open letter went on from stating the problem areas, to underlining the fact that the problems were no worse than one might find in other amateur sports organizations, yet it remained unacceptable that the same problems should recur so consistently for so long. In light of the problems and the increasing complexity of international sports administration it was evident that part-time administration was not adequate for the task. The letter advocated full-time paid professional administrators.

Although the letter stated that no *personal* criticism was intended, it was unfortunately taken as such. The only immediate response from the B.A.A.B. was an attack on the Sports Council. A scheduled meeting of the Sports Council took place immediately followed the release of the letter. At their meeting they endorsed the principle of the open letter, that full-time paid administration was required for the running of amateur sport today. The B.A.A.B. questioned the right of the Sports Council, as a grant-distributing body, to advocate a change in policy of amateur sport. Nevertheless my letter had also been addressed to the Sports Council – who would have to decide whether or not to establish any new posts. I later received confirmation that the Sports Council would be willing to fund 75 per cent of the cost of the posts outlined in the proposals presented to the Board at its meeting, November 19th 1972. These posts included co-ordinators for the following areas: (1) Domestic athletics, (2) coaching and development, (3) international athletics, (4) fund-raising and sponsorship.

Two months after the letter was issued there was the first full meeting of the Board. Alan Pascoe, the athletes' representative to the Board, put the open letter on the agenda and asked that I be present for its discussion. A letter was circulated to the Board members with the Chairman, Harold Abrahams, recommending that I should not be allowed to attend! I am thankful to say that the vote went for me to be there. So on November 19th I entered a marathon meeting. Unfortunately it turned into more of an inquisition than a discussion. There was a six-hour cross-examination to clarify and justify every critical point in the letter to the satisfaction of Arthur Gold and Harold Abrahams.

The points are virtually self-evident in amateur sport and the time of those present could have been used far more profitably. I asked that we not dwell on the criticism but discuss the positive proposals. However I soon discovered that this was not going to be allowed. Instead I was repeatedly forced on to the defensive. I was sorry that no representative of the Sports Council was present to see, for example, how an offer from over one hundred current and ex-internationals to act as liaisons with the Junior and Senior Internationals and the National Coaches under a new professional administration, was almost begrudgingly acknowledged. Also the point would not have been lost that paying someone makes them accountable. It is difficult to do anything but thank a person who is *giving* their time. I left the meeting feeling as though I'd run into a brick wall with my head down. I realized that the Board did not want to be seen to be bowing to pressure from anyone, be it from athletes, coaches, press or the Sports Council. I do not envy the Board Officers. They face some almost irreconcilable situations. Arthur is sitting on top of a fence. On one side are a large number of honourable amateur officials, coaches, and athletes who make up the majority of the sport. On the other side is a growing number of athletes, coaches, officials, and media men, whose professional dedication and attitudes towards their sport require more than part-time administration.

There is no doubt in my mind that the amateur official and helper will always be needed and appreciated. The selfless work of men like Arthur Kendall, Honorary Secretary of the Southern Counties A.A.A., holds the sport together, providing opportunities for thousands to compete and enjoy their sport.

There is also no doubt that the changes in sport, at international level, leave no option but to administrate at least *that* part of the sport professionally. For the senior officials who hold out against this, I believe it is just a race with time.

There is a sad parallel here with British Industry. Having also started this for the world, we have now been passed and out-dated. Parts of industry have recognized the need for change and are striving to keep Britain alive. It is hoped that our current 'do it yourself' approach to international representation will not kill our young people's opportunities at least to enter the Games arena with a fair chance.

Perhaps a turning point will come through the joint I.A.C./ B.A.A.B. Preparation Fund. The I.A.C. now under the Chairmanship of Derek Johnson, has taken strides towards substantial independent fund raising, through 'Superspike'. Derek, Mike Turner, and I, through many hours of discussions, brought into focus what positive and constructive role the I.A.C. could play in meeting the needs of our current and future international athletes. The requirement was for sound economic backing. With the cooperation of many current internationals and the help of Bill Oddie and John Cleese, giving their services free, the record and 'Superspike' campaign was launched in February 1976. This was followed closely by other entertainment and marketing ventures through 'Roger and Out Ltd'. The I.A.C. and B.A.A.B. partnership in this project is unique and I, for one, hope that it will lead to a new era of cooperation.

It is sad that so much wasted effort has gone into I.A.C. versus B.A.A.B. conflicts. For example, while I was Chairman of the I.A.C. from 1973–75 my main concern was a legal battle with the B.A.A.B. over the televising of the I.A.C./Coca Cola meeting. For six years the I.A.C. meeting had been covered by London Weekend Television, whose athletics commentator is the former Olympic athlete, Adrian Metcalfe. However, without any mutual discussion, and in full knowledge of our link with L.W.T., but also knowing that the B.B.C. badly wanted our meeting, the Board signed an exclusivity contract with the B.B.C. At the same time they added a rule to their books, stating that they would grant the right to televise and could stipulate any proviso which they saw fit. Of course, they saw fit only to grant us permission to televise on B.B.C. I spent many hours on legally fighting this gross injustice and inhibition of our freedom of choice.

It is some relief already to be able to look back and feel that these efforts and those of many others may not have been totally wasted. Changes in some areas are very encouraging. For example Liz Ellert was appointed Board Public Relations Officer at the end of 1972 and in the spring of 1975 she brought Board officers around a table with representatives of the athletes including myself. To me, this type of direct communication is a major step in helping to break down prejudices and hostilities. A working party has been formed and it is hoped that this will just be the start of co-operative interchange.

The aims and objectives of the I.A.C. and B.A.A.B. are not conflicting. The objects of the I.A.C. are varied. Basically it provides a medium through which international athletes can contribute constructively to the needs of the sport, particularly at international level. It also provides assistance to individual athletes and athletic clubs, for example, by providing athletic equipment, and specialist medical and physiotherapy services out of club funds, especially in cases of financial hardship.

The initiative to bring athletes and administrators together had to come from the B.A.A.B. Now that this initial step *has* been taken, the question is whether any action will follow. I sincerely hope so. We have all the right ingredients in Britain – not only in athletics but for most sports. For example, some of the world's most notable experts in sports medicine, sports psychology, and physiotherapy are scattered around the country. In addition specialists in management, coaching, marketing, public relations, and fund raising are all available. Is it not time that their knowledge be integrated on behalf of our national representatives? Our athletes are among the best in the world, but the individuals are getting there largely on personal initiative and/or independent subsidy, rather than a cohesively planned national development.

I had the opportunity of visiting Finland in the early part of

1974. In 1966 their senior man in athletics decided it was time to take a critical look at their country's athletics organization. Their problems then closely parallel ours now. Activity was too much in the hands of people who have another job. The organization was old-fashioned and worked only in the compass of one year. And the income for the association was too risk-influenced. An organizational plan and administrative structure was worked out with the help of management consultants. Athletes, coaches, and officers co-operated in the development of the national programme. They have now involved individuals who contribute specialized talents and have successfully integrated the old and the new. They are truly taking 'care' of their athletes. They check their blood every month and each has a complete physical every six months. They make sure that their diet is nutritious. They reimburse training expenses for their top senior and junior athletes. This is done on a graded system up to set limits. Careful planning goes into each season, with a tailor-made programme worked out with each athlete, his coach, and the National Coach with responsibility for that event. They use ex-internationals as liaisons in each event, working alongside their National coaches.

The list could be greatly extended but it is sufficient to note that another country outside of the eastern block area has decided to give their young men and women the assistance which could help them do better. Our national representatives are the heroes of our children. They follow them on television and on the field. Success breeds success. If we can help to keep our representatives in with a chance of being the best, our youngsters may be sparked to take part and, even become champions themselves.

APPENDIX 2.

COMPETITIVE CAREER

1953
May 28 Frinton-on-Sea   80y   11·6 (1) Frinton Prep School Sports
                    HJ   1·09 (1)

1954
June 3 Frinton-on-Sea   100y   14·0 (1) Frinton Prep School Sports
                    220y   34·6 (1)
                    HJ   1·14 (1)
                    80yH   14·0 (1)

1955
Apr 16 Motspur Park   100y   14·0 (1) Crusader Union Sports

1956
Mar 20 Colchester   2·5 mi. c-c   16·57 (1) Endsleigh School Inter-house
Apr 17 Motspur Park   440y   1:08·7 (1) Crusader Union Sports
May 31   LJ   4·13 (2)
May 31 Colchester   100y   12·6 (1) Endsleigh School Sports
                    150y   18·6 (1)
                    50yLH   8·2 (1)
                    HJ   1·27 (1)
                    LJ   4·37 (1)

1957
April Colorado Springs   50y   6·7 (1) Junior High School Sports
                    100y   12·6 (1)
                    120yH   16·7a (1)

1958
April North Quincy,
      Mass.   1mi   (3) Thayer *v.* North Quincy H.S.
April Holbrook, Mass.   1mi   (4) Thayer *v.* Holbrook H.S.

1959
April Braintree, Mass.   1mi   (1) Thayer *v.* Portsmouth Priory

1960
April Braintree, Mass.   880y   (3) Thayer *v.* Scituate H.S.
April Yarmouth, Mass.   880y   (2) Thayer *v.* Dennis-Yarmouth
May Braintree, Mass.   880y   (3) Thayer *v.* St Georges
May Rockland, Mass.   880y   2:15·8 (1) Thayer *v.* Rockland H.S.
May Braintree, Mass.   880y   2:09·7 (1) Thayer *v.* Holbrook H.S.
May Braintree, Mass.   880y   2:11·0 (1) Thayer *v.* Portsmouth Priory
May Braintree, Mass.   880y   2:13·0 (1) Thayer *v.* Silver Lake H.S.

1961
April Braintree, Mass.   880y   2:07·0 (1) Thayer *v.* Dennis-Yarmouth

April	Braintree, Mass.	160LH	19·0	(1) Thayer *v.* Scituate H.S.
April	Newport, R.I.	80yHa	11·1	(1) Thayer *v.* St Georges
		880y	2:10·0	(1)
May	Braintree, Mass.	440y	53·9	(1) Thayer *v.* Holbrook H.S.
		120yLH	13·7	(1)
May	Braintree, Mass.	880y	2:09·0	(1) Thayer *v.* Rockland H.S.
May	Yarmouth, Mass.	880y	2:07·8	(1) Area Invitational
May	Braintree, Mass.	880y	2:05·8	(1) Thayer *v.* Portsmouth P.
		80yHa	10·3a	(1)
May	Milton, Mass.	880y	2:06·6	(1) Thayer *v.* Milton Acad.
May		120LH	13·5	(1)

1962

April	Yarmouth, Mass.	440y	55·3	(2) Thayer *v.* Dennis-Yarmouth
		LJ	5·83	(1)
		120LH	14·4	(1)
April	Braintree, Mass.	440y	54·3	(2) Thayer *v.* Scituate H.S,
		LJ	5·83	(1)
		120LH	14·4	(1)
April	Braintree, Mass.	LJ	5·81	(1) Thayer *v.* St Georges
		120LH	14·9	(1)
		80yHa	10·9a	(1)
April	Braintree, Mass.	LJ	5·88	(1) Thayer *v.* Portsmouth P.
		120LH	14·9	(1)
		120Ha	16·5a	(1)
April	Braintree, Mass.	LJ	5·93	(1) Thayer *v.* Holbrook H.S.
		120LH	14·1	(1)
		880y	2:09	(2)
April	Milton, Mass.	LJ	5·83	(1) Thayer *v.* Milton Acad.
		120Ha	13·8	(1)
		880y	2:07	(2)
July 8	Smethwick	120Ha	15·5a	(1) Midland C.A.A.A. Jr Championship
Aug. 11	Welwyn Gdn City	120Ha	15·6a	(3) A.A.A. Junior Championship
Nov. 2	Stanmore	60Ha	8·1a	(2) Southern C.A.A.A. Open
Nov. 3	Stanmore	60Ha	8·1a	(2)
Nov. 11	Feltwell	60H	8·3	(1) heat Eastern C.A.A.A. Open
		60Ha	8·2a	(2)
		60H	8·1	(2)
Dec. 8	Stanmore	60H	8·0	(2) heat Southern C.A.A.A. Open
		60Ha	7·9a	(1) heat
		60H	8·1	(3)
		60Ha	8·1a	(1)

1963

Jan. 1	Stanmore	60Ha	7·9	(1) Southern C.A.A.A. Open
Jan. 12	Stanmore	60H	8·2	(2) Southern C.A.A.A. Open
		60H	8·0	(2)
Feb. 9	Stanmore	60H	7·9	(3) Southern C.A.A.A. Open
		60Ha	7·8	(1)
		60Ha	7·8	(1)

'a' following hurdle distance indicates the race took place over 3 feet 3 inches. hurdles.

June 22	Smethwick	120H	15·0w	(2)	Midland C.A.A.A.
		440H	58·6	(3)	
July 6	Birmingham	120Ha	14·7	(1)	Midland Junior C.A.A.A. Championships
July 13	White City	120H	14·7	(2)	heat A.A.A. Championships
		120H	14·9	(6)	
Aug. 10	Hurlingham	120Ha	14·6	(1)	A.A.A. Junior Championships
1964					
Dec. 11	Providence, R.I.	45yH	5·9	(1)	B.U. *v.* Brown Univ.
		440r	50·9		
Dec. 16	Cambridge, Mass.	40yH	5·4	(1)	B.U. *v.* Harvard
		440r	52·8		
1965					
Jan. 16	Boston, Mass.	440r	50·4	(1)	Knights of Columbus
Jan. 3	Boston, Mass.	440r	50·5	(1)	Boston A.A. Indoor
Feb. 3	Hanover, N.H.	60yH	7·4	(1)	B.U. *v.* Dartmouth
		440r	49·3	(1)	
Feb. 6	Boston, Mass.	45yH	5·7	(1)	B.U. *v.* Northeastern Univ.
		45LH	5·6	(1)	
Feb. 12	Cambridge, Mass.	40yH	5·2	(1)	Greater Boston Inter-col.
		40LH	4·9	(1)	
Feb. 20	Orono, Maine	45yH	5·8	(1)	B.U. *v.* Univ. of Maine
		60LH	7·6	(1)	
		50y	5·7	(2)	
		LJ	6·41	(1)	
		440r	49·8	(1)	
Feb. 22	Boston, Mass.	45yH	6·0	(1)	B.U. *v.* Boston College
		45LH	5·7	(1)	
		50y	5·7	(3)	
		LJ	6·56	(1)	
		440r	52·0	(1)	
Mar. 31	Brunswick, Maine	45yH	5·8	(1)	B.U. *v.* Bowdoin Univ.
		45LH	5·5	(1)	
		40y	5·0	(3)	
		LJ	6·51	(2)	
		440r	50·0	(1)	
OUTDOOR					
Apr. 9	Boston, Mass.	120H	14·3	(1)	B.U. *v.* Boston College
		440H	53·3	(1)	
Apr. 24	Boston, Mass.	120H	14·6	(1)	B.U. *v.* Univ. of Maine
		440H	54·7	(1)	
		LJ	6·39	(1)	
		TJ	12·57	(1)	
Apr. 28	Hanover, N.H.	LJ	6·44	(1)	B.U. *v.* Dartmouth
		TJ	12·99	(2)	
		100y	10·5	(1)	
		120H	14·5	(1)	
		440H	53·5	(1)	
May 1	Chestnut Hill, Mass.	120H	14·3	(1)	B.U. *v.* Boston College
		440H	53·5	(1)	
		LJ	6·40	(1)	
		TJ	12·93	(1)	

May 5	Cambridge, Mass.	120H	14·3	(1)	Greater Boston Inter-col.
		440H	52·8	(1)	
July 5	Medford, Mass.	120H	14·9	(1)	B.U. *v.* Tufts University
		440H	59·0	(1)	
		100y	10·3	(1)	
		220y	23·5	(1)	
		440y	50·8	(1)	
		LJ	6·65	(1)	
		TJ	12·76	(1)	
		DT	30·56	( )	
		JT	39·68	( )	
		HT	27·62	( )	

1966

INDOOR

Jan. 16	Boston, Mass.	45H	5·8	(3)	Knights of Columbus
		600y	1:11·4	(2)	
Jan. 27	New York, N.Y.	440r	48·5	(1)	Millrose Games
Jan. 29	Boston, Mass.	45H	5·6	(4)	Boston A.A.A. Indoor
		600y	1:09·8	(2)	
Feb. 2	Hanover, N.H.	600y	1:10·5	(1)	B.U. *v.* Dartmouth Univ.
		440r	48·6	(1)	
Feb. 5	Boston, Mass.	45H	5·7	(1)	B.U. *v.* Northeastern Univ.
		45LH	5·5	(1)	
Feb. 12	Cambridge, Mass.	45LH	5·5	(1)	Greater Boston Interc.
		45H	5·7	(1)	
Feb. 19	Orono, Maine	60y	6·5	(1)	B.U. *v.* Univ. of Maine
		60H	7·4	(1)	
		60LH	7·0	(1)	
		440r	48·0	(1)	
Feb. 22	Cambridge, Mass.	50y	5·6	(1)	B.U. *v.* Boston College
		600y	1:15·3	(1)	
		45LH	5·6	(1)	
		45H	6·0	(2)	
		440r	49·0	(1)	
Mar. 5	New York, N.Y.	60H	7·4	(1)	heat I.C.A.A.A.A.
			7·1	(1)	semi-final
			7·2	(1)	final
Mar. 12	Detroit, Mich.	60H	7·2	(1)	heat National Collegiates
			7·2	(1)	semi-final
			7·2	(2)	final
Mar. 19	Hamilton, Canada	50H	6·0	(1)	
		600y	1:12·5	(2)	

OUTDOOR

Apr. 18	Orono, Maine	120H	14·2	(1)	B.U. *v.* University Maine
		440H	53·1	(1)	
Apr. 22	Hanover, N.H.	440H	54·6	(1)	B.U. *v.* Dartmouth
Apr. 25	Boston, Mass.	440y	48·6	(1)	B.U. *v.* Northeastern Univ.
		120H	14·6	(1)	
May 4	Boston, Mass.	440H	52·5	(1)	Greater Boston Inter-col.
		120H	14·2	(1)	
		440r	47·5	( )	
May 7	Medford, Mass.	440y	51·2	(1)	B.U. *v.* Tufts Univ.

		220y	22·5	(1)
		120H	14·7	(1)
		440H	58·2	(1)
May 21	Boston, Mass.	120H	14·3	(1) heat New England Inter-col.
		120H	14·0	(1) final
		440H	53·4	(1) heat
		440H	52·5	(1) final
May 28	New York, N.Y.	120H	14·4	(1) heat I.C.A.A.A.A.
		120H	14·3	(1) semi-final
		120H	14·1	(1) final
		440H	53·6	(1) heat
		440H	51·8	(2) final
May 30	White City, G.B.	120H	14·5	(1) heat C.A.U. Championships
			14·3	(2) final
June 17	White City, G.B.	110mH	14·2	(1) G.B. *v.* U.S.S.R.
June 25	Smethwick	120H	14·6	(1) Midland Championships
July 2	Odessa, Russia	110mH	14·0	(1) heat Znamenskiy Mem.
			13·9	(2) final
July 8	White City	440H	53·2	(2) heat A.A.A. Championships
July 9	White City	120H	14·2	(1) heat
		120H	14·0	(1) final
		440H	52·5	(5)
July 16	Portsmouth	120H	14·3	(1) G.B. *v.* B.U.S.F.
July 23	Los Angeles	110mH	14·1	(4) Commonwealth *v.* U.S.A.
Aug. 11	Kingston, Jam.	120H	14·2	(1) heat British Commonwealth
			14·1	(1) final
Aug. 20	White City	120H	14·3	(1) British Games
Sept. 2	Budapest	110mH	14·1	(2) heat European Champions.
Sept. 3	Budapest	110mH	14·2	(5) semi-final
INDOOR				
Dec. 8	Providence, R.I.	45yH	5·8	(1) B.U. *v.* Brown Univ.
		50y	5·6	(2)
		88or	1:56·5	(1)
Dec. 14	Cambridge, Mass.	40H	5·3	(1) B.U. *v.* Harvard
		44or	50·6	( )
1967				
INDOORS				
Jan. 7	Lewiston, Maine	45y	5·2	(3) B.U. *v.* Bates Univ.
		45yH	5·7	(1)
		45LH	5·5	(1)
		44or		( )
Jan. 11	Boston, Mass.	45H	5·7	(1) B.U. *v.* Northeastern Univ.
		45LH	5·4	(1)
		50y	5·7	(3)
Jan. 14	Boston, Mass.	600y	1:11·2	(3) Knights of Columbus
		44or	49·1	( )
Jan. 26	New York, N.Y.	44or	49·0	(1) Millrose
Jan. 28	Boston, Mass.	600y	1:10·1	(2) Boston A.A. Games
		44or	48·8	( )
Feb. 3	New York, N.Y.	500y	56·7	(3) N.Y. K of C. Indoor
Feb. 12	Medford, Mass.	45yH	5·6	(1) Greater Boston Interc.
CROSS-COUNTRY				
Sept. 29	Franklin Park	4·8mi.c-c	26:18	(9) B.U. *v.* Tufts, Boston C.

Oct. 12	Providence, R.I.	5·3mi.c-c 29:16	(11)	B.U. *v.* Providence, Holy Cross, Central Conn. U.
Oct. 16	Waltham, Mass.	4·1mi.c-c 21:40	(3)	B.U. *v.* Brandeis Univ.
Oct. 25	Franklin Park	4·8mi.c-c 25:06	(9)	B.U. *v.* Northeastern U.
Oct. 28	Durham, N.H.	4·3mi.c-c 24:15	(7)	B.U. *v.* Bates, Univ. N.H.
Oct. 31	Franklin Park	4·8mi.c-c 24:37	(22)	Greater Boston Interc.
Nov. 13	Franklin Park	4·8mi.c-c 25:20	(74)	New England Intercoll.

INDOOR

Nov. 25	Boston, Mass.	600y	1:15·0	(2)	B.U. *v.* Northeastern Univ.
Dec. 7	Providence, R.I.	600y	1:12·7	(1)	B.U. *v.* Brown Univ.
Dec. 12	Cambridge, Mass.	600y	1:12·9	(1)	B.U. *v.* Harvard
		440r	50·1	( )	

1968

INDOOR

Jan. 13	Boston, Mass.	600y	1:11·8	(4)	Knights of Columbus
Jan. 20	Lewiston, Maine	600y	1:14·9	(1)	B.U. *v.* Bates Univ.
		440r	50·0	( )	
Jan. 25	New York, N.Y.	440r	49·0	(1)	Millrose Games
Jan. 27	Boston, Mass.	600y	1:12·5	(3)	Boston A.A. Games
		440r	49·0	( )	
Feb. 2	New York, N.Y.	440r	48·8	(1)	New York Athletic C.
Feb. 3	Boston, Mass.	600y	1:14·6	(1)	B.U. *v.* Northeastern
		440r	50·6	( )	
Feb. 10	Boston, Mass.	400r	51·5	( )	Greater Boston Interc.
Feb. 14	Hanover, N.H.	600y	1:12·5	(1)	B.U. *v.* Dartmouth
		440r	48·2	(1)	
Feb. 16	New York, N.Y.	440r	48·8	(1)	N.Y. K of C. Games
Feb. 20	Boston, Mass.	600y	1:14·3	(1)	B.U. *v.* Boston College
		1,000y	2:20·3	(1)	
		440r	51·0	( )	
Feb. 24	Orono, Maine	600y	1:10·2	(1)	B.U. *v.* Univ. of Maine
		1,000y	2:14·5	(1)	
Mar. 9	New York, N.Y.	600y	1:12·4	(1)	heat I.C.A.A.A.A.
		600y	1:10·8	(2)	final
Mar. 15	Detroit, Mich.	600y	dnf	( )	N.C.A.A. Indoor Champs.
Mar. 23	Hamilton, Canada	600y	1:12·1	(2)	Canadian A.A.U. Champs.

OUTDOORS

Apr. 10	Boston, Mass.	120H	14·0	(1)	B.U. *v.* Boston College
		440H	51·8	(1)	
April 13	Boston, Mass.	120H	14·4	(1)	B.U. *v.* Northeastern Univ.
			52·6	(1)	
May 13	Boston, Mass.	100y	10·3	(2)	Mass. C.Y.O. Open
		440y	49·2	(1)	
April 19	Boston, Mass.	120H	13·9	(1)	Boston College Relays
		440H	50·7	(1)	
April 20	Boston, Mass.	440r	46·9	( )	lead-off leg.
April 24	Hanover, N.H.	120H	14·7	(1)	B.U. *v.* Dartmouth Univ.
April 26	Philadelphia Pa.	440H	50·7	(1)	Penn Relays.
April 30	Cambridge, Mass.	120H	13·7w	(1)	heat Greater Bostons
		440H	52·7	(1)	heat
May 1	Cambridge, Mass.	120H	13·9	(1)	final Greater Bostons
		440H	50·6	(1)	final

May 4	Cambridge, Mass.	120H	14·0	(1) B.U. *v.* M.I.T. Tufts
		440H	54·2	(1)
		440r	47·4	(1)
May 18	Orono, Maine	120H	14·4	(1) B.U. *v.* Univ. of Maine
		440y	49·4	(1)
		220y	21·8	(1)
May 25	Boston, Mass.	120H	14·4	(1) heats New England Inter-col.
		120H	14·1	(1) semi-final
		120H	13·9	(1) final
		440H	52·8	(1) heat
		440H	50·5	(1) final
		440r	47·5	( )
May 31	Philadelphia Pa.	440H	53·1	(1) heat I.C.A.A.A.A.
June 1	Philadelphia Pa.	440H	50·4	(1) final I.C.A.A.A.A.
June 13	Berkeley, Calif.	400H	50·9	(1) heat National Collegiates
June 14	Berkeley, Calif.	400H	50·2	(1) semi-final National Collegiate
June 15	Berkeley, Calif.	400H	49·8	(1) final National Collegiates
June 25	Crystal Palace	400H	50·4	(1) S.C.A.A.A. Meet
July 12	White City	440H	51·6	(1) heat A.A.A. Championships
July 13	White City	440H	50·2	(1) final A.A.A. Championships
July 28	Poiana, Romania	400H	52·9	(1) heat Romanian Champs.
		400H	50·4	(1) final
		400r	46·5	( )
Aug. 24	Crystal Palace	400H	49·6	(1) I.A.C. Meet
		400r	47·2	( )
Sept. 2	White City	400r	46·5	( ) G.B. *v.* Poland
Sept. 12	Crystal Palace	400r	46·3	( )
Sept. 14	Portsmouth	325H	35·2	(1) G.B. *v.* The Rest
Oct. 13	Mexico City	400H	50·3	(2) heat Olympic Games
Oct. 14	Mexico City	400H	49·3	(3) semi-final Olympic Games
Oct. 15	Mexico City	400h	48·1	(1) final Olympic Games
Oct. 19	Mexico City	400r	45·1	(2) heat Olympic Games
Oct. 20	Mexico City	400r	44·6	(5) final Olympic Games

1969
INDOOR

Jan. 4	San Francisco	60H	7·3	(2) heat All American Games
Jan. 17	Los Angeles	60H	7·3	(2) heat L.A. Invitational
		60H	7·2	(4) final
Feb. 22	Cosford, England	60mH	7·9	(1) heat Cosford Championship
		60mH	7·9	(1) final
Mar. 22	Cosford, England	60mH	8·0	(1) heat Home International
		60mH	8·0	(1) final

OUTDOOR

Apr. 12	Oxford	120H	14·3w	(1)
		220H	24·8	(1)
		HJ	1·77	(3)
		JT	40·69	( )
May	Oxford	60mH		(1) *v.* Birmingham Univ.
		LJ		(1)
		88or		(1)
May	Oxford	100m		(1) Oxford *v.* Cambridge
		110mH	14·3	(1)
		LJ	23′5″	(1)

May 3	Crystal Palace	Pen.	3237	(1)	N.U.T.S. Meet
		LJ	7·11		
		JT	38·74		
		200m	22·1		
		PV	2·90		
		1,500m	4:22·8		
May 10	Sale	120H	14·1	(1)	National League
		PV	2·51	( )	
		LJ	6·60	(3)	
		HJ	1·67	( )	
		440r	48·2	( )	
May 17	Wimbledon	Dec.	6,560	(2)	Surrey Championships
18		100m			
		Sp	35' 2"		
		LJ	21' 5½"		
		HJ	5' 10"		
		400m	48·0		
		DT	92'		
		PV	8' 9"		
		110H	14·1		
		JT	146' 6"		
		1,500m	4:29·5		
May 25	Crystal Palace	110mH	13·9	(1)	heat C.A.U. Championships
May 26	Crystal Palace	110mH	14·2	(1)	final into 3·7 wind
May 31	Loughborough	110mH	14·5	(1)	
		200mH	23·5	(1)	
		440r	47·3	( )	
June 7–8	Vlaardingen,				
	Holland	Dec.	6893	(3)	Britain *v.* Holland *v.* Belgium
		100m	10·9		Decathlon
		LJ	22' 4¼"		
		SP	36' 1¼"		
		HJ	6' 0¾"		
		400m	48·0		
		110mH	14·0		
		DT	100' 4½"		
		PV	9' 2½"		
		JT	143' 5"		
		1,500m	4:19·1		
June 14	Leicester	110mH	14·1	(1)	Midlands *v.* Scotland
		HJ	1·83	(2)	
		400m	47·9	(1)	
June 21	Leicester	110mH	14·3	(1)	Midlands Championships
June 22	Crystal Palace	110mH	14·2	(1)	Sward Trophy
June 28	Crystal Palace	Dec.	6,768	(1)	Southern Championships
−29		100m	11·2		
		LJ	22' 8½"		
		SP	29' 9"		
		HJ	6' 1¼"		
		400m	48·1		
		110mH	14·4		
		DT	105' 11"		
		PV	9' 10¼"		

		JT	144′ 9″	
		1,500m	4:18·5	
July 5	Brno, Czech.	110mH	13·6	(1) G.B. *v.* Czechoslovakia
July 9	Ostrava, Czech.	110mH	13·9	(1) Czech International
Aug. 5	Belfast, N.I.	440y	48·5	(1)
Aug. 6	Belfast, N.I.	110y	–	(3)
		880y	–	(3)
Aug. 23	Nottingham	110mH	14·4	(1) National League
		400mr	46·5	( )
Sept. 1	White City	110mH	13·9	(1) G.B. *v.* France
Sept. 6	Crystal Palace	110mH	13·7	(1) I.A.C. Meet
Sept. 18	Athens, Greece	110mH	13·8	(1) heat European Champions.
Sept. 19	Athens, Greece	110mH	13·8	(1) semi-final European Champ.
Sept. 20	Athens, Greece	110mH	13·7	(2) final European Champions.
Sept. 28	Hamburg, Ger.	110mH	13·9	(1) G.B. *v.* West Germany
Oct. 8	Crystal Palace	110mH	14·2	(1) G.B. *v.* Finland
Oct. 22	Oxford	LJ	7·17	(1) Oxford freshmen *v.* sr.
		100m	10·9	(1)
Nov. 11	Oxford	110mH	14·4	(1)
		100m	11·0	(1)
		PV	2·39	(4)
		LJ	7·13	(1)
Nov. 19	Oxford	SP	10·84	( ) O.A.U.C. *v.* C.U.A.C. field
		DT	30·84	( ) events

1970
OUTDOOR

May 6	Birmingham	110mH	14·5	(1) A.A.A. *v.* B.U.A.C.
May 9	Crystal Palace	110mH	14·4	(1) O.U.A.C. *v.* C.U.A.C.
		100m	11·1	(4)
		200m	22·3	(2)
May 16	Cardiff	110mH	14·4	(1) National League
		100m	11·1	(3)
		200m	22·1	(2)
		100r	–	( )
		400r	–	( )
May 20	Motspur Park	110mH	14·5	(1) O.U.A.C. *v.* U.L.A.C.
		100m	11·2	(2)
		200m	22·3	(2)
		SP	11·29	( )
May 24	Leicester	110mH	14·3	(1) heat C.A.U. Champs.
May 25	Leicester	110mH	14·1	(1) final C.A.U. Champs.
June 6	Leicester	110mH	14·5	(1) B.C.G. Trials –4·7w
June 11	Crystal Palace	110mH	14·2	(1)
		200m	22·0	(2)
		100r	–	( )
June 13	Edinburgh	110mH	14·1	(1) British Games
June 20	Smethwick	110mH	14·4	(1) Midlands Champs.
July 4	Brighton	110mH	14·1	(1) National League
		100r	–	( )
July 5	Crystal Palace	110mH	14·2	(2) Sward Trophy
July 10	White Stadium	110mH	14·0	(1) G.B. *v.* East Germany
July 17	Edinburgh	110mH	13·7w	(1) heat Commonwealth Games

July 18	Edinburgh	110mH	13·8w(1) semi-final Commonwealth Games
			13·6w(1) final Commonwealth Games
Aug. 1	Zurich	110mH	13·4 (2) Zauli Cup
Aug. 8	White City	110mH	14·0w(1) A.A.A.
			13·9 (1) A.A.A. Champions.f.
Aug. 19	Portsmouth	110mH	14·3 (1) B.U.S.F. *v.* A.A.A.
Aug. 22	Crystal Palace	110mH	14·4 (1) National League
Sept. 5	Turin, Italy	110mH	14·1 (1) heat World Student Games
Sept. 6	Turin, Italy	110mH	13·6 (1) final World Student Games
Sept. 13	Warsaw, Poland	110mH	13·6 (1) G.B. *v.* Poland

1972
OUTDOOR

Apr. 28	Philadelphia	440yH	54·6 (2) fell, Penn Relays
June 11	Amherst, Mass.	440yH	50·2 (1) New England A.A.U.
July 14	Crystal Palace	400mH	50·8 (1) heat A.A.A.
July 15	Crystal Palace	400mH	49·7 (1) A.A.A. Champs. final
July 25	Helsinki, Finland	400mH	49·3 (1) G.B. *v.* Spain & Finland
July 26	Helsinki, Finland	400yr	47·4 (2)
July 5	Crystal Palace	400mH	49·9 (1) Invitational
July 28	Reading	400m	48·5 (1) National League
Aug. 1	Liverpool	400m	47·1 (1) National League
Aug. 1	Liverpool	400mr	46·3 (1) National League
Aug. 31	Munich, Ger.	400mH	49·7 (1) heat Olympic Games
Sept. 1	Munich, Ger.	400mH	49·6 (3) semi-final Olympic Games
Sept. 2	Munich, Ger.	400mH	48·5 (3) final Olympic Games
Sept. 8	Munich, Ger.	400mr	45·2 (2) heat 1,600mR
Sept. 9	Munich, Ger.	400mr	44·9 (2) final 1,600mR
Sept. 15	Crystal Palace	300mH	34·6 (1) Invitational
Oct. 1	Paris, France	400mH	49·3 (1) G.B. *v.* France

This chart was compiled by Peter Matthews (G.B.-A.T.F.S.) with assistance from David Hemery, Peter Hemery, and Fred Housden.

Index